Profit of Education

Profit of Education

Dick Startz

AN IMPRINT OF ABC-CLIO, LLC
Santa Barbara, California • Denver, Colorado • Oxford, England

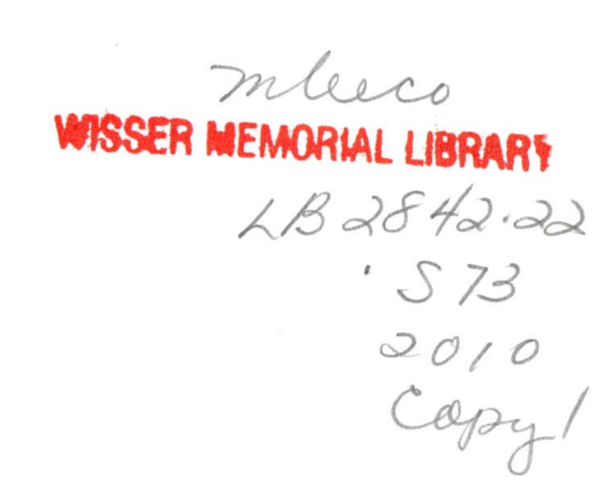

Library of Congress Cataloging-in-Publication Data
Startz, Dick.
Profit of education / Dick Startz.
p. cm.
Includes bibliographical references and index.
ISBN 978-0-313-39379-2 (hard copy : alk. paper) — ISBN 978-0-313-39380-8 (ebook) 1. Teachers—Salaries, etc.—United States. 2. Bonus system—United States. 3. School improvement programs—United States. I. Title.
LB2842.22.S73 2010
331.2'81371100973—dc22 2010025261

ISBN: 978-0-313-39379-2
EISBN: 978-0-313-39380-8

14 13 12 11 10 1 2 3 4 5

This book is also available on the World Wide Web as an eBook.
Visit www.abc-clio.com for details.

Praeger
An Imprint of ABC-CLIO, LLC

ABC-CLIO, LLC
130 Cremona Drive, P.O. Box 1911
Santa Barbara, California 93116-1911

This book is printed on acid-free paper ∞

Manufactured in the United States of America

To my late parents Arthur (father/non-profit executive/school board president) and Adele Startz (mother/school psychologist/UFT member). They believed in education and in justice, and that the two went hand-in-hand.

Contents

List of Tables

List of Figures

Acknowledgments

Bringing a book to fruition takes lots of helping hands. I have the world's best editor, Meredith Startz. Thanks Meredith for reshaping so much of *Profit*, and for doing it so nicely while being so firm with me.

Lots of folks have assisted on facts, exposition, and even on writing style and typos. Out of a long list I'd especially like to thank Dan Goldhaber, Bob Roseth, Barbara Startz, Kate Walsh, and Albert Yoon. Financial support from the Cecil and Jane Castor Professorship in Economics at the University of Washington is gratefully acknowledged. (I wish Jane was still with us; I think she would have liked the book.) Much of this book was written while on a sabbatical visit to the Federal Reserve Bank of New York. The hospitality is much appreciated, but of course neither the New York Fed nor the Federal Reserve System is responsible for any of the views expressed here.

Finally, I've been lucky enough to have had great teachers starting in kindergarten and first grade and going through graduate school with many more at all stages in between. I'm even lucky enough to be able to call on some of these teachers for advice to this very day. My hope for this book is that it'll help make future generations to be as fortunate in their teachers as I've been in mine.

Introduction

Perhaps you've read books that claim to have identified the silver bullet for the woes of American education—the one reform that will set schools back on the right track. You may have heard inspiring true stories of broken classes being repaired, stagnating schools brought back to life, and even whole school systems pulled back from the brink. In fact, if you have any attachment to the public schools, you've likely seen some great accomplishments up close and personal. I certainly have.

These many success stories leave me puzzled. A silver bullet is supposed to win the battle, metaphorically speaking, with a single shot. Each suggested reform is held out as the solution to most or all our educational problems. If there's a single right solution, why do we hear about so many *different* silver bullets? This is a puzzle, but it's a small one. The truth is probably that we have many workable solutions for the failings of our educational system, most of which have something to contribute to the battle, even if they can't end it in one fell swoop. Having lots of solutions is good news!

Yet the solution to this first puzzle only leaves me with a second, and bigger, question. If we have a silver bullet solution, or a plethora of smaller reforms that work, why are our schools still failing? This, in a nutshell, is the puzzle this book sets out to solve.

I'll get to the answer in a minute. First, let me share a story about my twelfth-grade social studies teacher, and now good friend, Vic. Vic is the sort of teacher lots of former students stay in contact with, me included. Several decades back, Vic became concerned about senior slump—students with one foot already out the door who waste the second half of their senior year. Vic and some colleagues designed a program that offers seniors a different sort of learning experience, one that motivates them to stay engaged and gain real skills they can put to use as adults. The program, called WISE,[1] asks students to design an individualized project on a topic of their choice, under the mentorship of a community member in a relevant field. Because Vic is one of those folks who make things happen, the program has run successfully for over thirty-five years and has reached over 25,000 students at more than eighty schools around the country.

Vic and I had lunch while I was researching this book. He told me of his frustration with a scenario he too often watches play out with WISE: some energized teachers start up the program in a new school and it's a big hit, but soon the innovators move on to a different job, and the program dies out. It struck me that this problem is not unique to WISE. Charismatic innovators build a successful program, some dedicated teachers pick up the idea and run with it, and then the initial burst of energy dies, and the program stalls not far from its starting point. It doesn't spread as far as it should, and it has no staying power.

This pattern is a common one: the small-scale success of local innovations, and the succeeding failure of systemic reform. We've seen myriad reforms that work, and work well. Curricular reforms, reforms in school organization, reforms in teacher qualifications, reforms in education funding. There's no shortage of successful tactics. At the same time, our public education system, which once led the world has fallen into mediocrity. The engine of economic growth and generator of a thriving middle class has stalled.

Early on in conducting research for this book, I realized that education doesn't need a new miracle cure. What we need is to ask a

> School reform has looked much like a field at twilight with some 85,000 fireflies in it—one for every public school in the country. For each effort at "reform" or "restructuring," a light blinks on, only to blink off again in a relatively short time.
>
> *Marshall Smith, Brett Scoll, and Jeffrey Link*[2]

different question. Why haven't the many local successes we see in our schools *spread*? There really are people working miracles in individual schools around the country. More important even than these superstars are the hundreds of thousands of classrooms where students and teachers may not work miracles, but are very successful on a routine basis. So here we sit, with both the occasional miracle worker and thousands of everyday heroes. Still, as a whole, our schools fail. What must we do to turn loose the energy and talent that drives these local victories, and spread it throughout the national education system?

Focus on teachers. Imagine an army that devoted all of its energy to clever tactics and new equipment, while ignoring the troops. Not a good idea. It's the same in the schools. New methods and different organizational designs do matter, but unless the troops on the ground—the teachers—carry through on reforms, we're forever stuck winning isolated battles while losing the war. How do we bring the focus back to our teacher-troops? The message here is simple. Hire good people by paying them well. Reward them for doing a good job.

Outside the education sector, America has found two rules that lead to success: (1) If something is really important, we pay more for it. (2) When we buy an expensive item, we expect to get good value on the dollar. This book's strategy is unremarkable: we're going to spend more money to draw in more teachers like the successful ones we already have, and we'll allocate that additional money by rewarding teachers who do their job well.

How is this solution different from all of those miracle cures already out there? If I offer a silver bullet of my own, it is the recognition that *there is no silver bullet*. There are many good approaches to offering a better education; different ones will work for different teachers and students under different circumstances. Rather than picking one and requiring that it work for everyone in our sprawling, decentralized, diverse education system, I offer a rather commonsense metasolution. Get good people and give them the right incentives, and they'll find the solutions that work for them, on their own steam, and with the advantage of picking solutions that meet local needs, as the best already do. The books that advocate for a particular reform? The successes you may have seen in your hometown? All these proven reforms? What we're going to do now is create the conditions on the ground to break through the barriers and turn loose all those great ideas. Then we're going to generate the power to make them flow through the whole system.

How do we get there? There are three million public school teachers in the United States. The public, their employers, needs to start thinking of teaching as a profession rather than an act of sainthood. Sure, dedication to students, passion for learning, and altruism are all part of the reason that a person becomes a teacher. Unfortunately, we've fallen into the trap of thinking that dedication and altruism replace all other considerations. Because we rely on dedication and altruism, we think we can get away with substandard teacher pay. This doesn't work. We also don't reward success, apparently on the theory that the warm, fuzzy feeling of doing good is reward enough for teachers. This doesn't work either. Instead, we need to treat teaching like other highly skilled professions: pay for talent, and then reward a job well done.

Spending money on teachers in this way is a one-two punch for fundamental reform. The first force for a breakthrough is to increase earnings potential and change who becomes a teacher. Put yourself in the mind of a college student making a career choice, or an experienced teacher contemplating a career change. Personal considerations will certainly enter the decision. Do I find the work rewarding? Will I be good at it? But how well the job pays matters too, as does the ability to advance through hard work and achievement. For many years now it has been true that, for a job that requires a college education, teacher pay is lousy. What's more, there is almost no opportunity for advancement within the profession.

In the past, teaching paid moderately well. Plus, teaching used to be one of the few professions open to women, giving schools a special advantage at hiring top people. Today, teaching pays poorly compared to other occupations open to the college-educated. Because teaching is inherently rewarding, we still get quite a few good teachers. But we get fewer good teachers than we used to, and not nearly as many as we need. That has to change. Just as we do everywhere else in the American system, we need to be prepared to pay for quality. To attract top people into teaching and to keep top teachers from jumping ship, we have to raise teacher pay. Without the right people in place, nothing else matters.

The second punch—paying for success—is the driving force that will start solutions flowing through the system once we've broken through the quality barrier. Teachers in every school will seek out solutions that work for them and their students, once they are given the extra little push to do so. Professionals search for new and better ways of doing things. Professionals also take responsibility for team results as well as their personal successes. In part, such professional action comes from hiring people with the right attitudes. Most professionals, though, also have financial incentives for seeing that things work right. Sometimes the incentive is a cash-on-the-barrelhead bonus; sometimes it's as indirect as a promotion years down the road.

Neither immediate nor down-the-road incentives currently apply to teachers. Unlike most people in the American system, teachers have zero financial stake in getting good results and making the system work. In teaching, almost everyone is paid according to a set schedule, in which pay increases only with seniority and formal credentials, not achievement. That's got to change. Those thousands of examples of successful local reforms will take on an entirely different level of urgency when one teacher turns to a colleague and says, "I know that changing how we do things is going to be a pain, but I need a big bonus this year. We've got to do this."

My goal in this book is to build the *business case* for teacher-centered reform, and to lay out the details of what that means in practice. When a business faces a tough problem, it has to run the numbers before jumping into a proposed solution. I'll do that with you. Of course, for a business, the numbers are dollars and cents. In the nation's education business, the *product* is helping our children become well-educated, successful young adults. The idea that we can run the numbers and that we have a responsibility to look seriously at the evidence in the same way we would in a business leads to the title *Profit.* The profit metaphor reminds us about a way of thinking through a tough problem; there's no intention to focus on financial matters as a goal. As we go along, there will be a fair amount of money talk, but remember that it's all in the service of doing right by our kids.

First, I'll show you evidence that teacher-centered reform will work. Then we'll talk about what it will cost, and address some hard questions about the practical details of using financial rewards in ways that are both fair and effective for teachers and students alike. Finally, I'll describe the real, measurable benefits to the nation as a whole of repairing our failing system of education.

To get started, I want to provide a very clear, measurable goal for what the plan in this book will accomplish:

Educational outcomes for students will improve, on average, by learning equivalent to one year of additional education.

Let me be quite clear that I don't mean that students will be in school for an extra year. What I do mean is that the extra amount students learn in their normal schooling will be the same as what would now take an extra year. First graders will learn a little more than first graders do now. Second graders, who'll start the year a bit ahead of where today's second graders begin, will add another few weeks worth of progress on top of their better starting point. Down the road, the typical eleventh grader will be performing at what is today thought of as a twelfth-grade level. Most high school graduates will have a real start on college-level material, and students who today would today drop out will succeed in earning that high school diploma.

There's nothing untested about focusing on teachers to achieve this goal. We have many teachers, right now, who already do well enough to produce an extra year of learning over a K–12 education. We're not talking about one teacher in a hundred. We're not talking about one teacher in ten. We're talking about *many* of today's teachers who have already figured out how to give their students that extra edge. These teachers do it with students from poor families and rich families, at all different grade levels, and across the country. The problem isn't that we don't know what this level of teaching ability looks like; it's just that we don't have enough people at this level. What our reform requires is raising the performance of the average teacher to the level already achieved by these above-average teachers.

The principle that we're going to pull up the performance of the average teacher by making teaching a financially attractive career and then rewarding successful teachers is hard to argue with, but to make it practical you have to actually attach numbers. We'll go through the calculations in detail later, but for now, I'll tell you the bottom line: we've got to raise teacher salaries by 40 percent. Since this money will be allocated largely through bonuses that reward achievement, that means that the *average* teacher's share of this new pot will be large enough to raise her salary 40 percent.

A 40 percent raise will cost the country $90 billion a year. That $90 billion is the size of a major national program, say, one-third less than what we spent on the wars in Iraq and Afghanistan in 2009. Ninety billion dollars is a lot of money, although it is *less* than what the federal government spent on education in the emergency stimulus package of 2009. A 40 percent increase in teacher salaries corresponds to a 15 percent increase in overall school spending. Saying it that way puts the increased cost into perspective, but it doesn't change the fact that we are talking about a very significant expenditure.

Getting our kids an extra year of education is desirable, but is it worth it? Later in the book I'll show you that this is a big upfront investment with an enormous long-term payoff. The payoff from reinvigorating schools is so large that over the long haul it will pay off half the national debt! A better educated workforce is so much more productive that, according to my estimates, in the long run:

> *$90 billion a year spent fixing schools under this plan will raise GDP by $900 billion a year!*

Will taxpayers go for a plan which requires some sacrifice now, even for major benefits down the road? I'll argue yes, for a combination of two reasons. First, people are well aware that our schools are failing our future. The public believes that school performance is poor to mediocre—somewhere between a C and a grade of B.[3]

The public is right. Some of our schools are first rate; others are disastrous. On average, our schools aren't terrible—they're mediocre. C+ quality schools portend a C+ quality future. I don't think there's

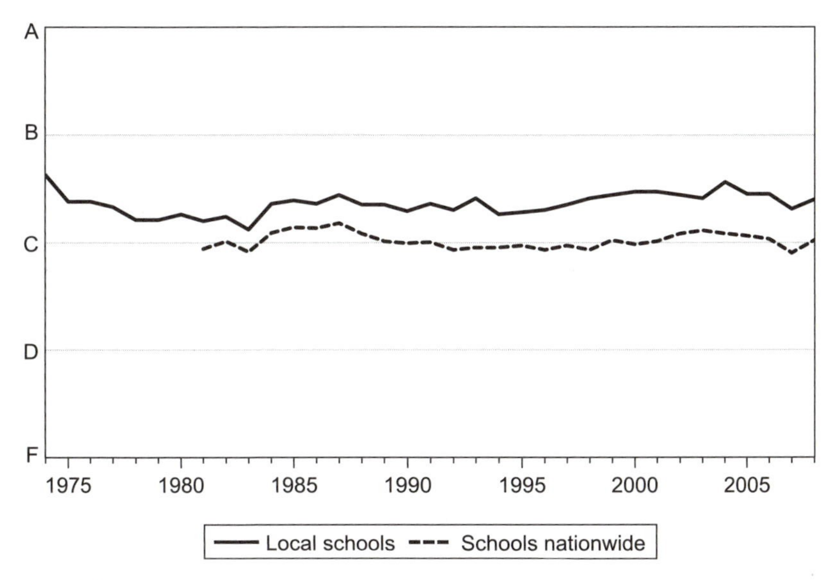

Figure 1 Public Opinion Grades of Public Schools

much disagreement about the need for fixing our broken-down education system. Education experts and the public agree. Yet, after decades of much sound and fury on the topic, we've seen little progress.

This has created a major political disconnect between the education establishment and the public. Here's my caricature of the education establishment's battle cry: "Kids are our future. Give us more money. Kids are our future. Kids are our future. Give us more money. Give us more money." Sometimes more money shows up in response to this plea. After all, it is true that kids are our future. But frequently, the public response—usually sotto voce—is "What the heck did you do with the money we gave you last time?"

Cynics say that we have put money into schools in the past, without great result. The cynics have a point. Over the last three or four decades, inflation-adjusted spending per student has nearly tripled. *But the spending has not gone toward higher teacher salaries.*

Taxpayers will ask—and given history, ask reasonably—why we should spend yet more money on schools. The answer, and the second reason I believe taxpayers can get behind this plan, is that unlike previous reforms, *Profit* comes with an implicit money-back guarantee. The plan is to raise teacher pay—which we have *not* been doing for the last forty years—while thinking very carefully about how the money is spent. We'll talk about the details later, but the heart of the deal for teachers is that while current base pay will be kept in place, large raises will be available to those who get results. The deal for the taxpayer is that schools are going to have to earn that extra money. If they don't earn it, *they don't get it*. There will be no bill for a failed program.

If you've walked into almost any school, you've seen tactics that work. And if you've read any of the innumerable books on school reform, or watched any of the *Blackboard Jungle/To Sir, with Love/Stand and Deliver* movie genre, you know that *some* of our schools succeed against all the odds. We have programs that *do* work and amazing people who make them succeed. We have hundreds of reforms that do work and thousands—tens of thousands—of local successes, and yet these true-but-local successes fail to translate into systemic reform. The goal of *Profit* is to make it possible for the successes we already have to scale up, to restore the world-class educational system that our kids—and our nation—deserve.

Profit is a big step, but a worthwhile one. After all, kids *are* our future.

READING NOTE

I come at this from a rather different aspect than most authors who write on education, as I employ the same kind of strategic economic analysis that we use for untangling other parts of our world. Can we apply the same techniques to looking at the ed-biz as we do to other fields of human economy? (Yes.) Can we identify a strategic knot that blocks conquering school failure? (Yes.) And do we have good enough scientific data to tell us how to swing the sword to cut that knot? (Yes.)

In the first instance, this book is about what it will take to have good teachers for all our kids. I present clear scientific evidence that points the way on broad issues. There are also sections on the nitty-gritty of resource deployment to effect change. Unlike many books that also attempt to persuade, I take care to explain when the scientific evidence is unsettled. The evidence isn't 100 percent clear, nor is it 100 percent one-sided. But the balance of the evidence is overwhelming. Critically important: the evidence is sufficiently clear to tell us what to do.

Because this is a book based on scientific research, and because I am an academic, I should explain that the research I present isn't *my* research. It's the distillation of the very careful work of others, the distillation of hundreds of articles by educational researchers in general and economists in particular. Because this is a book about strategy and actions for reform and not a research book, I have eschewed footnotes. If you want to see who figured out what, see the notes at the end of the book and the reference list. Those elements that are based on my own calculations are identified as such in the notes.

1

Teachers Make the Difference

> It's the Teachers, Stupid
>
> *Wall Street Journal Headline, 2006*[1]

> [Presidential candidate Barack Obama said] "The single most important factor in determining [student] achievement is not the color of [a student's] skin or where they come from. It's not who their parents are or how much money they have—it's who their teacher is." We couldn't agree more. To close the achievement gap, start with a three-word solution: Teachers, teachers, teachers.
>
> *Joel Klein, NYC School Chancellor, and the Reverend Al Sharpton, President of the National Action Coalition, Wall Street Journal, 2009.*[2]

For a child, the difference between a successful teacher and an unsuccessful teacher is all the difference in the world. It's the difference between a good education, one that not only imparts essential skills, but opens the mind and plants the seeds of a lifetime of thought, and no education at all. You've felt this difference if you, or a kid you love, have been inspired and motivated by a great teacher.

I began research for *Profit* believing that classroom teachers are the keystone on which the hope of our educational system rests. I could reel off the names of great teachers who'd done so much for my daughters, and I could even list the names of the excellent teachers who'd taught me so much several decades earlier. With Libby or Marie or Vic teaching a class, students burst into bloom.[3]

But was I fooling myself? Isn't it human nature to remember the extraordinary and let go of the ordinary? My warm feeling for teachers grew from experiences with stars like Libby, Marie, and Vic. Warm feelings are a fine motivator, but they're not a sound basis for reforming schools. We need facts. I needed to find out whether there is hard evidence that good teachers *routinely* make a difference in their students' lives. Is it just the superstars we all remember, or is there a solid corps of above-average teachers who produce the desired results? America has three million plus teachers. No matter what we do, they're not all going to be superstar, Libby/Marie/Vic–class, miracle workers. If teacher-centric reform requires all teachers to become miracle workers, then teacher-centric reform will be a dud, just one more feel-good program that doesn't deliver. So when I looked at the evidence, I needed to be sure that the evidence supported realistic, unmiraculous, change.

You, also, probably know teachers who are off the charts in talent and dedication, and as a result bring out truly spectacular results in their students. As important as these once- or twice-in-a-lifetime teachers are, *you can't build a system that requires every teacher to be a miracle worker.* To be blunt, if reinvigorating the teacher corps required off-the-charts success to work, then reinvigorating the teacher corps would be the wrong route to reform. That's kind of what off the charts means.

If change is proposed to be teacher-centric, then the evidence ought to be teacher-centric too. Teacher-centric evidence is different from the usual line of argument. Most calls for educational reform take the silver bullet approach, arguing for one specific change that will make all our problems go away. Math should be taught by "drill" or math should be taught by "discovery"; we should have more national standards versus encouraging local initiative; reorganizing school finance is what matters. These are critically important issues, although I have some doubt that there's a single answer that solves all our problems. But instead of me picking from among the proposed bullets, I decided to look directly for evidence that there already exists a sizeable group of teachers who've figured out how to get student results (perhaps implementing some of those reform bullets). This way we don't have to argue about whether a particular reform is doable or not. If there are lots of pretty good teachers already doing what we need, then pushing to get the average teacher up to their level makes sense. So I hoped the evidence would be that it's not just those few miracle workers who produce the required high level of student results.

The question, then, is "do we need to make teachers a little better or a lot better?" The answer about "a little" or "a lot" should be student results–centric and teacher-centric. This leads to organizing evidence in what my older daughter tells me I should describe as the teacher bobble-head approach.

Imagine one hundred bobble-heads representing one hundred teachers. Line them up from left to right in the order of how much their students learn, numbered from 1 on the left to 100 on the right. (Pretend you have a really big dashboard.) Now if one of the bobble-heads represents Libby, Marie, or Vic, that doll will stand way over to the right, in slot 99 or 100. For discussion purposes, suppose the doll has "Vic-100" painted on the base. Vic's a real name, but let's make up a name for the middle bobble-head, "Jack-50," and make up another, "Jill-70," for the doll in slot 70.

Jack-50 gets average results with his students; that's what it means to be smack in the middle of the line-up. *Today's average results aren't good enough.* (I hope that's sufficiently blunt.) Now let's use a red marker on the dash in front of each bobble-head to write down a number representing what the students of the teacher represented by that bobble-head learn in one year. In particular, a mark for what Jack-50's students learn, what Jill-70's students learn, and what Vic-100's students learn.

Teacher-centric reinvigoration of education is like moving all the bobble-heads to the right so that each bobble-head in the future gets better student results than today. Maybe Jack-50 gets incentives to look to his right and pick up teaching tips from the more successful dolls he sees there. Or maybe Jack-50 retires and his slot goes to Jack, Jr.-50, who's simply got more teaching talent. So here's the question, to fix education do we need to slide bobble-head 50 (sliding all the other dolls along with it) behind the red mark we made in front of Jill-70 or the mark in front of Vic-100? Jill-70 is a pretty good teacher; Vic-100 is a superstar. Getting tomorrow's average teacher to be like today's pretty good teacher is work, but eminently doable. Moving today's average teacher to superstar performance isn't.

In just a bit I'll drop the bobble-head metaphor in favor of statistical evidence. The bottom line is that moving the middle bobble-head up to the 70-mark does the trick. If tomorrow's average teacher (bobble 50 tomorrow) does as well as today's pretty good teacher (bobble 70 today), the average student tomorrow will pick up the equivalent of an extra year of education over the same K–12 years of schooling.[4]

Figure 2 A Bobble-Head Lineup

Our role model is *today's* pretty good teacher—Jill-70. There's nothing pie-in-the-sky here. We can see today's teachers in today's classrooms accomplishing tomorrow's task. We see lots of them. We needn't reorganize our entire educational system, nor rewrite the curriculum from top to bottom. And we don't need to invent a magic pill that prevents third graders from squirming, or teenagers from having hormonal spikes. As we move to a more teacher-reliant model, organization and curriculum will probably evolve as individual teachers and schools find ways to get better results. (Squirminess won't change; maybe it shouldn't.) All we need is to have more teachers do those things that their particularly successful coworkers already do day in and day out.

The purpose of this chapter is to attach a number to the size of the difference in Teachers Make the Difference. Of course teachers matter, *but how much?* Being *Profit*able requires being quantitative, so I'll attach numbers to "average" versus "pretty good," measured in terms of student learning.

HOW DO WE MEASURE SUCCESS?

Let's start putting some numbers on this average-to-pretty-good revitalization. I turn now to a quantitative analysis, beginning by establishing a unit of measurement for pretty good on the teacher side, and then moving over to do the same for the student achievement side. In the next section, I'll link the two together.

Join me in a more serious version of the bobble-head exercise, pretending that we could rank teachers in terms of their effectiveness at educating students. Of course, you can't rank individual teachers; one teacher is good at teaching math tricks, while another excels at getting at-risk students to show up for school each morning. Let me reassure you that nothing in this book will ever suggest that we ought to actually rank teachers. What we can do is take the millions of teachers out there, and ask how much a student learns from the average one. Even though ranking individual teachers is foolish, it's perfectly reasonable to talk about what an average teacher accomplishes because errors above and below the average will pretty much cancel each other out. This exercise lets us peg numbers onto the notions of average versus pretty good.

So, imagine one hundred teachers ranked from least successful (1) to average (50) to most successful (100). Or, if we had one hundred thousand teachers, the 1 percent at the bottom would rate a 1, the 1,000 teachers closest to the middle would rate 50, and the top 1 percent would rate 100. Statisticians call this kind of ranking a percentile. Teachers who rank at the 50th percentile do better than the bottom half of teachers and worse than the top half. Teachers who rank at the 95th or 99th percentile are extraordinary.

By definition, the average teacher ranks at the 50th percentile.[5] For our purposes, a pretty good teacher is one at the 70th percentile. That's quite a bit better than average. At the same time, our prototypical pretty good teacher doesn't make it into the top quarter of current teachers. That's why I've described moving teachers from average to pretty good as a big improvement, but nothing that requires a miracle. Our measure is completely teacher-centric, in that the standard of accomplishment is how well *other teachers do today.* There's no pie in the sky, no idealistic-but-unrealistic goal. Simply put, we're going to ask more teachers to do as well as successful teachers already do.

We turn now to the problem of attaching numbers to student achievement. The key here is to measure how much a student learns over the course of a year. That may sound obvious, but learning over a year is quite different from another measure that is sometimes used, level achieved at the end of the year. Consider two fifth-grade students. Dick[6] starts the year at a beginning-of-the-fifth-grade reading level and ends the year at a beginning-of-the-sixth-grade reading level. Dick has made one year of academic progress in one year; that is to say, average progress. Jane, in contrast, started fifth grade

HOW MANY MONTHS ARE THERE IN A YEAR?

While our goal is stated as one year of increased achievement over the thirteen years of schooling in K-12, it's sometimes easier to get a handle on how much more needs to be accomplished in a single academic year. In the education business, it's traditional to translate one year of academic progress into nine (not twelve) months of academic progress. So nine "months" of extra learning spread over thirteen calendar years comes to 0.692 extra months each calendar year. In other words, the goal of *Profit* is an extra three weeks of learning accomplished every school year.

reading at the beginning of fourth grade level (a year behind) and ends fifth grade reading at mid-fifth grade level. Jane has made a year and a half's worth of academic progress. Even though Dick is still ahead of Jane, Jane has learned more over the year.

Why is this "learning over a year" student gain approach so important? Teachers get handed classes with very different starting points, depending on family influences, community influences, school district resources, previous teachers, and even just plain randomness in students' innate ability. Looking at student gain provides a rough-and-ready adjustment for different starting points and allows us to better separate the contribution of the teacher from other influences. (More on this in Chapter 7, Effectiveness Pay: We Grade Students, Don't We?)

In practice, student gains are measured by test scores. While test scores are surely imperfect measures of accomplishment for individual students, the errors tend to average out when we look at large numbers of students, in the same way that errors in teacher rankings average out when looking at large numbers of teachers. But frankly, unless you're in the testing business, raw test scores don't convey much information. Is getting a 285 on the National Assessment of Educational Progress math test good or bad? In this book we'll measure gains in terms of "academic year equivalents." In other words, our illustrative student, Dick, who went from a fifth- to a sixth-grade performance level, gained one academic year equivalent in one academic year. Illustrative student Jane gained 1.5 academic year equivalents. As a

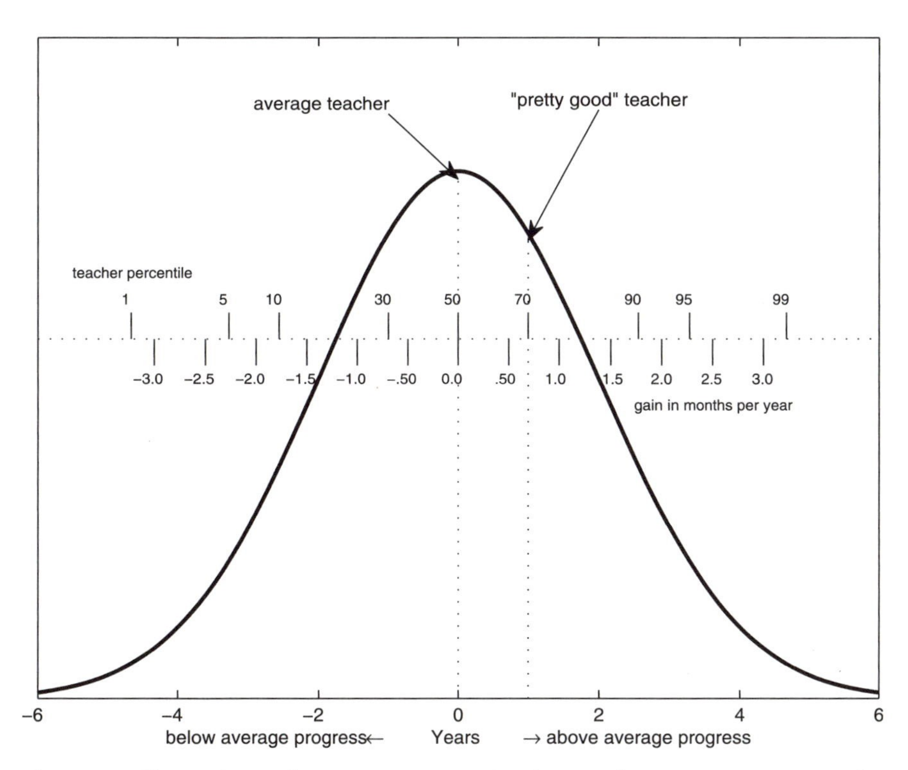

Figure 3 Effect of Teacher on Average Student Achievement, K–12, Relative to Average Gain of One Year

reminder, the goal of *Profit* is one extra year of progress for the average student spread over kindergarten through high school.

Coming up, we'll walk through the scientific evidence linking together teacher numbers and student numbers. Right now I'll show you the punch line in the form of a graph.

In Figure 3, I've plotted the distribution of teacher effects relative to student gains. The average teacher (aka Jack-50) isn't that far from a pretty good teacher (Jill-70). When looking across the spectrum of all teachers, the pretty good teacher isn't all that unusual. She's better than average, but by no means unusual. But in terms of student outcomes, the difference is quite large—large enough to realize our goal of an extra year of achievement over K–12.

More technically, the horizontal axis in Figure 3 measures *extra* gains over K–12 in academic year equivalents, so 1.0 means one extra year (our goal), 2.0 means two extra years, and so on. As a further comparison, the tick mark line midway up the graph marks horizontal units in both teacher percentiles and student gain months within a single academic year. The height of the curve represents the relative percentage of teachers at each position of student achievement.[7]

The one-year gain mark matches up with the 70th percentile of teachers: the "pretty good" teacher mark. This is doable and not miraculous. You can also see that if we wanted to improve education by the equivalent of three years, we'd need a reform that would make the typical teacher as successful as a teacher currently ranked 93 out of 100. That would take a miracle. We're not going there.

LINKING THE NUMBERS FOR TEACHERS AND STUDENTS

Once we measure teacher success and student achievement, we need to link the two by showing how much of the former is needed to produce the required degree of the latter. This is a major challenge for policy-makers of all sorts, and especially education researchers.

The first step researchers take is to track individual students' test scores from one year to the next.[8] Researchers then try to weed out differences in achievement that are due to outside factors that may affect what students learn. First and foremost, this is done by looking at the year-to-year gain for a given student just as we did in Figure 3. This automatically accounts for factors that have a large effect on academic accomplishment but don't change from one year to the next. For example, parents' education has a large effect on their children's education. Children of college-educated parents have, on average, a big head start over their peers. But the advantage doesn't change much from one grade to the next. Looking at how an individual student's learning changes from year to year accounts for this head start, and avoids mistakenly attributing it to background influences.

The next step is to link individual student records back to a particular classroom teacher.[9] The gains for a given teacher's students are then averaged. Once the gain is computed for each teacher, the teachers are sorted into order, effectively creating the bobble-head lineup we talked about earlier. Finally, we can look at the student gain for the average teacher compared to the student gain for teachers at a specified percentile—the 70th percentile for example—and see how big the difference is.[10] If the difference across teacher rankings is large, we conclude that teachers play an important role in student

Much of what's written about schools decries the "achievement gap." The gap between low-income and high-income students, or between white students versus black and Latino students, is both large and disgraceful. I don't talk much about the achievement gap simply because *Profitable* reforms will help everyone, students who already do well in addition to those now left behind. Rest assured that teachers do make an enormous difference for the kids at the bottom of the heap. Susanna Loeb, Cecilia Rouse, and Anthony Shorris write, citing work by Eric Hanushek:

> Indeed teachers are so important that, according to one estimate, a child in poverty who has a good teacher for five years in a row would have learning gains large enough, on average, to close completely the achievement gap with higher-income students.[11]

achievement.[12] In contrast, if the cross-teacher ranking difference had been minor, then we'd have to look elsewhere for fixing the educational system. As it turns out, the data shows that the range of student achievement across teachers is quite large. We're on the right track: *teachers make the difference.*

A wide range of scientific studies have consistently found this strong relationship between teachers and student achievement. Table 1 shows the results of nine studies conducted in a variety of places and grade levels. The first two columns present the effect of reinvigorating the teacher corps by turning pretty good into average, or moving the 50th to the 70th percentile. (In fairness to the authors of the various studies, I should tell you that I had to do some translating to get them all into the same units of student achievement. Translation details are given in the chapter notes and the Technical Appendix, but for the final authority, consult the original studies.) The studies are arranged from top to bottom in descending order of estimated teacher effectiveness.

Begin by looking at column (5), where you'll see the predicted effect on students over their school career. Of the nine studies, six show a considerably larger effect than our goal of one year. The other three suggest just a slightly lower effect than our goal, although the authors of one (Rivkin et al.) emphasize that they used statistical

> Teacher quality matters—a lot. Teachers' knowledge and skills are the most vital in-school factors influencing children's learning. And, for children from disadvantaged backgrounds or troubled home environments, quality teaching is even more important.
>
> *Andrew Leigh and Sara Mead*[13]

estimates to find a lower bound to the teacher effect. The real effect is probably larger. The middle study (Kane and Staiger) of the nine finds that reinvigoration will move us 60 percent past our goal. It turns out that this is a particularly interesting study for reasons that we'll discuss in a minute. This also suggests that our plan leaves ample margin for error, which we'll also discuss shortly.

Columns (4) and (5) present two views of the gain from a 20 percentile increase in teacher effectiveness. Educational gain over a K–12 career (column 5) is the number we need in the end to think about the long-run benefit to our kids, to our economy, and to our nation. But if you're a parent or a teacher (or maybe even an advanced high school student!), thinking about extra learning in terms of months in a single school year [column (4)] may be more relevant. It's certainly easier to visualize.

The middle study in Table 1 finds that students with a pretty good teacher advance by one month more than students with an average teacher, both over the course of one school year. As a parent, I can tell

> *Profit* calls for a reinvigoration equal to a 20 percentile point improvement in teacher effectiveness. I'm sometimes asked where this 20 point number came from? The answer is that it came from running through Table 1 "backwards," so-to-speak. What I actually did was look through the studies and ask for each estimate how many percentile points would be needed to reach the one year extra learning goal. The answers varied, as invariably happens with statistical studies, with 20 points turning out to be a reasonable middle ground. I then took the 20 point change and went back to each study and found the implied student improvement. That's what you see in Table 1.

Table 1 Effect of 20 Percentile Increase in Teacher Effectiveness

(1) Where	(2) Students	(3) Research authors	(4) Annual effect measured in months	(5) *Results:* K–12 effect measured in years *Col* (4) × 13 ÷ 9
Gary, Indiana	2,000, elementary	Hanushek[17]	2.3 – 3.4	3.2 – 4.9
Tennessee	5,000, elementary	Nye, Konstantopoulos, and Hedges[18]	1.5 – 2.0	2.1 – 2.8
San Diego	16,000, elementary	Koedel and Betts[19]	1.4 – 1.8	2.0 – 2.7
North Carolina	722,000, elementary	Goldhaber[20]	1.4	2.0
Los Angeles	3,200, elementary	Kane and Staiger[21]	1.1	1.6
Chicago	53,000, 9th grade	Aaronson, Barrow, and Sander[22]	1.0	1.4
New Jersey	10,000, elementary	Rockoff[23]	0.6	0.9
Texas	500,000+, grades 3–7	Rivkin, Hanushek, and Kain[24]	0.6 – 0.7	0.9 – 1.0
Los Angeles	150,000, elementary	Gordon, Kane, and Staiger[25]	0.6	0.9

you that's a big difference. As a researcher, I can tell you that the evidence is clear: many of today's teachers already make that difference.

A Quick Walk through the Evidence

For those who are interested, I'll walk briefly through the nine studies in Table 1. (If the gory details of social science research aren't your thing, feel free to skip ahead. The details aren't crucial to understanding the conclusions we reach in the end.) In addition to the summary reported in the table, there are some very interesting side results.

Gary, Indiana

Hanushek's pioneering study of the Gary, Indiana schools showed a very, very large effect of teacher differences. Hanushek writes "the estimated difference in *annual* achievement growth between having a good and having a bad teacher can be more than one grade-level equivalent in test performance."[14] Although he is talking about a notably bigger shift than that from the 50th to the 70th percentile, translating his results into our standard 20 percentile gain still shows an enormous effect.

Hanushek's study resulted in a quote widely cited in the educational research literature.[15]

> [T]eachers near the top of the quality distribution can get an entire year's worth of additional learning out of their students compared to those near the bottom. That is, a good teacher will

---

If you took a course in educational research some time ago, you might be surprised to learn how much modern research emphasizes the role of teachers. Following the enormously influential 1966 Coleman Report, researchers downplayed the importance of teachers in light of the findings that family and community influences mattered enormously. This turns out to have been a misinterpretation. Yes, family and community influences are enormous, but a sequence of good teachers can outweigh these factors. A recheck of the original Coleman data with modern statistical techniques reaffirms the importance of teachers.[16]

get a gain of 1.5 grade level equivalents, whereas a bad teacher will get 0.5 year for a single academic year.[17]

Tennessee

The most famous large-scale experiment in educational research was almost certainly the Tennessee STAR project. Originally designed to measure the effect of different class sizes, the project had students randomly assigned to classes, eliminating many of the statistical issues that confound nonexperimental studies. We want to be sure that what we measure as the teacher effect really is just that, as opposed, for example, to the effect of teachers in wealthier districts getting better student outcomes. The gold standard in such work is to run a randomized, controlled experiment, such as the STAR study.

Nye and coauthors took the data from the experiment and used it to measure teacher effectiveness. As reported in Table 1, the effect is large. The researchers found somewhat larger effects for math than for reading, not an uncommon result, and "[a] much larger teacher effect . . . in low socioeconomic status (SES) schools than in high SES schools."[18]

San Diego, California

Koedel and Betts' study of sixteen thousand San Diego elementary school students found particularly large teacher effects.[19] In their research they did something special which suggests that these particularly large effects appear for a sound reason. Other studies likely underestimate the importance of teachers due to an unavoidable technical issue: most are based on tests that have a ceiling on scores. With a ceiling on scores, once student achievement hits a sufficiently high level, more growth can't raise the test score any further. In essence, you can't get more than 100 percent on most tests. The result is that the difference that teachers make for students at the upper end doesn't get picked up in the score data. Koedel and Betts put together data based on the Stanford 9 test, which doesn't have a score ceiling. Thus, their finding of large teacher effects is especially credible.

North Carolina

North Carolina has a particularly effective system for tracking student achievement. As a result, Goldhaber was able to follow nearly all elementary school students in the state, where most other studies use a statistical sample. Goldhaber found that teachers have a very large effect. He also found evidence that students of teachers with a certification from the National Board for Professional Teaching Standards got better results, a topic we return to in Chapter 8, Qualification Bonuses: An Input Measure of Merit. Finally, Goldhaber's evidence shows that teachers with even one or two years of experience outperform novices, and that there is probably some further gain with a few more years of experience. Past that point teachers seem to have mastered their craft (or not, as the case may be), so there isn't further improvement with more experience. Goldhaber writes, "I find little evidence . . . of . . . productivity gains associated with increases in experience beyond five years."[20]

Los Angeles, California (Study 1)

Kane and Staiger looked at a relatively small number of teachers in Los Angeles, finding a large teacher effect. While this study includes fewer teachers than other studies, the results are particularly credible because the authors conducted a randomized, controlled experiment designed specifically to measure teacher differences. Kane and Staiger set up an experiment in which a pair of teachers teaching in the same school was chosen and two class rosters were prepared. A coin was flipped (figuratively) to choose which teacher got which roster. The research team later checked student gains for 78 teacher pairs, and found that the more common nonexperimental

If you want to escape from numbers for a minute, here's the overall conclusion from Gordon, Kane, and Staiger's research:

> [U]ltimately, the success of U.S. public education depends upon the skills of the 3.1 million teachers managing classrooms in elementary and secondary schools around the country. Everything else—educational standards, testing, class size, greater accountability—is background, intended to support the crucial interactions between teachers and their students. Without the right people standing in front of the classroom, school reform is a futile exercise.[21]

methods gave unbiased predictions of the experimental results—evidence that nonexperimental approaches provide valid evidence.

Chicago, Illinois

Aaronson and coauthors looked at Chicago ninth graders and found large teacher effects over a period as short as a single semester. Along the way, they made two important discoveries. The first is that measures of the teacher effect are quite consistent across a variety of statistical techniques, an important requirement if student achievement is to play a role in teacher incentive programs. Their second discovery is that having a good teacher is especially important for students who are the furthest behind their peers. Here's how the research team put it:

> [T]est score value-added measures for teacher productivity are not overly sensitive to reasonable statistical modeling decisions, and thus incentive schemes in teacher accountability systems that rely on similar estimates of productivity are not necessarily weakened by large measurement error in teacher productivity . . . the biggest impact of a higher quality teacher, relative to the mean gain of that group, is among African American students and those with low or middle range eighth-grade test scores.[22]

New Jersey

Rockoff's data on students in two New Jersey school districts had the advantage of tracking the same students for a number of years. These repeated observations allowed him to see how students performed with several different teachers. Additionally, more than a third of the teachers were observed for six or more different classrooms of students, giving a particularly powerful estimate.[23] Rockoff's study suggests it would take a smidgeon over a 20 percentile improvement in teacher effectiveness to achieve a one-year gain in student outcomes.

Texas

The Texas study by Rivkin et al. is notable for its huge sample size and statistical sophistication. The techniques the researchers deployed yield a lower bound estimate of the importance of teacher effectiveness, meaning that the real effect is no lower than their estimate and probably higher. Their techniques were also designed to eliminate, to the extent possible, any misleading evidence due to better students being assigned to better teachers—as opposed to better teachers producing better students. In particular, the research design completely discounted any teacher differences from one school to the next. This gives further reassurance that the differences they find reflect differences between teachers rather than differences between schools.

Los Angeles, California (Study 2)

Looking at a large number of students in Los Angeles, Gordon and coauthors computed an estimate of teacher effectiveness at the low end of our range. Fortunately, this low end is actually pretty darn high—just under our goal. The research team puts it quite forcefully,

> the average difference between being assigned a top-quartile or a bottom-quartile teacher is 10 percentile points. Moving up (or down) 10 percentile points in one year is a massive impact. For some perspective, the black-white achievement gap nationally is roughly 34 percentile points. Therefore, if the effects were to accumulate, having a top-quartile teacher rather than a bottom-quartile teacher four years in a row would be enough to close the black-white test score gap.[24]

ARE WE MISSING SOMETHING?

The scientific evidence is clear: teachers make the difference. Nonetheless, there are several elements not covered by these studies that deserve attention. Most important, what is the cumulative effect of the teachers who interact with a student over his or her thirteen years of school? Improving the average teacher doesn't mean that every student will have a great teacher every year. Does the effect of one highly successful teacher disappear if future teachers are less successful? In reviewing the evidence, we'll see that although this is a very legitimate concern, the effect of improving teachers is big enough to achieve our goals even with a significant margin of error.

Most of the studies presented in Table 1 look at student gains from having a particularly effective teacher during the course of a single academic year. This is a natural approach since, at least in elementary school, a teacher and a group of students typically are together for one year. In calculating column (2) in Table 1, the effect of having a particularly effective teacher every year from kindergarten through high school, I've multiplied the single year effect by 13, since there are thirteen years in K–12.

It is possible that the effect of having a good teacher gradually wears off, or contrariwise, that having a whole sequence of good teachers cascades so that the total effect is more than the sum of the parts. Unfortunately, we can't follow large numbers of students throughout their primary and secondary schooling. And we most certainly can't find students who have had thirteen teachers in a row who were each 20 percentile points above average. So there's not definitive evidence one way or another on cumulative effects.

Because this is an important question, researchers have started to look into it, and there are now several careful studies on the topic. Unfortunately, different results come down on different sides of the argument. Several studies use statistical methods to project out the effect of a single good teacher. These studies find that the effect fades out. One study actually tracked students for three years (rather than using statistical projections), comparing a group who had three good teachers to a group who had three unsuccessful teachers. This study found that the teacher effect does *not* fade out. Because the potential for fade-out or reinforcement is important, here are more details about several of these studies.

Kane and Staiger, in the experimental Los Angeles study discussed above, found evidence that the effect of a single good teacher appears to dissipate after several years. Rechecking student achievement one year after and then two years after the experiment, the researchers find a fairly strong fade-out effect, although they caution that students were no longer assigned in a random fashion in those subsequent years.

Josh Kinsler, at the University of Rochester, took a new look at North Carolina's data, building a model that statistically allows for the effect of a single good teacher to fade out over time. He found that the direct effect of good teacher for one year was quite large, about the same as the North Carolina results reported in Table 1. However, Kinsler also found that the effect of a good teacher had largely dissipated after three years.[25]

In a study looking at 60,000 students (again, in North Carolina), Princeton's Jesse Rothstein provides evidence that the kind of value-added measures that most of the (nonexperimental) studies rely on do an imperfect job of controlling for how students are assigned to teachers. As with Kinsler, Rothstein finds that gains from a good teacher in a single year are only moderately correlated with student achievement two or three years later.

Taken together, these three studies suggest that the effect of having one good teacher fades out. This is one good reason, among many, for leaving a margin of error in making our calculations. The middle estimate in Table 1 suggests that turning average into pretty good teachers results in a 1.6 year learning increase, 60 percent more than is needed to hit our goal. (The ubiquitous North Carolina results suggest an effect twice as large as what we need.) This suggests that meeting the one-year goal is realistic, even with a pretty large margin for error to compensate for at least some amount of fade out.

These studies don't address the potentially beneficial flip side of the fade-out problem: the cumulative effect of having *better* teachers over a number of years. One study does exactly that. Sanders and Rivers used the experimental Tennessee data from two school districts to check explicitly for the cumulative effect of teachers on future achievement.[26] They summarize their results by saying, "The effects of teachers on student achievement are both additive and cumulative." The researchers placed teachers in five groups based on how much their students learned. Then they compared the effect of having third, fourth, and fifth grade teachers all from the top group versus three teachers in a row from the bottom group. The cumulative difference in student gains with the highly skilled teachers was huge.

Since teachers make the difference, why not select and reward teachers according to those characteristics that matter most? The answer turns out to be that the characteristics that make a successful teacher are practically impossible to identify accurately. While I'm tempted to say that the best teachers are just magical, what I really mean is that whatever it is that a good teacher does is something that doesn't show up in quantitative measures available to outsiders. This is why the research discussed here has focused on outcomes—i.e., student achievement—rather than inputs into teaching.[27]

We do know a little bit about what identifies someone who is likely to be a good teacher. The teacher's academic ability as evidenced in her own test scores is a modestly positive signal, as is having gone to a highly selective college. With some limited exceptions, having more

While most research finds a modest effect from having gone to a selective college, a study of Philadelphia students by Anita Summers and Barbara Wolfe found a large effect, and an effect that was much larger for low-income students. The authors write that over a three-year period:

> A student whose family income was $5,000 [in 1970] grew 8.6 months more with a teacher from a higher rated college than with teachers from other colleges; a student whose family income was $10,000 grew 3.7 months more.[28]

years of education and getting a graduate degree does not lead to better teachers. The evidence on this is depressingly clear, as we'll show later.

More experience also doesn't seem to make for better teachers, with an important exception. Teachers improve a *lot* in their first few years. Two things follow from this observation. First, it suggests that great teachers are made, not born, since many who turn out to be fantastic have a rocky start. Second, stressed and disillusioned teachers exit the profession in droves early in their careers. This means that we have a massive inflow of novice—and therefore not yet very good—teachers. This is a circular problem: the difficulty of teaching in the first few years causes young teachers to leave, which leads to high turnover and a high proportion of teachers who are inexperienced, which leads to difficulty in teaching, and so on. We'd like to redesign our system so that teaching is an attractive career, not just something to do for a few years.

SUMMING UP THE DIFFERENCE

The evidence is clear: Teachers are incredibly important in determining student achievement. The shift in teacher effectiveness that we need to fix our education system is large, but eminently manageable.

Our next task is to figure out how much an improvement of 20 percentile points, the difference between an average and a pretty good teacher, is going to cost. But before looking forward at the cost of reinvigoration, we'll take a quick look back at how teachers are paid now and how current and historical practices compare.

I'll close this chapter with the words of one of my own superb teachers, Peter Temin, on the occasion of his presenting an honorary lecture:

> The lack of highly-capable teachers will impede the effectiveness of reforms. . . . Current reforms of school administration and evaluation take the quality of teachers as given; they simply rearrange the existing educational assets and have little or no effect. Only when we break out of the current equilibrium of teacher pay and quality will education in the United States show a marked improvement. . . . We are in danger of losing one of the great advantages we possessed in the twentieth century. Unless we raise the quality of teachers, we will experience an endless sequence of failed educational reforms. If the future of America is to be as bright as the past, we need to break out of our current equilibrium.[29]

2

Who Teaches?

America's children are educated in public schools (about 90 percent of children) by over three million women and men. Teachers are the single largest college-educated occupation, comprising almost 10 percent of the college-educated workforce. Almost all teachers have college degrees, and about half have graduate degrees. By most standards, this is an awfully talented group.

But the hard truth is that America hasn't done what's needed to attract enough top talent into teaching. Since the need for a reinvigorated teacher corps is a central theme of *Profit,* I want to share the evidence that we're not currently getting the talent we need. Compared to the population at large, teachers rate high on the ability scale—at least as measured by academic ability (which is pretty much the only available objective measure). Unfortunately, the pool of potential and actual teachers is the pool of the college-educated (not the population at large), and on average, today's teacher corps compares much less favorably with this group. The shortfall is particularly evident at the top end of the talent distribution. The most academically able college graduates rarely enter teaching.

This talent shortage is something of a historical anomaly. In the "good old days," teaching was more attractive to particularly able college graduates than it is today. In the next chapter, I'll document the economic reasons for this fall-off in attractiveness of a teaching career, but you probably already know the two main culprits. First, in those good old days, teaching salaries were a lot more attractive than is true today. Second, in the past (and perhaps we ought to apply the label "bad old days" here), jobs for women were very limited, and teaching was one of the few professions open. If we're to fix our schools, we'd better see to it that in the future teaching is once again attractive to particularly able college graduates. What that'll take is the subject of Chapter 4, Raises!

It's fine to make teaching more attractive, but for the attraction to have an impact, it has to change both who enters teaching and who leaves. It's not just that today's academically able college graduates aren't aimed toward a teaching career, it's also distressingly true that many of today's excellent teachers quit teaching and change careers to take advantage of better, alternative opportunities. The last part of this chapter takes a look at teacher churning.

TODAY'S TEACHERS

Who are today's teachers? If you want a single visual for the evening news, you ought to film a white, college-educated woman in her forties teaching elementary school, with over a decade of experience at her job.[1] Mind you, it might be wise not to rely on a single visual, since in many ways teachers are demographically diverse, with men, minority groups, and adults across the working-age spectrum all well represented.

One way in which teachers are not at all diverse (you'll have to forgive a "well, duh" moment here) is that they're well-educated. All teachers (99 percent) have a four-year college degree, compared to a quarter of the general population. The greatest number of those are degrees in education. U.S. colleges grant about one hundred thousand new bachelor's degrees in education each year. This number has been remarkably steady for twenty-five years, a period in which the total number of bachelor's degrees produced has risen by two-thirds.

You might think that teacher training would balance learning about pedagogy with learning about subject matter. Often it does, of course, but there's nothing in the system that mandates that it be that way. In today's credential system, with a few exceptions, one degree is as good as another. At the high school level in particular, teachers find themselves assigned to teach "out of field." About one core academic class out

> Thirty-five years ago, an education major was the most popular college major. Today, business majors outnumber education majors by three to one.[2]

> In private schools, 69 percent of secondary school teachers have a degree in an academic subject rather than in education. In public schools, only 47 percent have a degree in an academic subject.[3]

of four is assigned to a teacher who doesn't even have a college minor in the relevant field. You'll probably not be surprised to learn that this one-in-four average combines one out-of-field class in five in well-off schools and a much higher rate, one-in-three, in high-poverty schools.[4] Out-of-field assignment is also particularly acute in teaching math. What is more surprising is that the extent of the problem varies enormously from one state to another. In Minnesota only 7 percent of classes are assigned out of field. In Louisiana the number reaches 40 percent!

Another way in which teachers do not reflect population averages is that women outnumber men as teachers by a 3:1 ratio.[5] The fraction of teachers who are women has actually *increased* over the last four decades.[6] This is quite different from gender balances in the work force as a whole and something we'll have to give some attention to when we start looking at teacher pay in the next chapter.

WHAT DO TEACHER ACADEMIC SMARTS LOOK LIKE?

Let's turn now to the direct evidence on teacher ability, as measured by their own academic prowess. Teachers who are themselves better at academic work make better teachers on average. Sure, there is much that goes into motivating students that doesn't depend on a teacher's own academic ability. For instance, a teacher's emotional quotient (EQ) may be as important as her IQ. Nonetheless, pure intellectual ability does matter.

One of the big changes that has resulted from the combination of lower relative teacher salaries and the opening of labor market opportunities for women and minorities is that the teacher pool draws much less from the top of the academic talent distribution and more from the bottom than was true in the past.

Put yourself in the position of a college student considering teaching as a career. What you like to do matters. What a career pays also matters. The more academic ability you demonstrate, the more high-paying jobs will be open to you and the more likely you are to choose

In 1964, a third of young women were in the labor force. By 2000, 80 percent were. Over the same period, the fraction of young women with college degrees tripled, and the fraction of young teachers who were women rose slightly. At the same time, "In 1964, more than half of working female college graduates were teachers—by 2000, this percentage had dropped to 15 percent." The most remarkable change—in which women become teachers—is the drop-off in the top end of the academic talent distribution. In 1964, 20 percent of female teachers were in the top 10 percent of high school students; by 2000 this had halved.[7]

a path other than teaching. Since teacher salaries have lost ground relative to other jobs, it's even more likely now than in the past that an able college student will opt for something other teaching. The case of women and minorities is even stronger. It used to be that even the most talented women and minorities were systematically excluded from most good jobs, but a teaching career was allowed. With discrimination dramatically reduced, talented women and minorities are no longer forced into teaching. The free ride that the teaching profession had by grabbing talented women and minorities is long gone.

Before diving into the numbers I want to acknowledge that our measures of academic ability are somewhat limited. Teachers do need people smarts at least as much as they need a high IQ. But of course that was true in the past as well. There's no reason to think that the decline in the academic talent of teachers has been somehow offset by an increase in talents in other dimensions.[8] So while looking at measurable academic talent is imperfect, there's no reason to think that the results will be misleading.

Figure 4 compares the relative distribution of "intellectual ability" for college-educated teachers and nonteachers in their late forties.[9] (Intellectual ability is measured by scores on the Armed Forces Qualifying Test [AFQT], which is something like an IQ test.[10]) The dashed vertical line shows the average for all Americans (including those without a college education) of a similar age. As one would expect, teachers show much more intellectual ability than the population at large. Teachers are certainly smarter than the average bear.

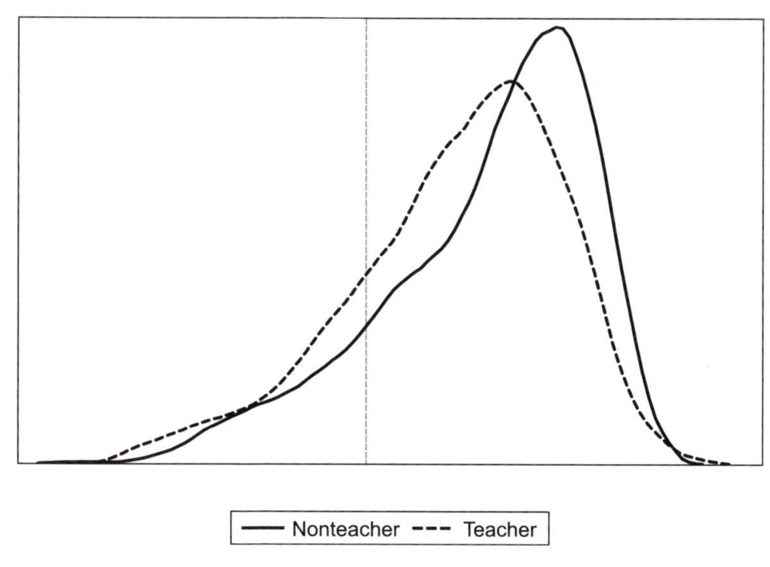

Figure 4 Intellectual Ability of the College-Educated

What's striking in Figure 4 is how the story looks when we compare teachers to other college graduates, the group from which teachers are drawn. The ability distributions of teachers and nonteachers overlap a great deal, but on average, ability is significantly higher for nonteachers. The median teacher's ability level hits at the 37th percentile of college-educated nonteachers.

I don't want to exaggerate the consequences of the picture in Figure 4. Most teachers fall within the ability range of the general college-educated public. However, there is an especially big gap at the upper end of the ability distribution (what statisticians call the "upper tail"). For example, if we look at the AFQT score needed to rank in the top fifth among nonteachers, it turns out that only eight percent of teachers score that high. It's not that all teachers need to be way above average academically, but there's something wrong when so few are.

It's not just that there is an ability gap, it's that the ability gap has grown over time. Marigee Bacolod has carefully pulled together data from a number of different sources to show what has happened to the intellectual ability of teachers over time.[11] Figure 5 shows what

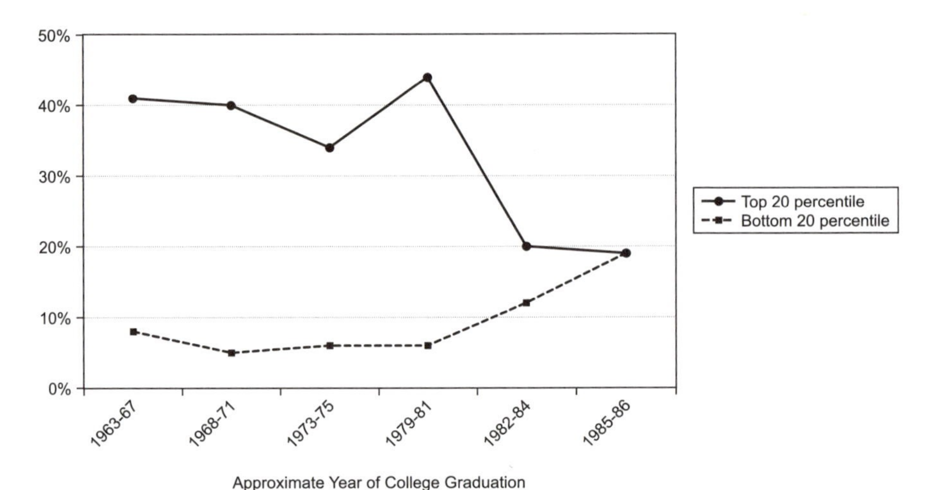

Figure 5 Percentage of Female Teachers Falling in Top and Bottom IQ Quintiles. (Based on Bacolod 2007, Table 3. Bacolod bases her calculations on birth cohort, which I have converted to approximate year of college graduation by adding 22.)

happened to IQ scores of female teachers before and after the women's labor market revolution. In the overall population, 20 percent of IQ scores fall in the top quintile and 20 percent in the bottom quintile (that being the definition of quintile). Teachers who came of age in the mid-1960s had twice that number at the top end of the IQ distribution and less than half the expected number at the low end. By the mid-1980s, when opportunities had opened up for women, teacher IQs looked pretty much like the distribution for the population as a whole.

So teachers look just fine compared to the general population. It's just that they used to look special. In the old days, teachers were twice as likely as others to be at the top of the IQ heap and half as likely to be at the bottom. Given the job we ask teachers to do, maybe the old days were better in a pretty important way.

Bacolod goes on to show that while higher salaries outside teaching discourage entry into teaching across the board, the effect is disproportionately high among the most able. Bacolod divided teachers into four groups ranked according to their ability and then estimated the effect of a 10 percent increase in salaries outside teaching. She found that a 10 percent raise in outside salaries cut entry into teaching by 3.7 percent in the group in the third quartile (the group ranked from 50 to 75). In contrast, the same raise cut entry into teaching by 6.4 percent among the top quartile.[12] In other words, the effect of salaries is twice as large in the group ranked 75 to 100 as in the group ranked 50 to 75.

> Looking at college graduates, researcher Matt Wiswall finds a near 60 point difference in SAT scores between nonteachers and teachers.[13]

Research by Caroline Hoxby and Andrew Leigh looked at SAT scores of teachers and nonteachers and came to similar conclusions.[14] The two researchers document a dramatic fall in the share of female teachers coming from the top group in academic ability, as measured by SAT scores at the college the individual attended (which is to be understood as a rough measure of the academic rigor of the college). In 1963, 16 percent of teachers came from colleges with SAT scores in the lowest five percent. By 2000, the fraction had more than doubled, reaching 36 percent. The draw from the top five percent had nearly vanished, dropping to one percent.

Hoxby and Leigh come up with a specific explanation for the declining draw from the top. Not only is teacher pay is low overall, the biggest gap is at the top end. Calling this "compression" (compared to the private sector, the distance between high and low teacher salaries is relatively small), the authors write "When we began this study, [we thought] that pay parity would play the major role, and pay compression the minor role. We had not recognized the implications of the fact that pay parity changed similarly for college women of all aptitudes, which makes its smaller role predictable. Put another way, outside of teaching, high-aptitude college women did not gain dramatically relative to low-aptitude college women: they all gained over time. However, in teaching, high-aptitude women experienced substantial relative losses."[15]

> In the late 1960s, academically talented college graduates were almost as likely to enter teaching as were college graduates of average ability. . . . By 1980 a college graduate with an IQ of 130 was only one fourth as likely to become a teacher as was a college graduate with an IQ of 100.
>
> *Dick Murnane and coauthors*[16]

Here's the take-away lesson:

You don't get above-average talent for below-average wages. Among the most talented, we've been coasting on the few willing to sacrifice their family's living out of dedication to teaching.

Let me say that again. *The drop in teacher salaries relative to other professions (carefully documented in the next chapter) hurts teacher recruiting across the board, but bites hardest in our ability to recruit the most able.*

TEACHER CHURN

Education lore has it that teaching has a very high turnover rate compared to other professions; consequently, the nation regularly replaces enormous numbers of teachers with newbies. The lore is somewhat overstated. In fact, many jobs have considerable turnover; teaching isn't all *that* different.[17] Nonetheless, understanding turnover is a key to thinking about reinvigorating the teacher corps by changing the "Who" in Who Teaches, i.e., the part of reinvigoration that occurs by replacing current teachers leaving the profession, as opposed to the part of reinvigoration that comes from changing the environment in which continuing teachers work. Because the teaching corps turns over rapidly, we have a ready-made opportunity for bringing in fresh faces. At the same time, we want to think about why so many of our best teachers choose to leave the profession.

In the latest year for which data is available, one teacher in seven with twenty-five years experience or more left teaching.[18] Presumably these are mostly retirements, and teachers do retire somewhat earlier than other professions. More startling is what happens at the front end of teaching careers: 10 percent of new teachers quit after a year. After three years, one in five is gone.[19]

> Following teachers for the first nine years after college graduation, researcher Matt Wiswall found that the average licensed teacher kept at it for about five years. (Unlicensed teachers stayed 2.5 years.)[20]

Because of the retirement issue, the age of current teachers is an important part of the churn picture. The average teacher is in her forties. The age distribution of teachers reflects both decisions teachers make and the changing demographics of school-age children, with hiring crests and troughs following the baby boom, baby bust, baby boom echo, etc. As a result, while the teacher corps is aging, there has also been a slight recent increase in the proportion of teachers under thirty, as more young teachers have been hired to accommodate the greater number of students in school. It's the aging that's a matter of concern as we head for a significant number of retirements. In 2003–04, one third of teachers were fifty or over.

Teachers' pension schemes tend to provide significant incentives to retire starting in the late fifties. As a result, teachers retire earlier than other professionals.[21]

Take a look at Figure 6. You'll see that the fraction of teachers approaching retirement age has increased noticeably over the last three decades. For better or worse, we're going to have to replace much of the teaching corps in coming years. Better would be better than worse, so it's well worth the effort to make sure that the influx of new teachers is as able as possible.

But leaving teaching isn't the only type of turnover. Teachers also change schools a lot. Between quitting teaching altogether and changing schools, one in four new teachers moves at the end of her first year! This constant churn causes considerable disruption in schools. How do you bring people together to make changes if many of them are on their way out?

Unsurprisingly, the churning is not random. New teachers get lousy assignments and move on to better ones when they can. Later, we describe better assignments as a method of compensation that comes about when the usual arrangement of compensating for a tough assignment, i.e., money, isn't available. The fact that teachers seek more desirable gigs proves they have the same healthy sense of

> You have in the schools, right now, among the teachers who are going to be retiring, *very* smart people. We're not getting in now the same kinds of people. In many places, it's disastrous. We've been saying for years now that we're attracting from the bottom third. This is hard for us to say because we represent all these people.
>
> *Sandra Feldman, late president of the AFT in an interview with Matthew Miller.*[22]

Figure 6 Percentage of Teachers Nearing Retirement, Ages 50+ and 55+. Author's Calculations. Teachers Reporting Full-Time Work, 20 or More Hours a Week, Annual Income Greater Than 1,000. (Based on King et al., 2004.)

self-preservation that the rest of do. It does not suggest that heavy churning is in the students' best interest.

Who leaves first? Teachers with good opportunities elsewhere leave first. Notably, it's teachers with a science background who find jobs outside education. Murnane and Olsen followed fourteen thousand North Carolina teachers for nine years. Five years after beginning teaching, over half of high school physics and chemistry teachers had quit teaching, compared to "just" a quarter of elementary school teachers.[23] Murnane and Olsen estimate that a 6 percent salary increase would lengthen the average teaching career by two to three years, by making other jobs less tempting in comparison to sticking it out.

> The fraction of teachers who change schools or quit teaching is higher by half in heavily minority schools (20.3 percent) than in mostly white schools (12.7 percent).[24]

Losing high school science teachers? That's just what our country needs to prepare kids to compete in the twenty-first century!

You know what else is signal of a likely short teaching career? Scoring well on the National Teacher Examination (NTE)! Does it seem that a system in which those who score best on a career exam are the first to leave that career is, to put it politely, a little screwed up? It's the teachers who score in the top quartile of the NTE who are disproportionately likely to leave early.[25] In other words, high-scoring teachers leave before low-scoring teachers, and really high-scoring teachers leave really early. This is a theme we'll return to again and again; while we need to improve conditions for all teachers, extra-special attention needs to be paid to getting and keeping the top performers.

What's Next?

You know where I am heading in the next few chapters. If we want to move to a world of pretty good teachers, we're going to have to pay for it. What we need is a system in which teachers who do an outstanding job—whether that's due to their own academic smarts, their ability to inspire kids, or just staying up all night writing lesson plans—are rewarded as they should be. It'll take us a couple of chapters to get there, but that's where we're headed.

3

Teacher Pay

Teaching is the downstairs maid of professions.
Frank McCourt, veteran teacher and Pulitzer Prize winner[1]

On most days, most of us get up and go to the same job we went to the day before. We occasionally dream about making a change. Once in a great while, we jump ship and choose a new career. (For a college student the time to choose a career is involuntary—graduation happens!) What we choose depends on our tastes or distastes for various kinds of work, what we're good at, and, of course, how good the pay is. This chapter is all about the pay element. Since we're thinking about getting the right people to jump into teaching, and not to jump out again, we need to compare the pay element to the pay available in an alternative career choice. Whatever the pleasure level someone takes from teaching, the more that teaching pays relative to an alternative career, the more likely a person is to enter or continue in teaching.

We need one more piece to connect up teacher pay with "who teaches." The more skills you have, the more well-paying alternatives that are open to you. As a consequence, careers that pay poorly get filled up by people who didn't have many better-paying choices. Obviously, some highly skilled people choose low-paid professions despite the low pay because a particular profession is so personally rewarding (think clergy). Anyone who's walked into a good school has met some teachers who have skills that would allow them to earn far more in another line of work, but fortunately for all of us, they just love to teach. Nonetheless, overall, the less you pay, the fewer top people you're going to recruit and the fewer top people you're going to retain.

Let me confess to a bit of initial ignorance. Before I started researching *Profit,* I thought that teachers were reasonably well-paid. Not that teachers are rolling in dough, but I thought they did okay compared to other college graduates. I was wrong. In 2008, it would have taken a 31 percent raise to move the salary of a typical teacher up to the salary level of a typical nonteacher college grad.

If you want a single take away from this chapter, that's it. *Teachers need a 31 percent raise just to catch up to alternative careers.*

If we want the best to teach, to pursue their dreams of inspiring our youth, we have to remove the financial barrier of low pay.

To be pointed, if we as a society really thought teachers mattered, perhaps teachers would earn *more* than the typical college graduate, no? In fact, in a later chapter, I offer evidence that that's exactly what's needed to get our schools working again. Teacher salaries should be 10 or 20 percent *above* average alternatives available to college graduates, not 31 percent below. For now, think of the average level earned outside teaching as a useful benchmark, but *not* as a target.

Keeping in mind that we're interested in teacher pay because it helps us understand who becomes a teacher and who remains a teacher (and implicitly, how we might change the "who"), I want to emphasize four aspects of teacher pay. The first aspect is historical. In the old days, teacher pay was much closer to salaries available to college graduates in alternative careers. It being unlikely that the nonfinancial attraction of teaching has increased, today's lower relative pay helps explain why we no longer attract and keep enough really good teachers.

The second aspect of pay I'll discuss is gender. The teaching corps is predominantly female, and for women the world of work today has opened to an enormous array of opportunities that were formerly closed off. In the past, education was sheltered from competition for women in the workforce. No longer.

The third topic in this chapter is the uniform pay schedule. Unlike most professions, teacher pay doesn't vary much with how well you do your job. It's not just that there is a predetermined scale, it's also that there isn't an opportunity for promotion to a higher job classification as there is in many other careers. I'll discuss the uniform pay schedule in part because it's unfamiliar to a lot of folks and in part because the uniformity is in and of itself a problem.

This uniformity is also the source of the fourth issue—teachers' salaries have insufficient *skewness.* "Skewness" is a technical term from statistics, but for our purposes, skewness can be thought of as a measure of the difference between high pay and average pay within a profession. In most professions, a high-flier earns quite a bit more than the typical pay rate. Even someone who's pretty good, although not exceptional, earns a fair amount more than average pay. Teaching is different. Really good teachers and average teachers earn pretty close to the same amount. Teaching salaries have less skewness than do salaries in other professions. So put yourself in the position of someone who can be an unusually good teacher or an unusually good something else. The teacher path gets you nothing extra for your extra qualities and the alternative career does. When choosing a career, if you're extra talented or extra hardworking you have an extra reason to choose not to be a teacher.

In other words while the average pay gap is big, the pay gap toward the upper end is even bigger. I've said the average gap is 31 percent. If we compare pay for relatively well-compensated teachers to pay for relatively well-compensated nonteacher college graduates, say at the 75th percentile, the gap doubles to 60 percent.[2]

If you want a second take away from this chapter, it's the uniformity versus skewness issue. At the 75th percentile of the pay scale, teachers need a *60* percent raise to catch up to alternative careers.

HISTORY

Teacher pay is very low compared to other college graduates. This hasn't always been true, at least not to the extent that it is now. In 1940, young women teachers earned the median salary for female college graduates.[3] By 1950 earnings had risen to the 55th percentile. But in 2000, the earnings of young female teachers had fallen to about the 37th percentile, so almost two-thirds of young women with college degrees were earning more than women teachers. Male teachers have always earned less than college-educated men in other professions but here too the gap has increased, with young male teacher salaries having fallen over the six decades from the 38th to the 29th percentile.[4]

The story of teacher salaries over the last forty years has some two main themes. Theme one relates to gender. From the 1970s through the mid-1980s, teacher salaries improved a little. But they didn't improve enough to offset the opening of the labor market to women. As a result, the teacher/nonteacher salary ratio for men went up a bit

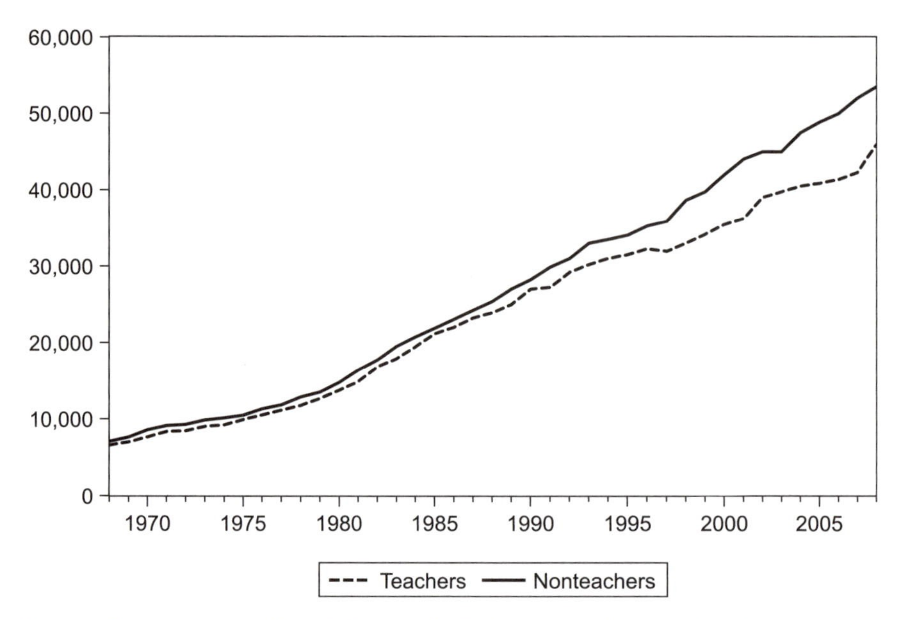

Figure 7 Median College-Educated, Full-time Salaries: Teachers Versus Nonteachers

while the teacher/nonteacher salary ratio for women dropped. Theme two is gender-neutral: starting around 1990, teacher salaries relative to other college-graduate pay fell for both men and women, as outside compensation for both genders rose more quickly than did teacher pay. By 2008, teacher salaries had gone from somewhat behind to way behind.

Since teachers are drawn exclusively from the college-educated, the pay of nonteacher college graduates is the right comparison group for potential teachers making a career choice. In Figure 7, I show teacher salaries compared to the salaries of other college-educated, full-time workers over the last four decades. The bigger the gap between the lines, the bigger the gap between outside opportunities and teacher pay.[5] While teacher pay has been below average for more than forty years, the last two decades have seen a further, slow-but-steady deterioration.

GENDER

Teaching is, and has been for many years, a predominantly female occupation. There are no doubt many reasons for this; one being that

SEX EVEN GETS IN THE WAY OF A SIMPLE NUMERICAL CALCULATION

The 31 percent pay gap reflects the gender composition of the workforce. But as everyone knows, the teaching workforce is disproportionately female. There's no perfect method of accounting for the gender imbalance. Ignoring gender, and using the 31 percent figure probably overstates the true gap. If we weight the pay gaps in rough proportion to the gender composition of teaching—three-quarters women and one-quarter men—the pay gap is estimated to be 17 percent.

teaching is a relatively child rearing–friendly profession and women continue to be the primary providers of child care. Nonetheless, a big part of the explanation for the gender composition is that the teacher/nonteacher wage gap is larger for men than for women. In the economy as a whole, men earn substantially more money than women. In teaching, the gender wage gap is quite small. Since men must accept a much larger pay gap with other men by teaching instead of picking another career, relatively few of them become teachers. Ignoring gender, the teacher/nonteacher pay gap is 31 percent. The teacher/nonteacher gap for women is only 7 percent, while the male gap is 46 percent![6]

More than just salaries have changed for women. The opening of the workplace since the 1970s has meant that women now have opportunities in professions that were formerly closed to them. Once, professions for college-educated women were pretty much limited to teaching and nursing. Today, most professions are mostly open, both by law and in reality. For example, the majority of law school students are women, as are nearly half of entrants to medical school. In the past, discrimination and cultural norms built a wall around teaching, protecting the education profession from competition for working women. The opening of the market to all means that education now must compete on a more level playing field without its historic, artificial advantage.

SKEWNESS

So far, this is a discussion about average salaries. While that's the most important element, looking at averages hides an important piece of the story. Most nonteaching professions offer a chance at substantially higher earnings for those who are most successful. As previously mentioned, statisticians call this skewness. Teaching salaries are insufficiently "skewey."

A comparison between high and average salaries for teaching and other professions is instructive. In teaching, a moderately high salary (75th percentile) is 22 percent above the median. For social workers, the jump is 28 percent. For paralegals it's 36 percent and for human resource managers it's 43 percent. For lawyers, the jump from median to moderately high is 60 percent![7]

In looking at pay ranges, I am by no means talking about the highest pay in any of these professions. The 75th percentile is the middle of the top half. That's why I've called the comparison point "moderately

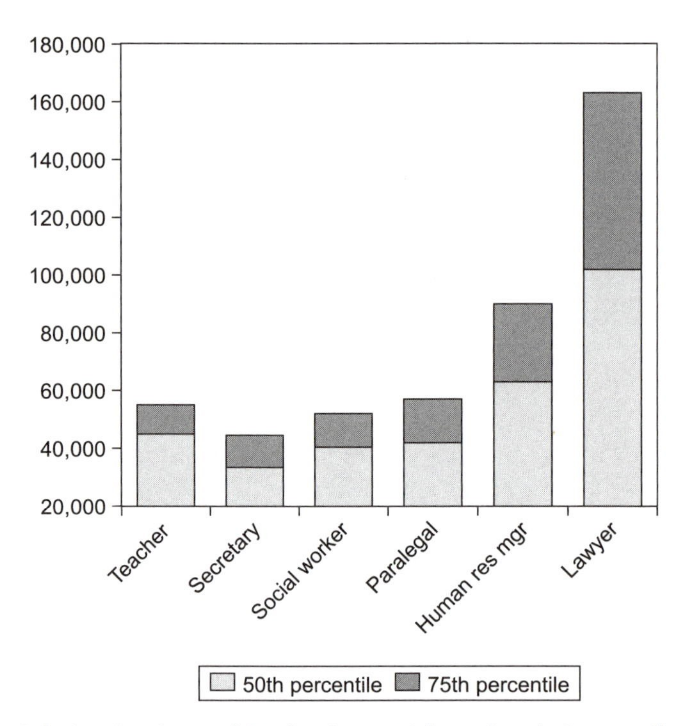

Figure 8 Salaries for Several Professions: 50th and 75th Percentiles of College-Educated Workers. (Author's calculations from March 2008 Current Population Survey. Sample is college-educated workers aged 22 through 64 reporting positive wages and full-time employment.)

high." Moderately high is a target that many of us aspire to, and aspire to realistically.

On the theory that one picture is worth a thousand words, I show the moderately high to average pay gap in several professions in Figure 8. The top part of each bar shows the gap between a median and 75th percentile salary. The bottom part of the bar is the median salary. You can see that the range of teacher salaries is notably more narrow than in other professions. Even among secretaries, who earn less on average than teachers, the range between average and moderately high is greater. The same is true of social workers. All these professions are more "skewey."

The compression of teacher salaries has two bad effects on the teaching corps: the "selection effect" and the "no incentive effect." Because of the selection effect, potential teachers who are particularly able/entrepreneurial/ambitious/saddled-with-many-mouths-to-feed look at how far they can advance financially, see that the answer is "not far," and select another profession.

Every profession needs to attract a mix of "get the work done" folks, and "take the lead" types. "Take the lead" types tend to be attracted by the possibility for career advancement—and corresponding pay increases. Fortunately, teaching has some inherent, nonfinancial rewards, so we get a good handful of the latter despite the financial disadvantage. Unfortunately, a good handful is not enough "take the lead" types to get the job done.

The second bad effect of compressed teacher salaries is the "no incentive effect." Once inside the system, good work—whether that means putting in extra hours or figuring out how to change an ineffective pedagogic approach—gets you a warm, fuzzy feeling of doing better by your kids, but it doesn't get another dime in your pocket. Warm and fuzzy feelings matter, but money is the usual major workplace motivator. At least, that's how the economy works for everyone except teachers.

Interestingly, starting salaries for teachers are not *too* bad. Teachers start their career near parity with other college graduates. However, a large wage gap opens with age as pay rises across a career much more strongly outside teaching than it does for teachers.

You can see in Figure 9 that, fresh out of college, teacher salaries start out roughly even with pay for college graduates overall.[8] Starting in the late twenties, a wage gap opens. The gap gets wider and wider through the prime earning years. This growing gap is one

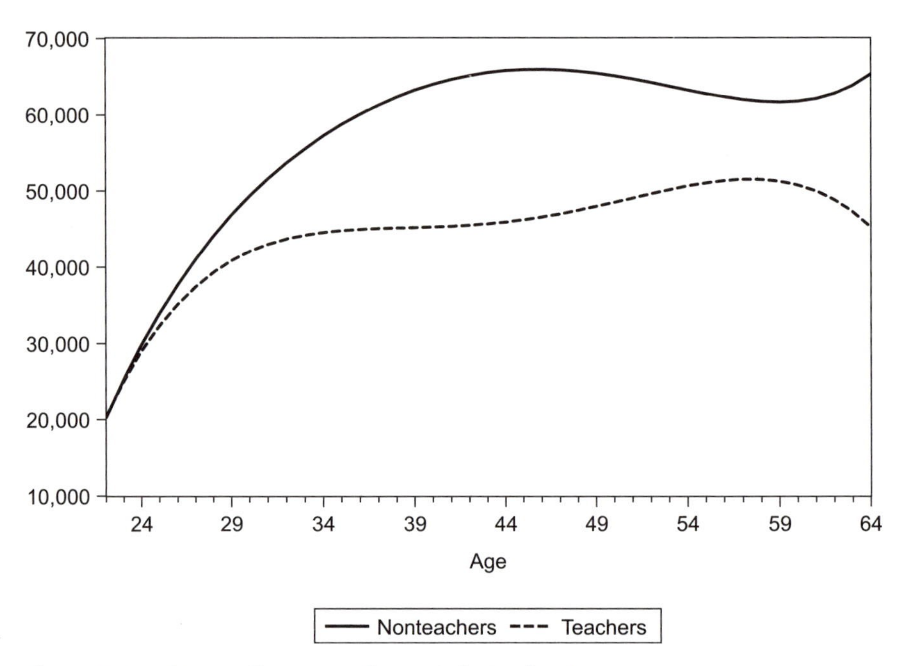

Figure 9 Median College-Graduate Salaries by Age

reason that teachers with good opportunities outside education are particular likely to leave the field. The teachers left behind are a combination of those who find working with kids especially rewarding and those who don't have attractive outside opportunities. One research team found that inflation-adjusted salaries of women teachers grew on average 17 percent between the beginning and end of a career, compared to growth of 50 percent for other college graduates.[9]

Another research team put this in a particularly pointed way. "A hypothetical female graduate from a top university with a technical degree . . . may actually earn more as a public school teacher upon graduation . . . but by the time she has about 10 years of labor market experience, she is estimated to be making over $10,000 less than she would in the non-teacher labor market."[10]

A Little Diatribe about the Short Hours Myth

One inevitable response to calls for higher teacher salaries is that teachers don't work very many hours a day, get summers off, and so on. The argument goes that although overall salaries are low, teachers are actually paid a high wage relative to the hours they spend on the job. Perhaps this is an interesting argument—albeit not a very accurate one, as I'll show you in a second—if you think salaries ought to be set according to some notion of fairness. If you're *Profit*-oriented, you pay enough to get the quality of motivated labor you need to get the job done.[11] Brain surgeons are well paid despite not spending many hours at the operating table. Microsoft pays well because it needs to in order to get skilled workers, not because it feels good. So whether the hourly wage rate for teachers is high or low by some abstract standard is fundamentally irrelevant. The point is, today's wage rate isn't high enough to get the teachers we need.

Here's another way of saying this: teachers aren't working fewer hours than they used to. They used to have summer off; they still have summer off. That hasn't changed. Irrespective of how many hours you think teachers work, the number of hours has remained steady over time while relative pay has dropped.[12] If you look at weekly pay during the school year, that *has* changed. One estimate is

Linda Darling-Hammond makes the point dramatically with what might be an honest help-wanted ad for teachers circa 1996:[13]

WANTED

College graduate with academic major (master's degree preferred). Excellent communication/leadership skills required. Challenging opportunity to serve 150 clients daily on a tight schedule, developing up to five different products each day to meet individual needs, while adhering to multiple product specifications. Adaptability helpful, since suppliers cannot always deliver to goods on time, incumbent must arrange for own support services, and customers rarely know what they want. Ideal candidate will enjoy working in isolation from colleagues. This diversified position allows employee to exercise typing, clerical, law enforcement, and social work skills between assignments and after hours. Typical work week: 50 hours. Special nature of the work precludes amenities such as telephones or computers, but work has many intrinsic rewards. Starting salary $24,661, rising to $36,495 after only 15 years.

that compared to other college graduates, the weekly pay of public school teachers fell 10 percent between 1996 and 2006.

In addition to stories about the number of hours that teachers work being pretty much irrelevant, they're also mostly wrong. Like many workers, teachers are required to work thirty-five to forty hours per week. But like many professionals, teachers put in far more hours than are required, averaging about fifty hours per week during the school year.[14] Ninety-nine percent of teachers put in uncompensated time grading papers, supervising clubs, and on other really fun activities such as bus duty.[15]

While the school year has fewer work days, about 188 (official) days for teachers versus 239 work days in a year-round job, the average teacher works more hours a week.[16] The two balance, so that teachers work roughly the same number of hours per year, something on the order of 1900, as other workers.[17]

The short teacher-hours canard is mostly a red herring. That doesn't mean that the current arrangement of working hours should be regarded as immutable. Let's be frank, there *are* teachers who drift in with the morning bell and take off like a shot at dismissal. It can't be good for morale for the fifty-hour-a-week teacher to see she takes home the same-sized paycheck as the laggards. Or to put this more positively, the system should offer extra money to those who regularly do extra work.

In the academic department in which I work, our administrative staff has a variety of working schedules both with regard to hours worked per week and time off during the summer—and of course, their pay reflects the quantity of work. (While the quantity differs, the quality is excellent across the board.[18]) Why don't teachers have similar choices? The answer lies in the uniform salary schedule.

Several well-regarded charter schools are set up for longer teacher hours and higher pay. KIPP (Knowledge Is Power Program) teachers work 7:15 in the morning to 5:00 in the evening plus some Saturdays, and earn an extra $10,000 a year. The TEP Charter School in New York City plans 8:00 in the morning to 6:00 at night workdays and plus six weeks of summer work—with salaries starting at $125,000 per year.[19]

THE UNIFORM SALARY SCHEDULE

Teachers, unlike most other professionals, aren't offered a career option that allows them to strive to improve their financial situation. This has as much to do with *how* teachers are paid as it does with *how much* they are paid. Fortunately, understanding teacher pay is made simple by the fact that almost all teachers are paid according to how long they've been teaching and whether they've gone back to school after their bachelor's degree. Schedules vary some from district to district, and sometimes there are a few dollars in sweeteners for hard-to-find specialties or extra duties. But basically, experience and degrees earned determine the bottom line.

The chart shows the Washington State teacher salary schedule for the 2008–09 school year. (Individual Washington State districts deviate from the state schedule, often adding local funds, but the basic layout of the pay schedule is pretty standard.)

2008–2009 Washington State Teacher Pay Schedule

Years of Service	BA	MA	PhD
0	34,426	41,274	46,369
1	34,889	41,733	46,847
2	35,331	42,195	47,321
3	35,786	42,632	47,801
4	36,232	43,091	48,295
5	36,693	43,558	48,791
6	37,167	44,036	49,264
7	37,999	44,932	50,265
8	39,218	46,341	51,797
9		47,765	53,374
10		49,265	54,993
11		50,807	56,656
12		52,410	58,389
13		54,069	60,162
14		55,778	62,003
15		57,227	63,615
16 or more		58,372	64,887

What you see is that Washington pays a fair amount more for extra experience and a fair amount more for extra education. What you don't see is any reward to being a better teacher, because there isn't any.

Let's talk about what's in this pay schedule that probably shouldn't be there, and then talk about what's missing.

If performance doesn't make a difference for an individual teacher's pay, what does? The first thing that matters is experience. In the case of Washington, teachers get small raises early in their careers, big raises midcareer, and then top out when a teacher hits sixteen years experience, usually at age forty or so. (Remember that all of these raises are in addition to cost-of-living increases or other across-the-board changes.)

Do we pay more for experience because experienced teachers are more successful with their students? This best scientific evidence is, not really. Statistical work has come to two conclusions about teachers and experience:[20]

- Beginning teachers are really lousy on average.[21]
- Teachers who make it through the first few years have pretty much learned the knack for the job. Once over the hump, further experience doesn't lead to much further improvement.

The typical new teacher underperforms massively when it comes to student achievement. Estimates vary, but a reasonable number is that students fall behind by the equivalent of a month or two when they spend a year with a novice rather than with an experienced teacher.[22] It seems to take about three years for new teachers to really catch on. Once they have gotten over startup bumps, there isn't much further improvement on average.

The key term here is "on average." Some teachers catch on quite quickly. My first-grade teacher, Mrs. Zeigler, was both new to the job and a great teacher from day one. Others never really take off. Paying for experience turns out to be no substitute for paying for a job well done.

This appears to suggest something of a conundrum. Figure 9 shows that the teacher salary gap is larger for teachers with more experience than for new teachers. At the same time, the evidence is that the benefits of experience flatten out early in a career. The former seems to argue for steeper raises with age while the latter seems to suggest that raises for experience are already too high.

The conundrum is more apparent than real. In most intellectual jobs, like teaching, people get better at their job with experience; the higher pay reflects increased ability. I suspect that in a teacher pay system where ability was rewarded, we'd find that more teachers would continue to add to their skills far into their careers. Pay would reflect this, and we'd still see that on average, more experienced teachers earned more. But for a very different reason than at present.

One can argue the merits of paying for experience. It does have some advantage in holding down teacher turnover, which is clearly desirable given that new teachers take a while to catch on. In contrast, paying for higher degrees is nothing more than good intentions gone wrong. Responding to financial incentives, the majority of teachers now have a master's degree. The scientific evidence on the value of this is quite clear: teachers with master's do no better by their students than teachers without. You can see above that Washington State pays about a 15 percent bonus for getting a master's and another 10 percent for a PhD.[23] Arguably, in light of the current low level of teacher salaries, any excuse to raise pay should be seized upon. However, in terms of direct student benefit, this is money down the drain. (As someone who's spent the last twenty-five years training PhDs, I am completely baffled as to why having a doctorate is thought to be a useful qualification for teaching elementary school.)

Children would be better off if the money spent on paying for advanced degrees was handed out instead to successful teachers. That said, there are a few caveats to keep in mind. First, teacher pay is determined more by politics than it is by market forces. Paying for advanced degrees is appealing to taxpayers, presumably because they believe (incorrectly) that advanced degrees get better teachers. It has served as an acceptable reason to raise average teacher salaries, even if the degrees don't improve teaching. Second, we—"we" meaning the representatives of the taxpayers—made an implicit deal with current teachers that if they went back to school we'd raise their pay. While we should cut way back on paying for credentials going forward, reneging on an existing deal is not good public policy. Extra pay for degrees needs to be honored for current teachers. Finally while most current higher-degree programs don't make teachers any better, that doesn't mean that more training can't help. If teachers were rewarded for success, they would begin to seek out those programs that really do work. It is entirely possible that teachers who do more continuing education will still be paid more, not as payment for the credential but because the education itself helped them improve their professional skills.

Paying for master's degrees is a mistake, but there is a policy lesson to be learned from it nonetheless. Some people seem think that teachers don't respond to financial incentives, apparently on the theory that teachers are warm, fuzzy, public-spirited types drawn from a different species than the rest of us humans. In reality, we see that in order to increase their pay, the majority of teachers are willing to spend thousands of dollars and hundreds of hours away from their families earning advanced degrees. Surprise! Teachers do respond to financial incentives, just like the rest of us. In later chapters, I look at how such incentives can be designed to achieve better results.

OTHER SALARY ARRANGEMENTS

It's not quite true that good teachers don't get compensated. What is true is that good teachers don't get compensated with *money*. Instead, they get compensated with easier assignments.

Some teachers love a challenge. But while turning around the hard-to-reach kid is the stuff of movie legends, teachers on average are just like the rest of us; all else equal, they prefer pleasant working conditions, a supportive environment, and, frankly, easier-to-teach students. With minor exceptions, teacher pay is the same whether the work is hard or easy. Absent an incentive to pick the hard slog, they tend to go for easy. You might call this "assignment compensation," as a substitute for financial compensation.

Assignment compensation gets implemented by giving novice teachers undesirable assignments and letting more experienced teachers move to more desirable jobs, although it's not part of any official policy. Unfortunately, "novice" tends to go along with "not yet such a good teacher" and "undesirable assignment" tends to go along with "students who need help the most." In Missouri schools, first-year teachers were located at schools with a 6 percent higher number of students on free-or-reduced lunch programs. If you look at teachers with less than three years experience, the number was even larger: 11 percent more free-or-reduced-lunch students. Similarly, novice teachers in the Houston school district were assigned to schools with 83 percent free-or-reduced-lunch students, compared to the district average of about 73 percent.[24] Interestingly, the assignment of inexperienced teachers to poor students results from within-district assignment practices rather than which districts teachers sign up with.[25]

Teachers who stick with the profession are mobile, changing schools and sometimes changing districts. This very high level of mobility leads to the second mechanism producing assignment compensation: experienced teachers move to easier assignments. One study tracking essentially every fourth- and fifth-grade teacher in Florida found that over a five-year period, 18 percent had changed schools and 4 percent had changed districts (with 27 percent no longer teaching in any Florida public school). When Florida teachers moved, even within a district, they typically moved to higher-performing schools with lower African American enrollments and fewer students receiving free-or-reduced-lunch.[26] (While we're supposed to be contrasting assignment with financial compensation, I can't help but note that when Florida teachers changed districts they moved to better-paying ones.) Similar work in Texas showed that teachers in Houston move to schools where students do better on standardized tests.[27] Yet another research team, studying North Carolina fifth-grade teachers, summarized their findings: "teachers with more experience, degrees from more competitive colleges, and advanced degrees tend to teach at schools serving more affluent, higher achieving and whiter populations. . . . even within schools, teachers with stronger credentials tend to teach more affluent students."[28]

None of this is criticism of the dedication of teachers. One group of teachers who are indisputably dedicated are the young college graduates employed by Teach For America (TFA). Selected from top colleges after having earned excellent grades, they sign up for minimum two-year teaching stints in tough schools. These young people could certainly make more money and find easier work! Nonetheless, the evidence from Houston is that, just like other teachers, TFA teachers who stay in teaching tend to transfer out of the most challenging schools into ones with higher achieving students. In fact, because TFA teachers are especially sought after—the evidence from Houston is that TFAers are unusually effective teachers—the test score jump from starting schools to the schools to which they transfer is as big or bigger for TFA teachers as for their non-TFA peers.[29]

Since we don't reward teachers monetarily, we end up rewarding teachers by moving them away from the students and out of the schools where they are needed the most.

Linking pay to performance has become increasingly common in the private sector, where the fraction of workers eligible for performance pay rose from 38 percent in the late 1970s to 45 percent in the late 1990s. Both the level and increase in performance pay over this period were greater among salaried workers, rising from 45 to nearly 60 percent.[30]

Almost all teachers are paid according to a simple schedule much like the one shown earlier for Washington State. *But there are exceptions!* Only 6 percent of traditional public schools reward teaching excellence with higher pay, but 36 percent of charter schools and 43 percent of private, nonreligious schools do so.[31] Additionally, about 8 percent of traditional public schools increase pay for teachers certified by the National Board for Professional Teaching Standards, a topic we'll return to later.

We've just seen that if you're a public school teacher, your pay is probably determined pretty mechanically, varying with the district where you teach, the number of years you've been in the classroom, and your education level. For college-educated professionals outside the public schools, life is usually quite different. Most professionals have a financial incentive to do a better job, a financial incentive that includes raises and bonuses on the one hand, and promotions into a new job on the other. The issue of promotions complicates thinking about teacher pay. One simple point is that in the private sector many a nominal promotion is largely an excuse for recognizing superior performance with little real change in duty. Since there's no parallel mechanism for teachers, the relative range of salaries for teaching is even narrower than the private sector range once title upgrades are accounted for. So the figures we've seen for skewness, which treat different titles outside teaching as different jobs, probably understate the real gap between average and moderately high pay.

The average principal earns 70 percent more than the average teacher and has eight years experience as a principal after thirteen years work as a teacher.[32]

A teacher who performs well enough to get promoted into a raise also gets promoted out of teaching and into administration. Much as we badly need great principals, there's something wrong with a system in which the only way to get ahead is to move away from students.

WHERE DOES THIS LEAD US?

We're have to pay teachers a lot better than we do today. We also have to work out a system that's more sophisticated than the one-size-fits-all, uniform pay schedule. What this is going to cost and how to be smart about how we do it is the subject of the next several chapters.

4

Raises!

There's very little incentive outside of pure altruism [to go into teaching].

Arne Duncan, then CEO of the Chicago Public Schools, now Secretary of Education[1]

Couching the discussion in the usual $1,000–2,000 increments so commonly proposed by state lawmakers and school boards does not begin to ameliorate the problems in teacher recruitment/retention or students outcomes. . . . it appears that increases on the order of $10,000–15,000, on average—depending on the state, will have the greatest effects on teacher and student outcomes.

Constance Bond, education researcher[2]

Teachers make the difference, and if we want more teachers to make more of a difference, we're going to have to pay them accordingly. Higher teacher salaries is the *sine qua non* of reinvigorating our schools. But simply saying "pay more" is a platitude, not a plan. To go operational, we need to answer the "how much" question. That's our first task in this chapter. How much will it cost to reinvigorate the teaching corps so that the average teacher looks like today's pretty good teacher, or more quantitatively, to boost teacher success from the 50th to the 70th percentile? (We'll need to be smart about raising salaries. "How" matters as much as "how much." I'll talk about "how" in detail in the next four chapters.)

I think the fact that higher salaries lead to better work is dead obvious. That's certainly the way it works in the economy at large.

TALKING ABOUT RAISING SALARIES ISN'T NEW

Matthew Miller, in *The 2% Solution,* proposed a 50 percent pay hike for the top half of teachers, plus 50 percent for teachers in low-income schools. In broad stroke, that's not too different from what's being proposed here.[3]

Nonetheless, there's a certain myth that teaching is different. Perhaps teachers and potential teachers, unlike the rest of us, ignore financial motivation. To put the myth to rest, in the second part of the chapter I'll go over the evidence on the response to higher salaries in education.

Figuring out salary changes isn't an exact science, but in what follows, you'll see that 40 percent is about right. I approach the evidence from several different angles. Some come in a little lower than 40 percent and others come in somewhat higher. If someone wants to argue for 35 percent or 45 percent, that's fine. But if someone tells you that a 5 percent raise will fix our schools, or that we just *have* to double teacher salaries, they're in the wrong ballpark.

The bottom line is that we need raises that are large, but not enormous. (In Chapter 12, Payback!, we'll see that while the required raises are large, they are likely to be self-financing.) Now let me show the evidence behind that 40 percent figure.

DOES A 40 PERCENT RAISE SOUND LIKE A LOT?

Here's what Tennessee Republican Lamar Alexander said two decades ago, as reported in *Education Next*.

> Governor Alexander, who would go on to become secretary of education under President George H. W. Bush and is now a U.S. senator, was more colloquial in his description, calling the [Tennessee] program "an old-fashioned horse trade" with teachers. Taxpayers said to teachers, "The state will pay you up to *70 percent more* based on your performance if you'll promise to be evaluated every five years."[4]

THE HISTORICAL APPROACH

I'll start by taking a historical approach to analyzing teacher pay, asking how large a raise it would take to restore teacher salaries to the way they used to be. The challenging part is deciding what the current equivalent really looks like. One possible target is to return pay for a teaching career to the same level of financial attractiveness compared to the rest of the workforce that it was on some date in the past.[5]

Of course, looking at salaries fifty years ago ignores the revolution in the job market for college-educated women. The expansion of opportunities in the 1970s and thereafter means a huge increase in competition for women professionals. Teaching (plus nursing) is no longer the only game in town for well-educated women. This argues that relative pay for women needs to be higher than in the past if we're to attract the same caliber of teacher, because talented women simply have more and better-compensated options than they used to. When we look at the change in relative teacher salaries over time, realize that we have to do somewhat better than just restoring salaries to how they used to be.

A lot has changed in sixty-plus years. Nonetheless, history may help get us some outer bounds. I'll show you that a 10 percent raise won't get us back to historical levels, while a 100 percent increase would be way beyond anything seen in the past.

In 1940, teachers earned more than the typical college graduate. Female teachers earned at the 69th percentile of women college graduates; in other words, they earned more than two-thirds of college-educated women.[6] Male teachers earned at the 53rd percentile of the male, college-educated wage distribution. In 1940, teaching was not a bad-paying job. Having said that, there is no magical reason for picking 1940 as the comparison year. At the next census, in 1950, female teachers had fallen to the 55th percentile and men to the 36th.

By 2008, teachers' salaries had fallen to about the 37th percentile. Or, returning to the gender breakdown, to the 29th percentile for men and the 46th percentile for women. Turning the numbers around, I calculated the increase needed to restore teachers to the same relative position in the college-educated wage distribution they had in 1940 or in 1950, done separately for women and men. (You can see the results visually in Figure 10. A 40 percent raise would bring women to the 1940 standard plus a smidgeon, but a 50 percent raise would be needed to restore men to their 1940 position. If we chose 1950 for a

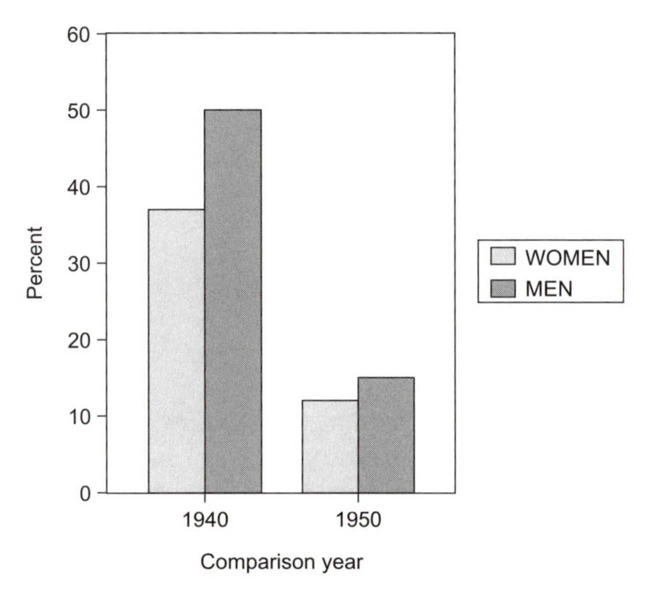

Figure 10 Percentage Increase in Teacher Salaries Required to Restore Teachers to Equivalent Positions in the College-Educated Wage Distribution. (Author's calculations from March 2008 Current Population Survey. See Technical Appendix.)

comparison year, a much smaller raise would be required, since by 1950 teachers had already lost significant ground.

TEACHER POSITIONS IN THE COLLEGE-EDUCATED WORK FORCE

Imagine lining up one hundred college-educated people in the labor force in order of their pay. To some extent, those people will also be ordered in terms of ability, ambition, etc. (Things other than talent and hard work determine wages too, but bear with me for a few paragraphs.) Based on your experience, you choose a number in that ranking that you think would have the right amount of talent for a pretty good teacher. You need to be a little hard-nosed—we're not going to pay brain surgeon wages to three million teachers. At the same time, remember that while some people will (and do!) teach for the love of it, we are not going to fill up three million slots on altruism alone.

Okay, have a number? Figure 11 shows where teacher salaries would rank compared to the college-educated workforce for several hypothetical raises. Table 2 provides the same information in numbers instead of a picture.

If your experience tells you that the average college graduate will be a pretty good teacher, then take a look at the second row in Table 2.

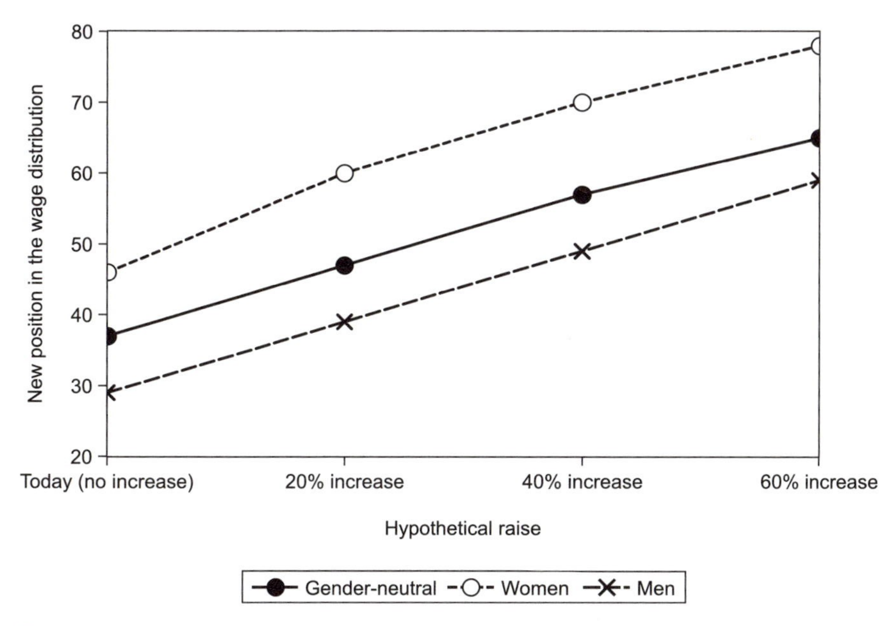

Figure 11 Position of Teacher Salaries among the College-Educated after Several Hypothetical Raises

Table 2 Position of Teacher Salaries among the College-Educated after Several Hypothetical Raises[7]

2008	Gender-neutral	Women	Men
Teacher percentile in wage distribution	37th	46th	29th
Teacher percentile in wage distribution after 20 percent increase	47th	60th	39th
Teacher percentile in wage distribution after 40 percent increase	57th	70th	49th
Teacher percentile in wage distribution after 60 percent increase	65th	78th	59th

A 20 percent pay boost won't quite get there. Or, considering gender, a 20 percent boost will get us woman 6 out of 10 rather than just 5 out of 10, but for men, we only reach 4 out of 10. On the next row, we see that a 40 percent raise gets us to the 57th percentile of the college wage distribution and a 60 percent increase in gets us to where teachers earn more than two-thirds of other college graduates.

Because I think that teaching requires more than the average amount of talent, my pick for a percentage raise is above 20 and below 60. That narrows the range, but it's somewhat subjective. Let's see if we can make a similar comparison with a little more objectivity by adding a new approach to our analysis.

THE COMPARATIVE PROFESSION APPROACH

The previous mental exercise asked you to think about what position in the salary distribution it will take to attract and retain the kinds of teachers we want. Let's now use a more concrete approach. Instead of picking a percentile that matches our subjective sense of how talented teachers need to be, we'll see what some other professions get paid. By looking at comparable professions, we can get a more objective context for what it takes to recruit people with talent levels similar to what we need from teachers.

The table below shows salaries for a number of professions where the typical college graduate earns about the same amount as a

Professions Earning about the Same as Teachers in 2008

Profession	Salary
First-line supervisors, retail sales	$47,000
Surveyors	46,000
Dental hygienists	46,000
Teachers	45,000
Bailiffs and correctional officers	45,000
Clergy	45,000
Food service managers	44,000
Paralegals	42,000

teacher.[8] Today the median teacher earns about the same salary as a member of the clergy.

Remember that we are not looking at fairness here. We're looking at what it takes in a competitive job market to attract a certain level of talent. In principle, how attractive a job is depends on working conditions as well as pay rates. Teachers have much nicer working conditions than correctional officers (in most schools, on most days), so when deciding whether the ratio of pay to desired talent is comparable between teaching and another profession, some informal adjustment is needed for working conditions. Note though that high-paid/high-talent jobs typically come with nicer perks than lesser-paid/lower-talent jobs. So the informal working conditions adjustment to required salary levels is small. We shouldn't expect to save very much on teacher salaries just because it can be a personally rewarding job.[9]

Now that we've seen who earns about the same amount as teachers under the status quo, let's look at what comparables would be after a 40 percent increase. (Remember here that we are looking only at college graduates in the other professions.)

A 40 percent boost would make teacher salaries match more closely to salaries earned by physical therapists and human resource managers and, interestingly, the current pay of educational administrators. These comparable jobs are notable for requiring academic smarts, general people skills, and the ability to deal with people in difficult, stress-laden, one-on-one situations—just like teachers.

For one more set of comparables, let's look at professions that pay 60 percent or greater more than current teacher salaries. What really pops out is that these jobs require a much more advanced level of academic

Professions Earning about 40 Percent More Than Teachers in 2008 (~$63,000)

Profession	Salary
Construction managers	$65,000
Detectives	65,000
Education administrators	65,000
Physical therapists	63,500
Human resource managers	63,000
Police patrol officers	63,000
First-line supervisors of production and operating workers	61,000

Professions Earning 60 Percent+ More Than Teachers in 2008 (~$72,000)

Physicians and surgeons	$150,000
Lawyers, judges	102,000
Pharmacists	100,000
Electrical engineers	80,000
Personal financial advisors	75,000
Management analysts	72,000
Computer programmers	70,000

training than teachers receive. These jobs also involve very high levels of responsibility to others. Teachers are responsible for students, but except on a very bad day—or a very good one—their responsibility for life and property isn't the same as that of a surgeon or a judge.

To my eye, the middle set of comparables (the 40 percent boost group) looks about right. These jobs require both some academic skills (for instance, needing to understand a particular area of legal issues) and strong people skills. That matches well with the requirements for K–12 teachers. In contrast, the first group does not require *both* advanced academic and people skills to the same extent. Jobs in the third group require much more difficult academic training. Matching job characteristics is a standard, although certainly not perfect, approach to salary determination. The examples we've seen support the 40 percent raise number as a sensible target.

We now have a 40 percent target raise. For those who still aren't so sure that higher salaries will help us hire and retain the best teachers, and for those think that teacher salaries and student outcomes aren't linked, let's look at the evidence.

DOES PAYING MORE DRAW BETTER-QUALIFIED TEACHERS INTO THE PROFESSION?

You might think that the answer to the question posed in the title of this section is pretty obvious. If you pay better, you hire better. Still, it would be nice to have scientific confirmation of the link between pay and skills. A recent Australian study by Andrew Leigh[10] tracked the decision to enter teacher training of *every* Australian university entrant for over a decade and a half. Some Australian states offer better pay to teachers than do other states, allowing Leigh to check whether academically able students were more likely to enter teacher training if they lived in a state with higher teacher salaries.

While America and Australia have much in common, Australian universities differ from American universities in one important respect. In Australia, students choose their major when they enter college and stay with it. As a result, the set of entrants who choose teacher training are pretty much the same young people who will become Australia's new teachers four years later. Ninety percent of Australian students attend university in their home state and few move after taking teacher training.

Leigh was able to link up test scores and starting teacher salaries. The result? A 1 percent increase in teacher salaries raises teacher aptitude by 0.6 percentiles. In other words, our proposed 40 percent salary boost would move the teaching pool up 24 percentile points in the ability distribution. You will remember that we found earlier that this salary increase would move teachers 20 percentile points through the income distribution. While academic aptitude and income are not perfectly correlated, and while academic ability is certainly not all that matters for successful teaching,[11] the close match is evidence that the suggested pay increase really will elicit the desired improvement in the teacher pool.

DIRECT EVIDENCE LINKING TEACHER SALARIES AND STUDENT OUTCOMES

We've seen that teachers are the key to better student outcomes and that the ability of teachers does respond to higher salaries. Still, before spending a great deal of money, we should ask whether there is direct evidence that higher salaries lead to better outcomes. There is indeed such evidence.

I'm going to share the evidence on two tightly coupled questions: (1) In general, do higher salaries lead to better student outcomes? And (2) Specifically, do salaries have a big or small effect on learning? The latter question lets us ask how large a salary increase is needed to meet our goal of increasing learning by the equivalent of an additional year of schooling. Answering this latter question means measuring student outcomes by test scores. But test scores are not the only thing we care about. So let's begin with a very careful piece of work that ties teacher salaries to dropout rates and college enrollment.

Salaries, Dropouts, and College Enrollments

The research team of Loeb and Page produced a particularly nuanced study linking higher teacher salaries to better student outcomes, which is helpful for a handful of different reasons.[12] Unlike other studies we'll discuss, Loeb and Page do not look at test scores. Instead they look at what higher teacher salaries do to dropout rates and to college enrollments. The first thing we get from their research is reassurance that raising salaries works on more than just a single indicator of student achievement. Even though test scores are not always a reliable indicator for a particular student, they're the best objective indicator for averages of large numbers of students. Nonetheless, some people just don't like standardized tests. Having positive results about dropout rates and college enrollment provides additional support and validation that increasing salaries will improve student outcomes in a holistic sense.

Students who drop out are, obviously, at the low end of the educational success ladder. At the other end, students enrolling in college have climbed well up on that same ladder. Looking at dropouts and the college-bound tells us something about the broad-spectrum effect of raising teacher salaries that we don't learn from looking at averages. While most other studies look at average results, Loeb and Page provide information specific to at-risk students and high-achieving students.

Loeb and Page also show that it's important how one adjusts for alternative labor market opportunities for teachers and for nonfinancial job characteristics. While this may sound like a merely technical detail, it's a critical advance in the science of the subject. A number of earlier of statistical studies (done by very respected researchers) failed to find much link between teacher salaries and student outcomes.[13] Loeb and Page were able to bring together data that previous researchers hadn't had. With this extra information in hand, they found that teacher salaries indeed do have a large effect on student outcomes.

Loeb and Page used four decades of census data to look at differences in salaries and outcomes across states. At the low end of the student achievement spectrum, the authors ask what higher teacher salaries do to the dropout rate, and find strong evidence that higher salaries indeed reduce the number of dropouts.[14] In fact, they estimate that a 10 percent increase in teacher salaries would lower dropout rates by 3 to 4 percent. Projecting this out suggests that a 40 percent increase in teacher salaries would reduce the dropout rate to near zero. While such a projection is an obvious overstatement, it emphasizes how much at-risk students would benefit from better-paid teachers.

What about the high-achieving end? The authors look at whether higher teacher salaries lead to more students enrolling in college. (Roughly, the top half of high school students currently enroll in college.) Here they estimate that a 10 percent increase in teacher salaries would increase enrollment by 1.6 percent. Projecting that again to a 40 percent raise suggests that college enrollment would rise about 10 percent. So, yes, the high-achieving end also benefits substantially, although the increase in college enrollment is less dramatic than the drop-off in the dropout rate.

What's important is that the evidence shows that students benefit from higher teacher salaries *across the spectrum.* The benefits are probably greater for those most in need of a lift up, but everyone moves up a step.

A Look at the Raw Data

In a moment, I'll tell you about more scientific evidence. First, I'd like to show you a simple picture of the relationship between teacher salaries and student outcomes. But I have a dilemma. Careful statistical studies relating teacher salaries to student outcomes have to do a lot more than simply look at raw data if they're to overcome confounding factors. Here's the simplest difficulty. Wealthy areas generally have higher-performing students without regard to teacher quality. Wealthy areas also typically pay teachers more. So simply finding that students perform better where teachers are paid better might be a statistical coincidence. It's hard to control for this kind of confounding factor on a picture. On top of these conceptual issues, it turns out that what the raw data show is sensitive to how you make measurements. For these reasons, you should take our look at the picture below with a grain of salt. In other words, while what you're about to see supports the salary/outcomes link hypothesis, I don't think you should give it too heavy a weight. In contrast, the serious scientific studies I'll get to in a minute *are* convincing.

Figure 12 shows fourth-grade reading scores on the vertical axis plotted against teacher salaries on the horizontal axis.[15] The reading score is from the fourth grade National Assessment of Educational Progress (NAEP), a low-stakes test constructed to be comparable over time and place. Teacher salaries are measured relative to average college-educated incomes within the state as a rough control for the position of teacher salaries relative to the state income distribution. The position of each state is shown by its two-letter abbreviation. The line through the data gives a statistical fit to the data.

You will immediately note in Figure 12 that salaries explain a great deal about student outcomes—the line drawn through the points slopes sharply upwards—but not everything. You will probably also note the enormous range of student outcomes across states. The average Vermont fourth grader reads at fifth grade level. The average Louisiana fourth grader reads at third grade level. Even after adjusting for higher income levels in Vermont, Vermont teachers are paid 44 percent more than teachers in Louisiana. These are enormous differences.

Vermont is, of course, a much wealthier state than Louisiana. A glance at Figure 12 shows that wealthy states (e.g., Massachusetts and Connecticut) tend to be at the top of the chart with high scores and

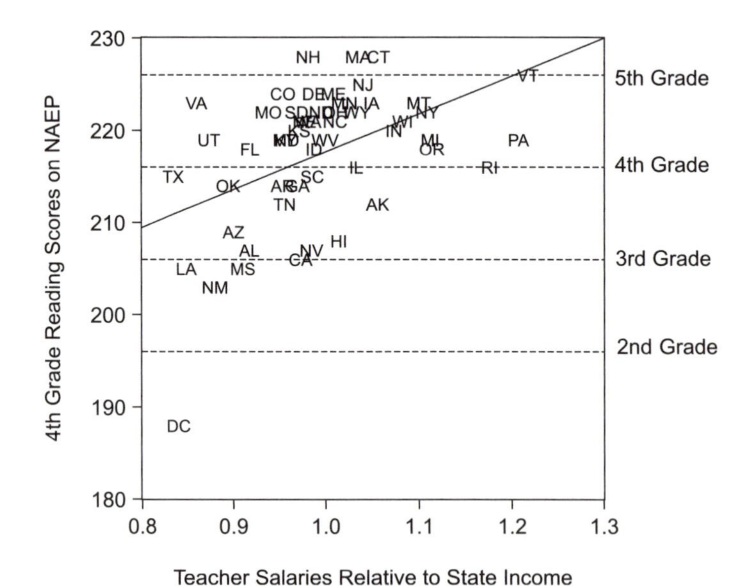

Figure 12 Reading Scores Versus Teacher Salaries across States

> In 2000, Texas had the lowest relative teacher salaries, 16 percent below average nonteacher, college-educated salaries. Washington, DC and Louisiana were right behind Texas. Vermont salaries were the highest, 22 percent above average.

poorer states (e.g., Mississippi and Georgia) tend to be at the bottom. So maybe part of the apparent effect of teacher salaries is picking up the coincidental effect of wealth. You can't easily fix the confounding effect of wealth in a picture, but you can in a statistical model. I've done that, and find that a 40 percent salary increase would lead to more than a one grade-level improvement.[16] And that's by fourth grade, not twelfth!

MORE SCIENTIFIC EVIDENCE

Several statistical studies provide careful evidence on the link between teacher salaries and student outcomes. I'll begin with a recent Columbia University Teachers College PhD dissertation.[17]

Cross-state Linkage between Teacher Salaries and Student Test Scores

Constance Bond modeled student outcomes and teacher salaries across states in the same general fashion as I did in the previous section—the difference being that Bond included controls for poverty, parents' education, and race. Such controls go a long way toward eliminating potential contamination from other factors that differ across states. Along the way, Bond finds strong evidence that higher teacher salaries greatly reduce dropout rates and increase teacher retention, but I'm going to concentrate on her findings on student test scores.

In Table 3 I've translated Bond's findings to show the effect of a 40 percent salary boost in terms of student outcomes measured in terms of grade equivalents.[18] As is usually true in statistical work, one ends up with a range of outcomes. Row (1) suggests a gain of 0.4 of a year by eighth grade. Since eighth grade is two-thirds of the way through school, that projects out to 0.6 years gain by high school graduation—which is a little under our goal of one extra year of learning across K–12. The estimate in

Table 3 Summary of Findings from *Do Teachers Matter?*

	Effect of 40% increase in teacher salaries	Test	Salary measure
(1)	0.4 grade level equivalents	8th grade math	Teacher/nonteacher salary gap at BA level
(2)	0.8 grade level equivalents	8th grade math	Teacher salaries at master's level
(3)	0.5 grade level equivalents	4th grade reading	Teacher salaries at master's level

row (2) is twice as large, projecting out to a 1.2 year gain—which is a little over our goal. The final row estimates a half-year gain in reading by fourth grade, well ahead of schedule.[19]

In other words, our 40 percent number is pretty much in the middle of my calculations based on Bond's work. Bond's own summary of her evidence reads, "While it is difficult to determine the actual dollar amount of the salary increase, it is clear that teaching salaries must be competitive with other professions in order to attract the required quality and quantity. At the present time, teacher salaries would need to be raised 40 percent, on average, in order to meet this goal."[20]

Teacher Salaries and Tracking Individual Student Achievement

The research team of Aksoy and Link used data from the National Longitudinal Education Study that let them track individual students, allowing them to control for differences in characteristics and behaviors of individual students.[21] This is a very powerful approach because it takes care both of observable factors (parents' education) and unobservable ones (family attitudes about school) that affect student learning. The researchers weren't actually looking for the effect of teacher salaries—they wanted to know if spending more time on homework and less time watching TV leads to higher test scores. (Guess what? They do.) Along the way, they also estimated the effect of teacher salaries on 2,756 students in eighth through twelfth grade.

Aksoy and Link find that raising teacher salaries has a statistically significant effect on student outcomes.[22] More usefully, we can compare the effect of higher salaries to the effect of other changes. For example, an increase in teacher salary has somewhere between three and nine times the effect of an equal increase in family income. Or a one thousand dollar increase in salary (about 5 percent) has roughly the same effect as cutting TV time by half an hour a day.

The tests the researchers studied aren't normed as grade level equivalents. So I've made the best translation I can. Projecting a 40 percent salary increase appears to cause a one and three-quarter to three year grade equivalent gain by the end of high school.[23] Even allowing for some translation error, this research suggests that our goal is eminently achievable.

PUTTING IT ALL TOGETHER

We've looked at some evidence that raising teacher salaries raises student achievement. I've asked you to focus on 40 percent as a target. This number lies somewhere in the middle of estimates of what is needed. A 40 percent average salary boost isn't out of the realm of experience. Put it this way: if the state with the lowest current teacher salaries raised pay 40 percent, it would still be behind the pay rates in 14 other states.[24]

These statistical studies provide critically important confirmation, but the relative wage evidence earlier in the chapter is what really gets at the heart of the matter. We simply are not going to get millions of pretty good teachers without paying them a wage that is competitive with what they could make elsewhere. Paying somewhat above the average pay for college graduates looks about right.

5

Paying for Success: The View from Thirty Thousand Feet

> One would think that schools with better results . . . would be widely imitated, that successful programs of any sort would be quickly identified by school boards and superintendents, copied instantly, and quickly improved upon. But nothing of the sort actually happens, as countless innovators, philanthropists, and government planners have discovered. Through decades of educational history in this country, programs of unquestioned effectiveness have spread very slowly, if at all. . . .
>
> The reason is not hard to find. Success in educating students is not reflected in the pay of teachers or principals, nor is it rewarded with opportunities for advancement in the system. These facts are merely indicators of a broader problem. School districts are not performance-oriented organizations. There is no bottom line and there are no rewards for achieving it.
>
> *Ray Marshall and Marc Tucker,* Thinking for a Living[1]

To save our schools, teacher pay must rise significantly, as I've just argued, on the order of a 40 percent increase. But that doesn't mean that we ought to open the fiscal floodgates, hoping that a rush of money will float education higher. We need to channel our spending wisely. We need to pay teachers more, but pay them more in ways that will lure talented people to enter the profession, encourage them to stay and make it a career, and help them to help students succeed.

In other words, our money should serve to (1) recruit and retain the best, and (2) realign incentives so as to reward teachers for working for the best student outcomes. This chapter offers a high-level description of these two mechanisms, and how they are going to drive student success through increased teacher pay. The details of how to do this matter, of course, but I'm going to defer much of the nitty-gritty to the next several chapters. This chapter is about *why* moving to a pay system respectful of these two mechanisms is vital. The chapters that follow are, if you like, the *how* chapters.

In talking about why, keep in mind a fact and a challenge. The *fact* is that the history of educational reform is littered with hundreds of successful reforms, almost all of which have been local and temporary.

These successes never scale up. Reforms thrive under the inspiration of a single charismatic teacher or the leadership of a small team, and then die out after the innovators move on. Without a broad base of teachers with the ability and incentive to run with the ball, educational reform will continue to be a series of one-offs that dazzle, but then fade. The *challenge* is to redesign teacher compensation so that successful reforms translate from one-offs to systemic change. Think of higher pay—channeled through the two mechanisms that will give it the power to recruit, retain, and motivate good teachers—as the bottleneck-remover that allows all other reforms to break out into the major leagues.

Americans are a productive people. Our economy isn't perfect, it isn't always fair, and it certainly can use improvements. Nonetheless, few of us want to dump our basic economic structure. We've found that aligning financial signals with desired goals works pretty well, including working well at getting people into positions where they can be productive.[2] So in broad brush I'm simply going to argue that we arrange teacher pay something closer to the way pay works in most of the economy. To build a first-class organization you have to pay employees well. If you don't, good people won't join up and

THE TWO MECHANISMS

I. Recruit and retain the best possible cadre for the teacher corps.
II. See to it that teachers have "skin in the game"—the game being student success.

your top performers will leave. Once a first-class organization has good people, it finds a way to financially reward those who push forward the organization's goals.

Sure, there's an occasional (usually small-scale) exception to the American system. Being an exception hasn't worked for the teacher corps and it never will. Quite simply, I want to revolutionize teacher pay by making it normal.

MECHANISM I: RECRUIT AND RETAIN THE BEST

How will we recruit and retain the best possible teachers? We'll pay them.

May I rant? No one asks how Microsoft or the New York Yankees hires top talent. They pay for top talent, that's how. Does anyone really think it's the offer of pinstriped uniforms and free spikes that attracts the best to the Yankees? Businesses, whether in high tech or sports, understand that talent costs and we're all pretty much okay with this. Somehow, when it comes to teaching our kids, we expect to pay in warm fuzzy feelings instead of dollars. That's a sad statement about what we *really* value, isn't it?

In every field of endeavor, some great people are attracted because they love the line of work. This group is the icing on the cake, though. The vast majority of us choose a career because we can earn a good living doing something that's a comfortable, personal fit. Teaching probably attracts more folks driven by pure inspiration than many other careers, but we're never going to get three million great teachers willing to sacrifice their family's standard of living for the pure joy of educating our children. That joy is real, but for most people it's not enough. That's why raising salaries is the necessary foundation for all other educational reform.

> According to a McKinsey & Company report that examined top school systems around the world, the *first* thing that makes a difference is "getting the right people to become teachers."[3]

Think of building a college football team. The coach's number one job is recruiting. Playbooks matter, the training table matters, but without the raw talent you don't compete in the big time. What's more, having a star player or two

"They pretend to pay us and we pretend to work."

This must be *the* classic Russian joke from the Soviet era. (Okay, American teachers do a heck of a lot better than workers did under communism. But you get the point.)

makes a big difference, but you can't win without strength across the whole team. A great quarterback behind a weak offensive line scores more bruises and contusions than touchdowns.

The same is true in schools. There are some real star teachers in the classroom and some real star leaders in the schools. There are lots of solid players, too. What we don't have, because we don't put out the bucks, is across-the-board strength. Without stepping up pay, we won't ever get it.

To understand Mechanism I, we need to put ourselves in the shoes of a person making the decision to become (or remain) a teacher. What are the rewards, financial and nonfinancial, of teaching versus some other career? Mechanism I is effective when the increased financial rewards draw in and retain the right set of people.

What we've seen in past chapters is that teacher pay is low compared to other careers available to college graduates. A college student today has to accept a significant financial sacrifice if she becomes a teacher. It's not enough for her to think she'll like teaching and be good at it. She'd better like it a whole lot, because she's not going to have the lifestyle her classmates will.

We've also seen that the pay gap at the top end is even bigger than the average pay gap. So if our college student is especially smart, or good at business or technical subjects, or extra hardworking, she'll have to accept an even bigger financial sacrifice to go into teaching. Fixing the teacher pay gap will level the playing field. We can no longer afford to artificially discourage talented students from entering teaching.

The same Mechanism I issue applies to current teachers considering switching out of teaching. We've seen that it's exactly the teachers with good outside opportunities who are most likely to leave, those with science backgrounds for example, and, depressingly, those with the highest scores on teacher tests! (People who score well on teacher tests are talented in other areas, too.) Put yourself in the shoes of a ten-year veteran teacher. You've gotten over the startup hump of learning your craft. You've also started to fall behind your neighbors and college friends financially. Perhaps you've started a family and are thinking the expenses of supporting your kids. Looking ahead, the uniform salary schedule means you can count on modest raises for a few more years, but you if keep teaching you're going to fall farther and farther behind financially. It's hard not to think about bailing out.

Becoming *Profit*able is going to require an upfront investment—there are no two ways about it. Incentive schemes, licensing requirements, charged-up Teach For America kids, forgiving student loans for teachers, de-bureaucratizing school district hiring, and for that matter, bringing an apple to the teacher are all good. I mean that sincerely. There are many important reforms that are already being carried out by teachers, innovative district leaders, and concerned parents right now. These efforts matter and we need more of them. But none of them are going to systematically and reliably build a three-million-strong corps of across-the-board superior teachers. The only recipe for that is to pay them what they're worth.

MECHANISM II: SKIN IN THE GAME

> A market system has lots of problems, but in the long run it gets people to be innovative. It gets them to be entrepreneurial. I'm not saying that the only thing that can move people to action is the prospect of making or losing money; there are other important and valuable incentives—the desire to do a good job or to solve a problem or to gain the respect of colleagues or to attain professional norms. But systems that have ignored financial incentives haven't worked. If a system is to be successful, it must use *all* incentives.
>
> How is all of this relevant to the breakdown of our traditional model of education and to school restructuring? The point is that our schools operate as command economies. Incentives, where they exist at all, are lined up the wrong way. People in schools are not rewarded for improving student outcomes. They're rewarded for following a bunch of routines.
>
> *legendary teacher union leader Albert Shanker*[4]

Caroline Hoxby put it succinctly in talking to the authors of *Teachers Have It Easy,* "I think there's a pretty simple solution. If you want to attract people into teaching, you have to pay teachers more like other professionals. . . . We have to reallocate money from other things and toward teacher salaries. But we've also got to be willing to pay teachers more if they look like they're better teachers."[5]

"Skin in the game" is code for giving teachers a financial stake in students' success. Skin in the game *requires* differential pay. This point is not deep. If there is no opportunity to earn differential pay—if teachers earn the same amount no matter what they or their school teams accomplish—then those teachers have no financial stake in producing better outcomes. That's the current system, in which nothing aligns a teacher's incentive or a school's incentive with our goals for students. No potential for differential pay means no skin in the game.

If the very words "differential pay" set off alarm bells or sirens in your head, something which is true for many teachers, please stick with me for a while.

First, I'm talking about differential pay as an add-on to a solid base pay, not as a substitute. The vast majority of teachers will see a nice raise in their paycheck. Second, please, please, differential pay is not code for paying for student scores on standardized tests. Tests will play a role—something I will be completely unapologetic about—but only a role. There need to be multiple paths for a teacher, or a group of teachers, to demonstrate their success with students.

Mechanism II is all about aligning teacher incentives with student outcomes. Skin in the game is shorthand for workers sharing the wins

Support for paying for success receives support from sometimes unexpected quarters. New York City school chancellor Joel Klein and activist leader the Reverend Al Sharpton wrote an open letter to President Obama published in the *Wall Street Journal,* advocating a number of reforms, including "we oppose . . . antiquated pay structures that . . . stop good teachers from earning substantial, performance-based pay raises."[6]

and losses of their organization, in this case shorthand for teachers being rewarded when they lift up their students.

In education, as in all industries, it's hard to measure success and it's hard to know how much credit should go to each particular employee. Because measurement is so imperfect, in the greater economy, individual compensation is moderately linked to success measures, not completely linked. That's how it should be in education, instead of our current no-link-at-all system. So after a little more on the why of Mechanism II, I'll talk about the two areas of measurement relevant to education: (1) *input measures,* where we see what a teacher has done to enable her to do a better job, and (2) *output measures,* where we see what results the teacher gets with her students.

Fundamentally, the why of Mechanism II is obvious. Teachers respond to incentives exactly like all the rest of us humans. We need to stop pretending that teachers are from an alien race and start paying them as you pay any normal human: for achieving valuable results. Our current one-size-check-fits-all system is plain abnormal.

All of us respond to incentives by modifying our behavior. Sometimes we put in extra hours; sometimes we study up to qualify for a promotion. But doing a good, rewardable, job isn't usually a solo act. Sometimes we make a suggestion for improving the work process. And sometimes, although it isn't much fun, we have a little chat with a coworker whose performance is dragging down the whole team.

In the case of teachers, some of the behavior modifications in response to financial incentives—or their absence—are obvious. Most teachers put in lots of off-the-clock hours, but a fair number don't.[7] With money at stake, some teachers who are now clock-punchers will

MECHANISM II OUTSIDE TEACHING

There are no official statistics on the use of "performance pay" in the economy at large. The best estimate is that between the late 1970s and the late 1990s the use of some component of performance pay among salaried workers increased from about 30 percent of jobs to about 50 percent. Higher-paid workers are more likely to be in jobs with some element of performance pay.[8] In addition to direct performance pay, most workers find good work rewarded by promotions to higher-paying jobs.

put in more time. Most teachers rework lesson plans as needed, but some don't bother. With money at stake, more will go to that extra effort. These are just examples, of course. The key is that teachers are the boots-on-the-ground professionals of the educational system. Give them an incentive to overcome the inertia in the system, and they'll find a way.

Difficult Conversations

Precisely because teachers are professionals, the talk-to-coworker response is especially important. Teachers don't work in isolation. Yes, teachers spend time as the sole adult present in the classroom, but the school environment matters a great deal. The support of other staff matters, and the accomplishments of the teacher who taught your students last year matter. Teachers who care about results have good reason to care about the work of those around them. Despite this, teachers are reluctant to have unpleasant conversations with their colleagues. Unless you have something personally at stake, it's rarely worth the discomfort of confronting a coworker with whom you have to coexist.

Having skin in the game provides a huge personal motivation—your pocketbook—for initiating that unpleasant conversation in the teachers' lounge. Imagine, if you will, Ms. Good Teacher sitting in the teachers' lounge when her colleague, Jack, who is neither a good teacher nor terribly pleasant to his colleagues, walks in with a rented DVD in hand. Let's eavesdrop on the conversation going on inside Ms. Good Teacher's head.

> "Good gracious. That's the fourth time this month Jack's shown a Harry Potter movie in class instead of teaching. I know those kids have proficiency exams coming up. That lazy slug shouldn't be let near students." [Rolling eyes and shaking head, Ms. Teacher exits lounge.]
>
> *Thought bubble in today's compensation system*

> "Good gracious. That's the fourth time this month Jack's shown a Harry Potter movie in class instead of teaching. I know those kids have proficiency exams coming up. That lazy slug shouldn't be let near students. I have a $10,000 bonus riding on

our school's performance this year. He's not going to ruin it for me." [Out loud: "Jack, you and I need to talk . . . *right now*!"]

Thought bubble in tomorrow's Profit-oriented compensation system?

Difficult conversations are about administrators as well as about colleagues. Ask a teacher how often in-service training days help her innovate versus how often in-service training days help check off an annual requirement. Sometimes this kind of continuing education turns out to be valuable, but far too often it has become just another bureaucratic requirement. No administrator ever intends in-service training to be nap-inducing. When teachers have skin in the game, they'll be the ones demanding that training be useful—precisely because teachers as individuals and as a team will see the results in their paychecks.

Difficult conversations are also about successful teachers supporting administrators when they try to get unsuccessful teachers moving, and standing firm against administrators who engage in personal politics instead of looking for results. There's nothing like money at stake to refocus school politics toward results and away from personalities.

A critical element of Mechanism II is that teachers (and administrators) become advocates for change. At that boots-on-the-ground level, teachers are the professionals with the detailed knowledge to separate reforms that work from reforms-for-reform's-sake. Working together, teachers have the weight to push changes from within. Attaching significant financial rewards to success can go a long way to breaking down reluctance to engage in those difficult, but necessary and professional, conversations.

> School leaders genuflect when the idea of modifying the way schools do their work is brought up, but change is almost never put on the table in a serious way. . . . The political dynamics appear to require accepting current structures as the natural order of things. Reform in this framework is something that is welcome as long as it changes nothing of major consequence to the adults in the system.
>
> *Educational reformers Paul Thomas Hill and James Harvey*[9]

Measuring Input/Measuring Output

Offering differential pay necessarily means measuring something on which to base the difference. What that something should be is a critical and controversial component of a reinvigoration program. Few really object to differential pay in principle. Even today, a teacher with a PhD and thirty years experience might earn twice the starting teacher salary.

That's pretty differential! No, what gets people upset is linking differential pay to something they don't want it linked to. The next few chapters explore a variety of options. To set the stage, I want to talk about an overarching concept. We care directly about the output of education, where "output" means what students learn. We care about inputs, such as teacher credentials, only indirectly—only to the extent that those inputs lead to better student learning. Nonetheless, we want to link pay to both inputs and outputs. The reason for this two-prong approach is that we can't measure output perfectly. Incentivizing inputs that lead to more learning mitigates the imperfect measurement problem.

Think about contract negotiations with a professional football player, say a defensive linebacker. The contract might include a bonus for every quarterback sack; sacks are a measure of output. But we know that we want more from the linebacker than just dumping the quarterback. Some of what we want, the key block, even team leadership, are tough to put a number to. So what we offer in a contract also takes account of inputs, speed in the forty, coming in at optimal weight, etc. We don't care about the linebacker's speed directly, but we know that faster linebackers on average do a better job disrupting the offense.

Notice though that we don't offer the linebacker higher pay to reward good grades in his college economics courses. Some of us think that doing well in college economics courses is incredibly important, but the evidence linking good econ grades to quarterback sacks is kinda weak . . .

The *sine qua non* of an effective compensation system is that we pay for success. Success means neither that Mr. Chips is a nice chap nor that he has a long list of merit badges covering everything from blackboard techniques to mastering the Delaney Book.® *Success means that students learn.*

The principle is the same for teachers, or at least it should be. We care about student learning, but since we can't measure it perfectly we should partially compensate teachers for the elements of student learning that we can measure, partially compensate teachers for their activities and accomplishments that generally lead to student success (but not for accomplishments unrelated to student success), and, of course, include a very hefty element of straight base pay, just as everyone else gets.

People tend to be pretty comfortable with linking pay to inputs. One reason for that comfort level is that workers have a fair amount of control over inputs. For example, in most jobs if you put in extra hours you get paid overtime or you increase your chance for a raise or promotion. (Except for teachers, who get neither pay nor promotion for extra hours.) As another example, an American soldier proficient in a foreign language can earn "foreign language proficiency pay (FLPP)" adding as much as $300 to $1,000 to monthly pay. (How many teachers get this kind of raise for foreign language fluency?)

The problem with linking pay to inputs is precisely that they are just inputs, not results. Unfortunately, there is a strong tendency to reward inputs that sound attractive and are easily measured, without asking for evidence of their efficacy. Historically, we've paid extra for inputs that are very easily measured (such as graduate degrees; more on this in a later chapter) but which we now know *don't* lead to better results.

Outputs are measures of student success. If you're a commissioned sales rep you may receive base pay, but the bulk of your compensation depends on what you sell. Compensation for commissioned salespeople is almost completely output-driven.

Compensation for commissioned salespeople illustrates the idea of linking pay to results, but it's a more extreme example than how most of us get paid. Nonetheless, partially linking pay to results is very common, sometimes explicitly and sometimes implicitly, in the form of bonuses, raises, promotions, and continued employment. Here's how Ed Lazear, the nation's leading expert on personnel economics, put it: "Variable pay simply means tying a worker's compensation to some output-based measure of performance. . . . In the real world there are many forms of variable pay. Indeed it is possible to argue that almost no job's pay is truly fixed. Poor performance over a substantial period of time results in lower future pay, and at the extreme, termination."[10]

BUZZWORDS

A teacher is deemed *highly qualified* based on having a college degree, state certification, and other measures of input. Teachers are deemed *highly effective* based on her students' test results or other measures or student achievement. Current federal law emphasizes the use of highly qualified teachers.

Discussions among reform advocates about the appropriate balance between qualifications and effectiveness (read: inputs and outputs) get pretty testy. Education professors tend to lean toward qualifications, economists toward effectiveness.

Both major teachers' unions, the National Education Association (NEA) and the American Federation of Teachers (AFT), lean toward qualifications.[11] While reformers have strong views on the relative merits of rewarding qualifications versus effectiveness, the bottom line is that both offer improvements over the current system, there is evidence demonstrating this, and both have a role to play.[12]

Arguments often are made against linking pay to output, claiming that student achievement isn't measurable and student achievement isn't under a teacher's control. Both are false. Or perhaps more accurately, both are mostly false with a modest grain of truth. Focusing on the limitations of output measurement has led us into a system that 100 percent ignores outputs. We've built a system in which teachers have almost zero accountability for their prime mission: teaching kids.

Let's confront the "accountability" word for a moment. While there has been much talk about accountability in the last few years, most of the talk has taken the form of threats and negative reinforcement: take a bunch of underpaid teachers, the majority of whom do a good job, and then threaten to punish them. All that negative reinforcement has accomplished is to put up teachers' backs and stiffen resistance to reform. Why do we persist in such negativism? We go negative because threats are cheap. Positive reinforcement, i.e., cash for accomplishment, costs money. Putting down teachers doesn't fix schools. It's just plain mean-spirited.

I'm not naive; there is a role for negative reinforcement. The problem with current attempts to weed out weak teachers is that sticks reasonably aimed at the 5 percent of bad apples damage the morale of 95 percent. Effective negative reinforcement is best applied by insiders. That's the role of difficult conversations.

Some argue that because success in teaching is hard to measure perfectly, rewarding success with positive incentives just isn't possible. The fact is that private schools—where the mission isn't that different but the political arena is—often use differential pay. As Dale Ballou writes, "Merit pay is used in a large number of private schools. Awards are not trivial; nor is it the case that merit pay is awarded to nearly everyone. Reasons for the failure of merit pay are not inherent in teaching."[13] By 1993, 38 percent of teachers in private, nonsectarian schools were covered by some sort of merit pay plan.[14]

Measurement of both input and output is certainly imperfect. But imperfect doesn't mean unusable. Join me in a thought experiment. Suppose we picked a wise, experienced, fair-minded teacher, and sent her to evaluate educational outcomes in a school where she didn't have any personal connections or biases. Let her read through all the student records at the beginning of the year, tell her about each student's family background and individual strengths and weaknesses, chat one-on-one with students, see all the standardized test results at the end of the year, read student portfolios, and generally spend some time hanging out and observing. Do you think that the evaluator-teacher we're imagining could do a reasonable job of identifying which teachers had made a really big contribution to student learning over the year and which were just coasting? I do.

Would you object to distributing a hefty differential pay pool, say one adding 40 percent to base pay on average, based pay on our fair-minded evaluator recommendations? It works for me.

THE GREAT "YOU CAN'T MEASURE A TEACHER'S CONTRIBUTION" RED HERRING

I have news for doubters. Except in special circumstances, businesses also can't perfectly measure the contribution of an employee or a group of employees. But they can measure the contribution *imperfectly*, just as we can imperfectly measure the contribution of a teacher or a school. So businesses base *some* elements of compensation on these imperfect measures and schools need to do the same.

In practice, we don't have such a pool of wise evaluators. We have to rely on less perfect methods. In other words, we're *in exactly the same situation as most private businesses.* Most pay will always be base pay. Nonetheless, the idea of zero linkage between results and compensation has to go.

For a concrete example of linking pay to output versus input, let's do a compare and contrast example: two tasks, each of which there are many ways to accomplish.

Task 1: Teach a typical class of third graders their times tables.

Task 2: Teach at-risk teens coping skills for staying out of trouble.

There are many different ways to teach multiplication. When I Googled "times tables" Google responded "came up with about 538,000 results." Should we pay teachers for mastering a particular pedagogic technique for teaching multiplication? Of course not. Let a teacher use whatever techniques work best for her and for her students. Measuring the output of learning the times tables is pretty straightforward. Give the class a pretest early in the year and a posttest later, and then a small piece of the teacher's annual bonus depends on how much the class has improved. Whether a kid's multiplication skills have improved is pretty straightforward to measure. In this case paying for output is the way to go.

Contrast teaching times tables with counseling at-risk teens. The latter is important, but the results are much harder to measure. There's only one right outcome to three times three, but the best outcome for at-risk youth varies from teen to teen, and even from month to month. Since measuring results is very difficult, it may make much more sense to reward teachers who acquire relevant extra training. In this case, paying for inputs—for instance, getting a credential from a program with proven results—may be sensible, even though paying for a credential in times table pedagogy isn't.

Valuing What We Measure Versus Measuring What We Value

Some things that we care about (for instance, knowing the times tables) are far more easily measured than others (say, appreciating art and music) that we also care about. It is extremely easy to fall into the trap of basing differential pay on what's easiest to measure instead of what's most valuable. There is no magic solution, but awareness of the problem and vigilance buy us a degree of protection.

This is a politically sensitive subject with a powerful, and perhaps unexpected, constituency. Upper-income parents of academically successful students are among the most resistant to the adoption of output measures. These parents, generally very supportive of education, understand correctly that their kids will master the basics, which are easily tested, regardless of what most teachers do or don't do. They're more worried about enrichment and the teaching of more subtle, and harder-to-test, skills. There is a legitimate concern that enrichment will lose out in favor of more easily measured aspects of the curriculum. Differential pay systems need to respect the concerns of these parents. This is not merely a political issue. Those more subtle curriculum items really are vitally important, especially to high-achieving students.

Pain and Gain

Keep in mind that we're asking teachers to accept a shocking restructuring of their compensation. Unsurprisingly, many teachers prove unenthusiastic about disruptions where the rewards are largely symbolic. Attempts to implement Mechanism II on the cheap fail because they mess up Mechanism I. Disruptions that make teaching less attractive (at least until people are used to new approaches to compensation) while offering very little extra pay don't help to attract and retain top teachers. For example, a much-heralded reform in Denver[15] included a student achievement growth component: "Each year, teachers will set two student growth objectives, in collaboration with principals or supervisors. Teachers who meet both objectives will receive a 1% addition to their base salaries, while teachers who meet one objective will receive a 1% bonus."[16] In a Dallas reform of the early 1990s, about one teacher in five received $1,000 for student test score gains. In a school-based award program in South Carolina, winning schools might win $15,000–$20,000—for the whole school. Schools were also given a colorful flag to display.[17]

Would you dive into a new career or help restructure your current job for a 1 percent raise? How about for a *really* colorful flag? No? Me neither. Teachers are not different.

In contrast, consider a rare example in which differential pay was large enough to compensate for disrupting the status quo. In 2004, Little Rock, Arkansas, adopted a pilot program in which teachers could win quite large bonuses for increasing student test scores. While only a small number of schools participated, student improvement was

A MECHANISM II SUCCESS

A pure Mechanism II experiment was conducted in Israel in 2000 and 2001. Teachers in forty-nine high schools were offered large bonuses, potentially 25 percent of pay—or sometimes even more, depending on student performance on standardized exams. Students of the incentivized teachers showed significant gains compared to other students. Given the design of the experiment, there was no opportunity to change who was in front of the class, so we know this was a pure Mechanism II effect. What made the difference? According to Victor Lavy's study of the experiment:

> Improvements were mediated through changes in teaching methods, enhanced after-school teaching, and increased responsiveness to students' needs. No evidence was found of manipulation of test scores by teachers.[18]

impressive and continued the longer a school stayed in the program.[19] Math and reading scores rose by the equivalent of an extra month in the schools offering bonuses.[20] Participating teachers were more satisfied with their salaries and rated their own effectiveness more highly.

That's the pain side. There's also an overlooked gain side to Mechanism II, especially with regard to output measures. Greater reliance on output measures (that is, greater than the current level of reliance: zero) offers the perhaps unexpected effect of empowering teachers and liberating them to use their professional skills. Students have different learning styles. Teachers have different teaching styles. Use of output rather than input measures favors diversity, in place of endless debates over choosing a single, one-size-fits-all pedagogic technique. Here's how Eric Hanushek, a world leader in education research, put it:[21]

> The simple reason for the failure to define best practice among teachers would seem to be that there is none. No single set of teacher characteristics, teacher behaviors, curricular approaches, or organizational devices guarantees a high probability of success in the classroom. Instead different teachers succeed, or fail, in very different ways. . . . One teacher may be

particularly effective by employing word games with children from well-to-do backgrounds who have reading deficiencies; another may be able to motivate students by recounting personal experiences from living in Southeast Asia; yet another may be energized by close, interactive contacts with other teachers in the school.

Suppose one goal in a school district is third-grade reading ability, and let's further suppose that we're looking at a district where most kids stick with one elementary school all the way through K–5. One school might decide to teach reading using the whole language approach and another might emphasize phonics. The district would choose a standardized reading test that would determine a hunk of each school's bonus pool. The output measure would be standard across schools, but the inputs (i.e., pedagogical approaches) would be diverse. Both techniques might be valid, but one might be better for a particular group of students, or it may even be that a particular set of teachers is more comfortable with one technique rather than the other. Instead of arguing over whether phonics or whole language is a universally better technique, we let teachers and schools use whatever technique works for them, so long as the evidence shows that it works for the kids they teach.

ZOOMING IN

I've talked in broad brush about Mechanism I and Mechanism II, and within Mechanism II about input versus output pay linkages. Looking back to earlier chapters, we talked in detail about what it's going to require in Mechanism I tools to get the teacher corps we need. That's where the 40 percent number came from. Looking forward to the next chapters, I'm going to talk in much greater detail about implementation of Mechanism I. The next chapter is about knowing when an input is worth paying for. The following chapter takes a frank look at output measures, with serious attention to their warts. Then I'll turn to sorting out individual versus group incentives.

6

Qualification Supplements: An Input Measure That Matters

In the last chapter, I talked about extra pay for highly qualified teachers as one of the two broad avenues for rewarding successful teachers. "Qualification" is an input measure where we link pay to some measurable aspect of a teacher's skills, in contrast to an "effectiveness" measure that looks at student results—an output measure. In this chapter, I'm going to go into more detail about paying for qualifications. Primarily, I want to tell you a little about what's arguably the most important current program for identifying highly qualified teachers, the National Board for Professional Teaching Standards (NBPTS). Then I'll talk about some widely used qualification measures that are unfortunately less helpful.

One of the things you'll see in this chapter is that the NBPTS isn't just any standard—it's *tough!* As we'll see in a minute, there's solid evidence that it works. The NBPTS is interesting in its own right, but it's also a good example of the fact that we can validate qualification programs. Some reformers react negatively to any proposed use of qualification measures because current measures are badly flawed. This leaves the reformers advocating output measures only. The NBPTS is proof that qualification measures have a role to play.

In contrast to the views of such reformers, qualification supplements are relatively popular with people inside the system. The reason is understandable: with a qualification supplement you know exactly what you have to do to earn extra money. The reformers' objection is that the certainty is all about how to earn the money, leaving the uncertainty about whether a particular qualification works for getting better student outcomes. So part of the value of the NBPTS as an example for using qualification supplements is that there *is* solid evidence linking NBPTS certification to student results. Solid isn't the same as airtight. But in the economy outside education we're usually good with making decisions based on "solid." Airtight is too high a standard. So I'm suggesting, using the NBPTS as an example, that when someone proposes paying for a particular qualification, we do ask for solid evidence of its efficacy, but hold short of requiring airtight proof.

BOARD CERTIFIED: THE NBPTS

This one modest-sized program—the National Board for Professional Teaching Standards—has brought together a wide-ranging set of players in producing a new mechanism for certifying highly qualified teachers.

NBPTS-certified teachers are rewarded with higher pay nearly everywhere in the country. As a metric for identifying teacher success, the NBPTS has received considerable attention, a lot of money, much controversy, and a good measure of acceptance. As we shall see, there is solid (but not airtight) evidence that the program works.

Some of the commendable characteristics of the NBPTS are: rigor, serious intellectual standards, accomplishment rather than preparation focus, and manipulation resistance. These characteristics are a key to the success of the NBPTS and a clue to what to look for in other qualification programs.

First, a bit about the NBPTS program, then a look at the evidence.

Possibly the most telling characteristic of the National Board program is its rigorous evaluation of individual candidates. To be eligible to even apply, a teacher needs three years of classroom experience. Becoming a National Board Certified Teacher (NBCT) requires two steps: (1) the submission of four teaching portfolios, and (2) passing six computerized subject area tests. The portfolios include video tapes of classroom teaching and samples of student work. Portfolios are evaluated by

> Legendary labor leader Albert Shanker, president of both the American Federation of Teachers and the UFT (the AFT's New York city local), is credited with proposing the NBPTS.

NBPTS PROFESSIONAL STANDARDS REVOLVE AROUND FIVE CORE PROPOSITIONS

"I. Teachers are committed to students and their learning.
II. Teachers know the subjects they teach and how to teach those subjects to students.
III. Teachers are responsible for managing and monitoring student learning.
IV. Teachers think systematically about their practice and learn from experience.
V. Teachers are members of learning communities."[1]

at least twelve experienced, NBPTS-trained teachers. The certification process costs over three thousand dollars and can take three years to complete. It's estimated that a teacher spends four hundred hours on the process of becoming certified.

Rigor

You can see why these are called *professional* standards. Tough? One estimate is that about 50 percent of applicants fail their initial attempt at certification!

The NBPTS regularly says no to candidates who haven't made the grade. This adds to the visible credibility of the program. That tough-mindedness, and the credibility to be won, is doubtless part of the reason rejected applicants are willing to try again.

Serious Intellectual Standards

At the specific skills level, the NBPTS offers certification in twenty-five areas of education. Subject matter tests require demonstration of content knowledge (not just pedagogical technique). For example, the math standards require an understanding of calculus, which is generally thought of as the first college-level math course. Understanding calculus is required for the

Only 2 percent of America's teaching force has achieved NBCT status.

math certification for teaching seven- to fifteen-year-old students as well as fourteen to eighteen year olds. So while the math standard is much less than would be required of a university math major, even teachers of middle school students are required to demonstrate an ability to understand and explain beginning college-level math.

In other words, certification requires subject area knowledge well beyond the level that the teacher's students are expected to master.

Accomplishment Rather Than Preparation Focused

Notice what kind of evidence the NBPTS looks at: proof of what a teacher does in the classroom and how the teacher approaches teaching (portfolios and videotapes), and proof of subject area knowledge (content tests). Specifically, the portfolio that candidates submit must include videos of the teacher in action and samples of student work. Note that the NBPTS doesn't review coursework in either pedagogy or subject area. In fact, the only eligibility requirements to apply are a college degree, a teaching license, and three years teaching experience.

Manipulation-Resistant

One reason for the wide acceptance of the NBPTS is that neither applicants nor administrators can manipulate the process; the NBPTS provides external control.

Portfolios are evaluated by a dozen experienced teachers. Portfolio evaluation is necessarily subjective, so the NBPTS arranges for the portfolios to be examined by outside, arms-length evaluators who have no vested interest in the outcomes for specific applicants.

There is a related complaint about the NBPTS worth noting. It's an expensive program. After a decade in operation, the NBPTS had certified 47,500 teachers at a total cost of around $637 million.[2] That comes to upwards of $13,000 per certified teacher.[3] That's a lot of money that might otherwise have been spent on teacher salaries or other

> NBPTS certification has wide political support. Both North Carolina and New York pay $2,500 of the certification fee. In granting a teaching license to out-of-state applicants, California waives all skills and other credential requirements for NBCTs.

educational purposes. Serious measures of qualifications may be unavoidably expensive. Perhaps in quality certification, as in so much of life, you get what you pay for.

By the way, the evidence is that the NBPTS identifies already excellent teachers, as opposed to the application process changing how the applicant teaches. That makes it more a Mechanism I than a Mechanism II device, which is just fine. The research team of Goldhaber and Anthony showed this, writing "We find consistent evidence that NBPTS is identifying the more effective teacher applicants and that National Board Certified Teachers are generally more effective than teachers who never applied to the program. . . . We do not find evidence that the NBPTS certification process itself does anything to increase teacher effectiveness."[4]

What's the Reward?

Becoming a NBCT is tough, time-consuming, and expensive. Why do teachers do it? No doubt there are many reasons, prestige not being the least of them, but NBPTS is upfront about this being a "pay for performance" model. More than two-thirds of states offer some kind of financial compensation for becoming a NBCT.

In some states, raises come straight in as higher paychecks. Others have special compensation for NBCTs for teaching in high-needs districts or for agreeing to take on roles mentoring other teachers. Financial

SAMPLE FINANCIAL REWARDS FOR BECOMING A NBCT

North Carolina: 12 percent annual bonus.
Florida: Up to a 10 percent annual bonus.
Washington: $5,000 annual bonus; additional $5,000 annually for teaching in a challenging school.
California: One-time $20,000 bonus for teaching in a low-performing school.
New York: $10,000 annual bonus for three years for teaching in low-performing school and mentoring new teachers.
North Carolina, Florida, and Washington have an above average number of NBCTs and relatively high differential pay. State numbers are below the national average in California and New York, which offer relatively low differential pay.

incentives range from modest to significant; some examples appear in the box on page 89.

Does the NBPTS Really Measure Teacher Success?

Clearly, NBCTs are held to a high standard. But is it a *relevant* high standard? Bottom line, is there evidence that students of NBCTs learn more? While the certification process does look at samples of student work as submitted by the applicant, certification is fundamentally based on teacher knowledge rather than student outcomes. This input-rather-than-output orientation is one reason that NBPTS is controversial in the education reform community. Some reformers view professionalization as exactly the right way to go. Other reformers regard anything not based on student outcomes as fundamentally irrelevant.

From a compensation system design point of view, the question is not whether the NBPTS looks directly at student outcomes for individual applicants. It's whether the NBPTS is validated by better average student outcomes for NBCTs. The answer is in the affirmative.

The most direct evidence on student outcomes comes from a series of studies that look at improvements in student test scores for NBCTs versus other teachers. The balance of the evidence is that NBCTs really do better, although not all researchers agree—a point acknowledged by the NBPTS.

North Carolina is a favorite locale for researchers both because North Carolina has an unusually high number of NBCTs and because the state maintains an excellent database that it makes available to the research community. Two researchers, Dan Goldhaber and Emily Anthony, looked at test score improvements from year to year for nearly four hundred thousand North Carolina students, comparing results for students taught by NBCTs to the results for students who were not.[5] The bottom line answer is that NBCT-taught students learn more. The authors find that spending a year with an NBCT gets a student the

One informal piece of evidence in favor of the NBPTS is that NBCTs regularly win far more than their share of teaching awards. For example, the 2 percent of the nation's teachers who are NBCTs walked off with 25 percent of the state "teacher of the year" awards in 2008. And then did it again in 2009.

equivalent of one to two weeks extra learning.[6] That's fairly big, suggesting that if every student could have a board certified teacher, we'd be about halfway to our goal of an extra year's learning for each student.

In a second North Carolina study following essentially all North Carolina elementary school students over a ten-year period, Goldhaber provided a particularly useful metric by comparing the gains of students of NBCTs versus non-NBCTS to the gains of students of experienced teachers versus novice teachers.[7] A student gets something like half the boost from having a board certified teacher as from having an experienced rather than a novice teacher. Or, since all NBCTs are also experienced teachers, we might say that NBCTs provide an extra 50 percent boost over that provided by other experienced teachers.

Both these studies show that the NBCT advantage is greater in math instruction than in reading, a finding confirmed in an independent examination of North Carolina data by Clotfelter, Ladd, and Vigdor.[8] These same researchers come up with another useful comparison: having an NBCTs certified teacher provides an advantage to students equivalent to that of a five-pupil reduction in class size.[9]

Yet another researcher, Linda Cavalluzzo, examined one hundred thousand high school student records in Florida and compared math results for students of NBCTs and other teachers. She found similar results to Goldhaber and Anthony's North Carolina results. In fact, Cavalluzzo found an even larger impact than appeared to hold in North Carolina. Her results suggest the NBCTs add three to four weeks worth of schooling to student outcomes.[10] Moving west, Vandevoort, Amrein-Beardsley, and Berliner looked at results of having an NBCT for Arizona elementary school students. Although the number of teachers involved was quite small, their results were consistent with other studies. These researchers estimate that an NBCT is worth a month of extra schooling.[11]

This seems to all add up to fairly strong evidence that NBPTS really works. However, two studies come to a different conclusion. An influential study by Douglass Harris and Tim Sass

While most research is based on standardized tests scores, Tracy Smith and colleagues compared student writing samples from a small number of classes taught by NBCTs and other teachers and found that students of NBCTs wrote deeper responses.[12]

looked at a million student records in Florida. NBCTs do better, but by much less than appeared to be true in the North Carolina studies.[13] Despite having a very large sample, the apparent NBCT advantage is not statistically significant. Unlike the other studies, which find strong evidence of a moderate-to-large effect, Harris and Sass find only weak evidence of a fairly small effect.[14]

A second study that looked at two large North Carolina school districts, by William Sanders and colleagues, found "a student randomly assigned to a NBCT is no more likely to get an 'effective' (or an 'ineffective') teacher than a student assigned to a non-NBCT."[15]

Interestingly, the Sanders et al. study with negative results was commissioned by the NBPTS itself. That deserves major props! There's an important lesson here to apply to future proposed input certifications. Being open to, in fact encouraging, independent evaluation is a sign that the certification provider has faith in its product. Arguably, differential pay should be linked only to qualifications vetted in this way.

But more recent work by Cantrell, Kane, and Stagier looked at a controlled experiment in Los Angeles where students were randomly assigned to NBCTs or non-NBCTS; the result supports the general finding that certification is a good predictor of student success.[16] Interestingly, however, the authors also found evidence that knowing how well a teacher scored in the NBPTS process didn't add a great deal of information to what you could have learned by looking at how well her students had done in earlier years.

It is frustrating when scientific studies disagree, but that's sometimes the nature of the beast. The bottom line is that while the evidence is not conclusive that NBCTs are more successful teachers, it leans heavily in that direction.

Evidence on a Couple of Other Qualification Programs

The National Board for Professional Teaching Standards is the 800-pound gorilla of programs to vet qualifications, but it's not the only such effort. Increased student success has also been validated for two short-lived programs, one in Tennessee and one in South Carolina. The most convincing evidence comes from the Tennessee STAR experiment, where students were randomly assigned to teachers. Some of the teachers had been marked as highly qualified by earning promotions on Tennessee's Career Ladder Evaluation System. (These career promotions came with relatively large financial rewards.) Students randomly assigned to teachers who had moved up the career ladder performed much better in both math and reading.[17,18] Similar results, although without the random assignment of students, were found for a South Carolina teacher bonus plan in which teachers identified as "meritorious" achieved higher student test score gains in both reading and math.[19]

QUALIFICATIONS THAT *DON'T* IDENTIFY EFFECTIVE TEACHERS

There is good evidence that teacher board-certification is correlated with student success. But the most common, nearly universal in fact, "pay for qualifications" program is linking pay to teacher experience and to earning a graduate degree. Unfortunately, there is good evidence that both experience and further education are *un*correlated with student success. The latter is particularly distressing, as rewarding teachers for advanced degrees has received wide support among people who really care about education.

Experience on the Job

Experience pay is a form of qualification supplement, where being more experienced is treated as being more qualified. Unfortunately, the evidence is clear. On average, teachers don't get better with experience—with one very big exception, newbie teachers.

Six percent of teachers are in their first year teaching, and 12 percent have less than three years experience.[20] Beginners rarely teach as well as their more experienced counterparts. The difference is very large. Students taught by novice teachers lose out compared to students taught by teachers with three-to-five years experience by the equivalent of half a month to a full month of schooling.[21]

Don't misunderstand; none of this is a criticism of new teachers. If it were true that experienced teachers were no better than beginners, it would be a sad statement about teachers' ability to learn from their own successes and failures. Saying that teachers improve with experience and that beginning teachers underperform experienced teachers

PULITZER PRIZE WINNER, NEW YORK TIMES BEST-SELLING AUTHOR, AND THIRTY-YEAR VETERAN TEACHER FRANK MCCOURT POETICALLY DESCRIBES HIS FIRST DAY OF CLASS[22]

Here they come.
And I'm not ready.
How could I be?
I'm a new teacher and learning on the job.

are exactly equivalent statements. The bottom line is: *Teaching is hard to learn, except on the job.*

The fact that novices underperform more experienced teachers has implications for the discussion in Chapter 2, Who Teaches? Today, America needs to hire about a quarter of a million teachers each year. About three-fourths are complete novices and the other fourth are former teachers who have been persuaded to return.[23] If teacher turnover were lower, schools could spend much less energy hiring massive numbers of mostly beginners and we'd have fewer students taught by new teachers who are engaged in on-the-job training.

But once past the break-in period, teachers don't get better—or least don't better by very much. (This average result probably reflects some balance between teachers who continue to grow as teachers and others who burn out.) Researchers looking at teachers in New York City schools report "There are few gains to experience after the third year of teaching."[24] Researchers looking at hundreds of thousands of students in Texas schools found "beginning teachers and to a lesser extent second and third year teachers in mathematics perform significantly worse than more experienced teachers. There may be some additional gains to experience in the subsequent year or two, but the estimated benefits are small and not statistically significant in both mathematics and reading . . ."[25] Similarly, a study of North Carolina elementary school teachers found "little evidence, however, of statistically significant productivity gains associated with increases in experience beyond five years."

Longevity raises are automatic. If a teacher sticks around, she gets raises. She gets them if more experience makes her a better teacher, and she gets them if more experience doesn't make her a better teacher. Compare this system with the NBPTS, under which teachers have to present evidence of ability. Perhaps it's not surprising that the evidence shows board certification is correlated with student outcomes and that experience (after the startup period) isn't.

If you look back at the sample pay schedule in Chapter 3, Teacher Pay, you'll see that experience is the most significant determinant of higher pay. Now, I'm in favor of (almost) anything that raises teacher pay, because this is required to get Mechanism I in gear. But I sure wish that we had a system in which more experienced teachers grew their salaries through demonstrated ability.

Graduate Training

If you talk to a teacher, there's a good chance that she either has a graduate degree or is working toward one. Most teachers continue their education after graduating college. Half have further degrees, mostly master's degrees in education. A graduate degree comes with a hefty raise. In fact, more master's than bachelor's degrees in education are granted every year, the ratio being not quite two-to-one.[26] A small number of teachers go on to earn an EdD or a PhD, but while these are the most common doctoral degree in the United States, only one teacher in a hundred holds a doctorate.

Why do so many teachers put in long hours and write large tuition checks for further education? Because going back to school is pretty much the only thing teachers can actively do to raise their salaries! (Who says that teachers don't respond to financial incentives?)

Rewarding graduate degrees should be a Mechanism II path, since the idea is that more advanced training causes teachers to develop better teaching skills. Here's the unfortunate issue with most master's degrees, particularly degrees in education: they don't work. We encourage teachers to get a master's, sometimes we even require them to get a master's. But usually students of teachers with master's are no better off than other students. Given that teachers go to enormous expense to obtain graduate degrees, both in tuition dollars and in time away from their families, this is awfully discouraging.

The evidence is clear: on average, teachers with master's degree produce no better results than teachers without master's degrees.[27]

Masters in education continue to outnumber graduate degrees in other areas, accounting for over a fourth of all degrees. MBA degrees run a close second.[28]

Curiously, the highest proportion of teachers with doctorates can be found in Washington, DC (nearly triple the national average.) Next comes Louisiana. Neither DC nor Louisiana is renowned for the excellence of its schools. (In fairness, Connecticut—which does have above-average schools—is next on the list.)[29]

Dick Murnane and Jennifer Steele summarize the evidence by saying bluntly "most studies find that whether a teacher holds an advanced degree does not predict student achievement gains."[30]

Marguerite Roza and Raegen Miller of the University of Washington's Center on Reinventing Public Education write in a similar vein, "On average, master's degrees in education bear no relation to student achievement. Master's degrees in math and science have been linked to improved student achievement in those subjects, but 90 percent of teachers' master's degrees are in education programs. . . . Because of the financial rewards associated with getting this degree, the education master's experienced the highest growth rate of all master's degrees between 1997 and 2007."[31]

The fact that the typical graduate program doesn't work does not mean that no graduate programs work. There are almost certainly some that do. For pay raise purposes, graduates of useful graduate programs are currently lumped in with graduates of largely useless ones. Since teachers have no financial incentive to shop for effective programs, the providers of these graduate degrees don't have much incentive to foster the good ones. This discourages the graduate schools themselves from doing the hard job of weeding out ineffective programs and nurturing the ones that work.

To borrow a buzzword from economics, the inability to distinguish among graduate programs for teachers is called a "lemons problem." Here's the analogy. Getting a fair price for a used car is tough. No one wants to buy a lemon, and it's hard for potential customers to tell that your car is a cream puff. In the same way, providers of high-quality graduate education and other certifications can't easily demonstrate that their programs are the ones that are really worthwhile. This makes it hard for the best programs to prosper and grow. Finding a way to vet programs that claim to turn out particularly able teachers, for example by requiring evidence on how well program graduates teach, would give successful programs a big leg up in the market. We could then sensibly offer differential pay to graduates of programs of proven efficacy. That generates a virtuous circle, as teachers would have an incentive to spend their time and money on the proven graduate programs. *Quis custodiet ipsos custodies* is neither a new dilemma nor one that has a magic solution.[32] I'm pretty sure that the solution will have to come from leadership from those in education schools and education policy who have created some of the programs that do work. For now, if you're looking over proposals to link differential teacher pay to graduate work—be skeptical.

CONFIDENCE IN QUALIFICATIONS

Almost everyone is comfortable with the principle of paying for extra qualifications. We've seen that rigorous programs such as the NBPTS can identify really good teachers who can then be paid accordingly. Doing it right is tough, and apparently expensive. Unfortunately, schools today mostly tie pay to experience and graduate training, neither of which has much to do with better student learning. My suspicion is that it's not so much that experience and graduate training aren't worthwhile, as that schools indiscriminately lump together all kinds of experience and lump together all different graduate programs. Somewhere down the road, I'd like to see much wider use of experienced teachers with demonstrable track records as mentors and as troubleshooters for especially difficult teaching assignments. And that they get paid accordingly. Suppose graduate programs had to post information about their students' success rates, and that schools offered significant extra pay to graduates of programs with high success rates—and only those programs!

Paying for qualifications is part of the solution, but even when well done it's not the entire solution. In the next chapter we'll turn from looking at qualifications (input) to effectiveness (output).

7

Effectiveness Pay: We Grade Students, Don't We?

[T]ry to have any necessary employees on some kind of incentive pay. . . . We were THE PAINTING TEACHERS. I'd usually . . . give the teachers an hourly salary plus some fixed percentage of profits. In any business, it's the profit that is the incentive to work harder and more efficiently.

How To Teach School and Make A Living At the Same Time, *high school math teacher Patrick Crowe's fun and sometimes poignant 1978 "how to" book on running businesses as a sideline to teaching*[1]

The question isn't whether to use effectiveness pay—I hope if you've read this far you're convinced about the principle—the question is one of practicality. How do we make it work? An upfront warning: I devote this chapter almost entirely to discussing *problems* with implementing effectiveness pay. While the *principle* of differential effectiveness pay is a slam dunk, the *practice* of differential effectiveness pay, in contrast, is full of pitfalls. Worries about teaching to the test, fairness to all concerned, measurements difficulties, and misplaced incentives leading to unintended consequences are all quite real and legitimate sources of concern.

If we're to reward teachers for success we want to be smart about the way we do it, and that means being open about imperfections. That's why this chapter concentrates on the blemishes. Nothing here should provide solace to those who think the right amount of measurement is zero or that teachers don't deserve financial rewards.

The two hard parts of rewarding teachers for successful student learning is that we first have to decide *what* we want students to learn and then we have to find reasonably good measures of *how much* of that learning has taken place. Hey, the hard part of grading students is that teachers first have to decide what students should learn and then find reasonably good measures of how much of that learning has taken place. So let's take our cues from the teachers. Relate tests to the material. Use a variety of signals of accomplishment, rather than a single high-stakes test. Encourage a variety of methods of demonstrating accomplishment suitable for different situations. Emphasize success rather than failure. In the end, acknowledge that neither grades nor effectiveness pay will ever be perfectly accurate, or even perfectly fair. But just as is true with grades given by teachers, effectiveness pay for teachers needs to be as accurate and fair as we can manage. At the end of the day, we do assign grades to students and the grades matter. (If you think grades don't matter, tell it to the student held back in ninth grade or the student turned down by Harvard.) Despite all the bumps and warts in measuring student success, those who say we can't do it had better explain how it is that we *do* grade students.

To focus on addressing the objections to effectiveness pay, I'll begin with a caricature of an effectiveness pay system. The caricature here serves to magnify potential real problems so they can be avoided or mitigated

STRAW MAN PAY SYSTEM

At the end of each academic year, students in the Nowheresville School District will sit for a four-hour standardized test. Students in grades 1–12 will be tested on their memorization of vocabulary and rote knowledge of basic arithmetic operations. Kindergarten students will be supplied with crayons and tested on their ability to color inside the lines.

Teachers will be rated according to the percentage of their students demonstrating proficiency at grade level. The top 10 percent of teachers will each receive $25,000 bonuses. The bottom 10 percent of teachers will face a disciplinary hearing.

Sounds like a system designed by someone with a screw loose, doesn't it? In fact, a compensation system like this one is probably as nutty as a compensation system based zero percent on student outcomes—like the one we have.

Count the things wrong with this straw man: (1) Everything depends on a single high-stakes test; (2) The test focuses on the wrong things; (3) Teachers get no credit for students who excel, since the goal is "proficiency"; (4) Teachers get no credit for students they help climb from low starting points if the teachers don't get the students all the way to the announced standard; (5) Very few teachers get a bonus; and (6) The punitive aspect is completely misguided. (Feel free to add to the list.)

Let's break this down into three major pieces. First, we must have tests that do a good job of measuring the student results that we care about. Second, recognizing that students start in many different positions, we need to use metrics that tell us about the contribution of the teacher rather than the student's previous education, the student's background, or other student factors that the teacher can't control. Third, in any situation where there's significant money at stake, some folks will be tempted to bend the rules. Some countermeasures are required.

TEST SENSIBLY

The first design rule for a smart compensation system is to reward the thing you want to get more of. If you want third graders to learn their times tables, reward teachers whose students learn their times

YOU GET WHAT YOU PAY FOR

Randy Eberts and colleagues have a great example of "you get what you pay for." The researchers compared two Michigan high schools, one with a bonus system that offered potentially quite sizeable bonuses to teachers, and one that used a traditional pay scale. Bonuses were based on the percentage of students completing a course (this was an "alternative-education" high school, so course completion was a real issue) and student ratings of teachers on a fifteen-item questionnaire. The effect of bonuses for course completion was a large increase in the number of students who completed courses. Attendance didn't improve and neither did grades.[2]

tables. (We don't do this now.) If parents like to brag that their third graders are being taught by a PhD, then raise the pay for third-grade teachers who earn a doctorate. (We *do* do this now).

Some things are easier to measure than others. For example, it's easier to test whether a student has memorized a long vocabulary list than whether that same student can produce a clear, well-written expository essay. We just have to get past the mindset that the only knowledge we can test is the most mechanical kind. Put it this way, teachers test a wide variety of material before assigning grades. The same needs to be done at higher levels of testing.

A big part of the answer to the mismatch between tests and our goals for our kids is something that educational reformers have long worked toward—and this is so obvious that saying it is going to sound dumb—we should design tests that are matched to our goals for student learning. Instead of teaching to the test we should test what we want to teach.

If this is so obvious, why do we still have too many problematic standardized tests in use? Because making up good tests is expensive. Most of the expense of test creation is a one-time, fixed cost that remains the same whether the test is used in one small school district or it's used across the nation. There's no reason the U.S. can't afford to have ten (or fifty!) different standardized fifth-grade geography tests available, each one validated so that a district or school or teacher can freely choose to be evaluated by using any one of the ten tests. With enough variety, the issue of teaching to the test largely disappears. The school gets to pick a test that closely matches with its curriculum. Once the expense of test preparation is spread widely, the cost is low enough to not much matter.

Nothing gets around the fundamental need to decide what our society values. What about teaching art and music? At the college level, these are generally taught as academic subjects and learning is evaluated pretty much as it is for history or botany. Our art and music goals in K–12 are different from those at the college level, and are not easily measured by paper-and-pencil test. Care must be taken not to abandon areas we value just because the output is hard to measure.

Moulthrop et al. describe an example bonus objective from the pilot program for Denver's ProComp.[3]

> For example, a high school French teacher discusses possible goals with her principal. They agree they should set a goal for her first-year students of acquiring 1,000 new words over the course of the year, in addition to mastering the simple past, present, and future tenses of regular verbs. She gives her students pretests and posttests and aims for 80 percent of her students getting a C or better on the posttest. If that happens, she has met her goal, and she receives $750.

Spending money to prepare extensive test banks also combats teaching to the test in its most literal meaning, where a teacher who knows the questions that are going to appear on a standardized test teaches the answers to those questions rather than teaching the underlying material. If a test ought to be thirty questions long, three thousand questions can be prepared. Then the test sent to a school consists of thirty questions drawn randomly, where the school doesn't know in advance which questions have been chosen. (If a teacher prepares her students for all three thousand questions on a single point, there's a good chance she's succeeded in teaching the underlying concept.)

A useful buzzword to look for in reference to "test what we teach" is "curriculum-based." One state, New York, has long had a curriculum-based external exit examination system (CBEEES)—the Regents Exams. In this case, long is about 130 years! These statewide subject matter exams test high school level mastery in a variety of areas. According to one study, there is a direct relation between the use of these exams and the fact that New York students perform about one grade level higher on NAEP and SAT exams than do students in other states, after controlling for socioeconomic background.[4] (More on the external part of CBEEES later.)

Parents care about reading and writing and learning biology, all of which are quite objectively measurable. Parents also care about self-discipline and self-confidence, etc., which you can see but which you can't easily put a number on. We want a compensation system to reflect that which we value, not just those things to which one can

Just because you can't objectively measure something doesn't mean that you can't observe results. One measure of how terrific my daughters' completely flaky elementary school was is the observation that if an adult wandered down the hall with his arms full, it was likely that a random, loud, eight-year-old boy would interrupt whatever game he was playing long enough to hold open a door. And then unselfconsciously dash back to play. Take my word for it, this is not typical eight-year-old boy behavior.

attach an objective numerical score. The conflict between these goals is more apparent than real. If you teach kids self-discipline and confidence, the results will show up indirectly when we measure learning reading and writing and biology.

Of course, some of the benefits of learning to be a good learner don't show up until sometime down the road. Consider the situation in a K–3 elementary. It's not unreasonable to do some testing of what third graders have learned in reading, writing, arithmetic, etc., and to link a piece of teacher pay to measured outcomes. While we might do some testing of kindergarteners for diagnostic purposes, we probably don't want to much link teacher pay to the results. So we might have more differential pay at the third-grade level than at the kindergarten level. Or we might have equal amounts of differential pay, but have third-grade teacher effectiveness pay depend half on testing of the teacher's students and half on the schoolwide average, while kindergarten teacher effectiveness pay depends 90 percent on the schoolwide results and only 10 percent on class results (a weaker link between outcomes and results). Or perhaps kindergarten effectiveness measures don't have anything to do with objective tests; instead each kindergarten class is evaluated by several different master teachers (a more subjective approach to measurement) who look to see whether the kindergarten kids are excited about school and getting ready for first grade.

A word of caution, though. There's a lot of evidence that the early years of schooling are especially critical. The more important a particular educational stage, the more important it is to find a valid way to measure the results at that stage. The kinds of measurements that make sense for young students may well be more expensive than the kinds of tests that can be used at a later stage.

Academics matter, but they're not all that we expect from our schools. Teachers at the kindergarten level, for example, have a bigger effect on teaching social/behavioral skills than they do on teaching academic skills. While there is a correlation between those teachers good at imparting the former and those good at the latter, the available statistical evidence is that many teachers are better at one than at the other.[5]

At the least, we should consider whether early stage measurement might be a high-payoff investment.

Learn from the Way Teachers Use Tests

Teachers have been evaluating what their students learn for a very long time.

You'll note that teachers (in America at least) rarely think the way to do this is with a single high-stakes test. One technique that teachers use that I find particularly adaptable for our purposes is the use of multiple low-stakes tests in place of a single high-stakes test. Teachers routinely use multiple low-stakes tests—pop quizzes, weekly exams, midterms, final exams—in evaluating students. Teacher evaluation should go as far down this same path as possible.

Using many small tests relieves very understandable stress on all parties. What's more, teachers and students have different strengths.

[T]eachers don't like the idea of judging performance and compensation based on a test because they suspect it can be unfair. They oppose being judged by their students' performance on a single school day (or week). It would be an interesting proposition for a district to consider a distributed test strategy, with more tests of shorter length, scattered throughout the year, reducing the annual stress the current tests produce. Not only would multiple measures yield relatively stable assessments of teacher performance, but teachers would have much more opportunity to make midcourse corrections with more data.

Kate Walsh, President, National Council on Teacher Quality[6]

REWARD MULTIPLE PATHS TO SUCCESS (BUT DO INSIST ON SUCCESS AS THE BOTTOM LINE)

Mrs. Zilembo taught me how to write a formal mathematical proof in her high school geometry class. Alas, no one is ever going to be able to teach me the approach to geometry that depends on perceiving spatial relations; apparently my brain just isn't wired that way. To this day, when I teach PhD econometrics I either stick to the algebraic approach or ask a colleague to give a guest lecture on geometric interpretations. Mrs. Zilembo gave me a good grade for getting the right answers, even though I had to get those answers through logical reasoning rather than understanding spatial relations.

When teachers are awarded points for a variety of different student success measures, they can emphasize their own strengths and look for different strengths in different students.

In the greater economy a good manager is usually someone who brings out the best strengths of each of his or her employees, not someone who treats employees as if they should be clones. A system that in part rewards teachers for their students' successes should similarly reward multiple kinds of success. When testing confuses high standards with narrow standards, it has wandered astray.

Using multiple evaluations is a good idea; it's also a politic idea because it makes effectiveness pay enormously more palatable to

LOW-STAKES TESTING FOR HIGH-STAKES RESULTS

You may have noticed that high-stakes tests are not exactly popular. The "high" in current high-stakes testing ain't nothing compared to what we'll see as effectiveness pay spreads. With rare exception, current high-stakes testing has consequences for students but the consequences for teachers rarely exceed some mild embarrassment. Once in a great while a school gets reorganized. You *never* see any rewards for those all those teachers who bring their students successfully through the testing process.

teachers and teacher unions. Here's what the American Federation of Teachers says:[7]

> AFT locals have developed schoolwide differentiated pay based on a combination of academic indicators, including standardized test scores, students' classroom work, dropout rates and disciplinary incidents. Teachers reject being evaluated on a single test score.

Let me repeat that last sentence—it's important. *Teachers reject being evaluated on a single test score.*

Testing and Dumbing It Down

Why so much resistance to paying for measured results? Frankly, one cause is that some educators privately fear they can't produce results, so they don't want anyone checking up on them. But a legitimate source of resistance is parents' fear that a test-heavy system will emphasize the wrong goals. In particular, parents of educationally successful students worry, with some cause, about education being dumbed down. Here's what Julian Betts and colleagues found:

> Much of the most vocal opposition to standards-based reform, however, comes from a completely different segment of the population—that of generally high achievers. For example, according to recent reports, "Wisconsin scuttled plans for a high school exit exam after a protest lodged mainly by more-affluent parents." Similarly, efforts in Massachusetts to boycott the statewide exams have been concentrated in affluent and high-achieving suburbs, as well as high-spending communities such as Cambridge, rather than such urban areas as Boston. State representative Ruth Baiser told a group of Brookline test critics that most of her legislative colleagues support the exams. "It's just those of us from districts that were already doing really well, like Lincoln-Sudbury, Brookline, and Newton, who feel that our systems are at risk of being dragged down by ed reform," she said.[8]

In a similar vein, Tony Wagner, in *The Global Achievement Gap*, interviewed corporate CEOs reporting

> concern about their children's suburban public schools—schools that many of us consider to be among the best in the country: too much time teaching to the test, too much time memorizing,

at the expense of spending time on thinking skills that are more important.[9]

If you'll forgive another "this is so obvious it's going to sound dumb" suggestion, the way to avoid dragging down high-achieving programs is to be sure that teachers and schools get rewards for students' highest achievements. There's no reason everyone has to take *all* the same tests. If a student can score well enough on the Advanced Placement (AP) calculus test to earn college credit, then making that student take low-level math tests is a waste of school resources as well as a waste of the student's time.

Standardization and Innovation

Creating suitable ways to measure what students have learned will have to be an ongoing process, because what we want students to learn evolves. It's important that the use of measurement doesn't freeze what schools do.

Effectiveness measurement sometimes provides a boost to new teaching approaches. If someone invents a new pedagogy for teaching times tables, we can reasonably insist that students do well on standard math tests. Either students know how much two times three is or they don't. Because we can validate the output, application of the innovation needn't

Overstandardization risks killing all the quirky programs that contribute to making each school unique. As an example, my daughters' Seattle high school offered a course in marine science that was notoriously tough. There was a clear, objective measure of student learning: the final exam took students to the waterfront aquarium where they had to identify and state facts about dozens and dozens of aquatic life-forms . . . with their parents looking on. A great, kinky, course taught by a couple of inspired teachers. All well until Washington State announced a new statewide science test focusing on the more traditional high school science subjects, killing the marine science course.[10]

Standardized testing is a good tool for pulling up the bottom and middle of the distribution. Used carelessly, standardized testing risks lopping off the top, too.

wait for someone to approve the new pedagogy. In such a case, rewarding student results liberates teachers to use their own judgment in picking an approach that works for them and for their students.

But what happens if you want to teach something new or teach in a way that isn't measured by existing tests? For example, if a high school wants to teach a Latin course based on Virgil's *Aeneid*, it can use the College Board's Advanced Placement test as a tool for evaluating how well the course goes. If the high school instead wanted to teach a Greek course based on Homer's *Iliad*, well, since no AP test is available, evaluation would be much more difficult.

A piece of the *quid pro quo* for linking part of pay to test results should be a greater investment in evaluation tools for unusual and innovative course objectives.

STUDENTS DON'T ALL HAVE AN EQUAL START

Go into most any classroom, certainly almost any school, on the first day of school. Some of the children have already mastered most of the work expected for their grade level.

Others start two years behind. (And if the teacher hasn't figured which student is which on day one, she will have by day two.) With a bonus riding on the level of student test scores, how would you like to be the fifth teacher who gets handed a class who are mostly two years behind? If you do a great job in the nine months you have, your

WASHINGTON, DC SCHOOL CHIEF MICHELLE RHEE ON SOME OF HER GOALS FOR A TEACHER CONTRACT

Measuring excellence. We cannot rely on test scores alone. Good evaluations of teaching practices must be well rounded. Only some of our teachers work in grades or subjects in which tests are given, so we must use many assessments to measure student growth.

A growth model of achievement. Many teachers inherit classes of students who are far behind academically. Yet some teachers, even with minimal support, move their students two to three grade levels ahead in a year. Teachers will not be evaluated on an absolute measure but on how far they take their students.

Washington Post, *February 2009*[11]

kids might close the gap from two years behind to only one year behind. That's not going to get you a penny of bonus. Purely financially, you may as well go home.

The situation at the top end is no better. Suppose a teacher gets handed a fifth-grade class that's already been accelerated by two years. As far as financial incentives go, the teacher could simply coast. This set of kids will have no trouble achieving fifth-grade test scores even if they're mostly ignored.

While there's no perfect fix for different starting points, you can mostly handle the issue by rewarding teachers for how much they move their students along rather than the absolute level the students reach. Economists measure contributions to output by "value-added." This approach, Value-added Measures (VAM), has been widely adopted in educational research and needs to be used as part of any effectiveness pay system.

What's VAM? If a neighbor at a party told you he'd bought a little vacant lot, worked every weekend over the summer to clean it up, and then sold it for a million dollars, you might think him a pretty clever fellow. Later you learn that the chap bought the lot for $999,000. Suddenly he looks a lot more ordinary. Economists would say that the neighbor's contribution to the value of the lot, his *value-added,* was only $1,000. Another way to say this is that what impresses is the *improvement* in the value of the asset, not its final level.

The parallel for deciding on bonuses is to try to capture how much a teacher helps students *add* to their ability. This means you need at least a rough way of measuring how much a student gains over a year, not just where the student ends up. If we simply pay for high test scores, then everyone is going to want to teach only the very best students—clearly not what we want.

One approach to creating a VAM is to look at how much a student's score changes from one year to the next. So if a fourth grader begins the year reading at first-grade level and ends the year reading

> When 35,000 Texas teachers were asked their preferences about performance measures for teacher compensation incentives, improvements in student test scores ranked first. The level of student test scores, while viewed favorably, came in way down the list.[12]

TEXAS ALREADY USES A VAM-LIKE MEASURE TO COMPARE SCHOOLS

Texas uses the Comparable Index (CI), which measures students' annual progress in math and reading—a value-added measure. A school's average CI is then compared to other demographically similar schools.[13]

at the third-grade level, the student's teacher's effectiveness pay reflects two years value-added. The simple year-over-year VAM is pretty straightforward although it does increase recordkeeping requirements, especially in areas in which many students move between school districts.

A somewhat more flexible, albeit more complex, approach uses statistical methods to assign to each student a base score that reflects how easy or how difficult it's likely to be to teach that student. Such a formula can reflect individual histories, but may also account for low-income status, for whether the family is English speaking, and for other socioeconomic factors that affect a student's teachability. VAM is then measured as improvement relative to each student's base score. In theory, this more flexible approach is better than simply looking at changes in test scores over time. The flexible approach is more expensive to implement and harder to explain to stakeholders. There is a legitimate discussion about a particular school district choosing to go with the simple or more flexible VAM.

Without VAM, teachers are placed in the miserable position of being penalized for teaching students who are furthest behind. Value-added measures are imperfect,[14] but they at least give us an approximate

ADJUSTING FOR WHERE STUDENTS START MATTERS

My late mother worked as a New York City school psychologist in the 1950s and 1960s. One of her first assignments was to work with a group of students who had been identified as mentally retarded by a standardized IQ test. It didn't take her very long to explain to the relevant administrators that if you give an IQ test in English to kids who only speak Spanish they do tend to get kind of low scores.

> Critics of value-added assessment tend to embrace the concept but don't want the results gleaned from such analysis to be used for accountability purposes. . . . But teachers are the dominant school input, in terms of both spending and impact on student learning. Excluding them essentially leaves the education system without accountability.
>
> *Anita Summers*[15]

leveling of the playing field. Almost any value-added measure is better than using raw test scores.

MAKING IT HARD TO BEND THE RULES

One of the real problems in measuring successful teaching is the pressure inside the system to manipulate results. Sometimes, manipulation takes the form of outright cheating, as was the case when a number of Chicago teachers were caught faking their students' answers on standardized tests.[16] That's a rare extreme. More commonly, manipulation is more subtle, such as encouraging weaker students to opt out of standardized testing. Such problems arise now, in a world where relatively little is at stake for teachers or schools. Imagine the games that would be played if significant money rested on demonstrating results. As pay and results become more tightly linked, it becomes even important to pick measurements that are not easily manipulated. In other words, we want to make sure that when we see a signal of teacher success we're seeing a real success and not just a manipulation of the signal. If we decided to reward teachers for every student who got an A, it's a pretty good bet that a lot more A's

> Student test scores [among other indicators] should ALSO be considered—NOT by comparing the scores of last year's students with the scores of this year's students, but by assessing whether a teacher's students show real growth while in his classroom.
>
> *Randi Weingarten, President of the AFT*[17]

Saying that teachers will game the system when significant money becomes involved isn't a knock on teachers. Teachers, as is true with most professionals, take pride in a job well done. Teachers, as is true of nearly everyone, also respond to incentives relevant to feeding their family.

There is an easily seen example at the college level, where an increasing portion of the faculty is untenured and whose continued employment depends significantly on student evaluations. One documented path to better student evaluations, although not one faculty take pride in, is to inflate grades. The result is as one would expect: higher grades.

would be given out. Whether more students would have *earned* an A is a different question. The general point is that we want to separate the people with the incentives for student success from the people who measure that success.

For example, rewarding schools for better high school graduation rates is dicey. On the one hand, some schools have very successful efforts that reduce dropout rates. Dropping out of high school is an economic disaster for a student, so this is really important. On the other hand, if the student gets a diploma but can't read or do basic math, nothing's really been solved. If a school prevents dropouts *and* the students can pass an external test, then we've good reason to believe the school and its teachers should be rewarded.

8

Team Bonuses: We're All in This Together, Sometimes

Share-and-share alike, or to each according to her work? Should all teachers share equally in a schoolwide effectiveness pay pool? Would it be better for each teacher to be rewarded solely in accord with her own students' performance? There's no single best answer for all schools and all situations. There are, however, some useful guidelines that keep our focus on two (sometimes clashing) ideas. On the one hand, any kind of sharing has to maintain individual incentives. On the other hand, teachers and teacher unions look at sharing as a kind of protection against individuals being singled out for unfair treatment.

The middle of this chapter is devoted to some rough rules for sharing. I offer these for you to use as starting points in thinking about specific compensation plans. As bookends, I'll discuss two real-world compensation plans. It's not that either plan is perfect for team bonuses in schools, but I find them to be illuminating examples.

The first example is not exactly from the schoolyard.

CHAMPIONS OF AMERICA'S PASTIME

Like many Americans, I enjoy taking in the occasional ball game. It's an excuse for a hot dog, maybe a beer, and summer evenings at Seattle's Safeco Field tend toward the gorgeous. Unlike more serious fans who follow the insides of the game, my knowledge of how major league baseball players are paid could be summed up by the phrase "a lot, I guess." A friend who's much more serious about baseball than I am suggested taking a look at how baseball players are paid to stimulate thinking about how teachers might be paid; not so much because the answers will be the same (I was right about the "a lot" part. We're not going that far for teachers.) but because baseball has had to answer many of the same questions. The analogy between schoolwide bonuses and extra pay for players in the World Series and play-offs is especially interesting.

The master contract governing baseball is negotiated between Major League Baseball and the players' union, the Major League Baseball Players Association. The contract specifies a minimum salary covering all players for a season in the majors ($400,000 for the 2010 season). Players are free to negotiate for higher base salaries, and most of them do. The master contract is also quite explicit that it allows "Special Covenants to be included in an individual Uniform Player's Contract, which actually or potentially provide additional benefits to the Player." In other words, players and teams can sign up for bonuses for hitting a given batting average, etc. It's interesting that baseball allows for lots of individualized incentive pay, although I'd be surprised to see as much individualized incentive pay for contracts in public schools.

What's the reward for the ultimate success in baseball, winning the World Series? The short version is that a pool is created from the gate receipts from the first four World Series games, the first four league championship games, and the first three division series. Sixty percent of the gate receipts then goes into the players' pool. The team that wins the Series gets 36 percent of the players' pool, with smaller amounts going to the other teams who made it into the postseason.

Notice several elements. First, the postseason bonus is entirely a form of effectiveness pay. You have to win to get it. Second, the size of the bonus pool is entirely objective; in fact, it's derived by a prespecified, mathematical rule. Third, the award goes to the players as a group, not to individuals. That's analogous to a schoolwide bonus.

So how does the team pool—worth several hundred thousand dollars per player—get divvied up? Simple, the players on the team vote. Management isn't present during the vote and there aren't any contract restrictions on how the players can give out the money. As it works out, players on the active roster during the series typically get equal shares but the players vote full shares to a few nonroster players. Partial shares and straight cash awards are also voted, some of it given to nonplayer staff of the winning organization.

In other words, there's no formula at all. Champions sit down together and figure out what's best for the team.

It's not that I think the baseball solution is likely to fit many schools; still it's interesting to see how the system uses individual incentives in some places, team incentives in others, and a combination of objective and subjective decision-making. But it's time to go back to talking about schools.

ROUGH RULES FOR SHARING

Rough Rule for Sharing 1

> Effectiveness pay goes to those who produced the effect (better student outcomes), whether a person or team.

If the world were simpler than it is, then it might be true that what a student learns in a year depends entirely on the work of a single classroom teacher. Alternatively it might be true that what a student learns in a year depends equally on every adult in the building. If the world were simple in either of these ways, divvying up effectiveness pay would be an easy task. In the first case, the money would go to the single teacher in response to her success with her class. In the second case, the money for the entire school would be split equally among all.

The world not being simple, what a typical student learns depends heavily on his or her own teacher, but other people have an important influence, too. This leads to the *Rough Rule for Sharing 1*, which opens this section.

Most of what most teachers contribute is their direct work with students. Sometimes it's pretty clear which teacher ought to get the credit for student achievement. Sometimes who made the contribution is

---

TEACHER BONUSES IN TEXAS

The Texas Governor's Educator Excellence Grants require three-quarters of grants to go to classroom teachers and allow flexibility in how the remaining quarter is distributed. Schools have generally used that last quarter to reward nonclassroom staff rather than spend the money on professional development or other activities.[1]

---

clear to everyone on the scene, but not in a way that's objectively measurable. As a concrete example, suppose we look at a high school where much of the school's effectiveness pay rests on student scores on standardized math tests. Let's say the high school has half a dozen algebra teachers and one athletic coach. Sometimes coaches are in a position to influence a teenager's behavior in ways that a classroom teacher can't. Our hypothetical high school might very well take a piece of the effectiveness pay earned by high scores and use it to reward that coach for getting the athletes to class. If done wisely, the algebra teachers will encourage the school to divert part of the math-related bonus to the coach. Why? The coach gets the kids to class, so the algebra teachers can do their stuff, so the students can learn their stuff, so the size of the pay pool in which the algebra teachers share goes up. It's a lot like ballplayers sharing their World Series bonus with a trainer who never bats, but who helps them do their job better.

In the coach example, the link between what the coach does and student test scores would be pretty hard to measure. Even where accomplishments are easily measured, there should be room for thoughtful flexibility in allocating bonuses within a school. Sometimes a teacher takes one for the team, raising everyone else's success rate at her own expense. Here's an example taken from the economic literature on what might be called "the rotten apple spoils the barrel" phenomenon.[2]

Think about a school with six teachers and one hundred fifty students at a particular grade level. One hundred forty-four students are spread across the standard range of abilities and behaviors. Six students are totally disruptive. In a traditional arrangement, each teacher has twenty-four typical students and one rotten apple—twenty-five students in all. As the rotten apples ruin it for the rest, nobody learns much and all six teachers get pretty minimal bonuses.

Instead, we might give five teachers larger classes, twenty-nine students apiece, and have the sixth teacher take all six disruptive students. With only six students, if that teacher has the right gifts, the disruptive kids might actually learn something. Whether they do or not, the five larger classes will make far greater progress and one hundred forty-four kids will come out way ahead.

The point isn't whether separating kids or lumping them together is the wiser course; that depends on the situation. The point is that in the standard arrangement no one learns and no teacher gets rewarded, while in the second situation at least 96 percent of the students flourish. But who deserves a bonus, five teachers or all six? Clearly, the sixth teacher deserves a full share of the credit and a full bonus, even though the six students may turn in an abysmal performance. We can't link her pay just to the performance of the six bad apples simply because that's easily measurable. She has to share the credit and reward for the schoolwide gain.

Rough Rule for Sharing 2

> Effectiveness pay should create incentives to *directly* improve student outcomes, and also create incentives to assist or prod other team members in order to *indirectly* improve student outcomes.

In addition to teaching their own students, the other thing that teachers do—and probably do less of than we would like—is to help other teachers along. The positive side of teamwork is obvious. Less pleasantly, schoolwide incentives play an important role in engendering the difficult conversations we spoke of earlier. Getting those difficult conversations to occur is critically important. Let's think about a classroom situation where 95 percent of the school's total contribution to student learning comes from the classroom teacher and only 5 percent depends on other school team members. Suppose now that we linked differential pay 95 percent to a particular teacher's student outcomes. While that sounds logical, consider the following. Sometimes we're going to run into a slacker teacher who's willing to do a mediocre job for mediocre pay. That's not fair to the students stuck in that class. A lousy teacher who worked for free would be a lousy deal. So we want the other teachers in the school to be pressuring our hypothetical slacker. That means we want those teachers to have a financial stake. Part of having teachers' skin in the game is that the playing field extends past the four walls of the individual teacher's class. Schoolwide sharing incentivizes difficult conversations in a way that individual effectiveness pay doesn't.

Is a team only two teachers working in tandem, or the whole school? There is no single right answer, but *Rough rule 2* suggests a useful guideline about making teams too large. Teams need to be small enough to allow for meaningful accountability within the team. Call this the "difficult conversation rule." On those occasions when a teacher isn't pulling her weight, the team should be small enough that a teammate will talk with her. Here's an example. Suppose a $10,000 bonus for the team is in jeopardy. If the team has five members, one of them is likely to decide the $2,000 share is worth a difficult chat. In fact, several team members are likely to speak up. If, instead, there are fifty team members, it's more likely that for a $200 share, no individual will want to be the bad guy; hence no difficult conversations. Think of the difficult conversation rule as being that teams have to be small enough that even though rewards are shared, teachers still have the individual incentive to make the whole team succeed.

Rough Rule for Sharing 3

> The bigger the team, the bigger the share of effectiveness pay that's allocated at the individual level. The smaller the team, the more that effectiveness pay is shared team-wide.

Big teams tend to dilute the reward from team bonuses that individuals earn as a result of their own activity. Since this dilution works against the incentive effect, team bonuses don't work as well in big teams. In other words, size matters.

Let me illustrate a case in which complete sharing would fail. Imagine a crummy school with unmotivated teachers. Maybe a fairly large school, one with two hundred teachers in the building. A new, enthusiastic principal arrives with a turnaround plan that begins with re-seeding the school with half a dozen Teach For America veterans. But this is a world in which the effectiveness bonus is split equally among all teachers. No matter how well half a dozen out of two hundred teachers perform, realistically six of two hundred teachers aren't going to have much impact on the average score of the school's students. The average score is still going to be crummy and the school bonus pool will be negligible. As a result, hiring those six special teachers is going to be a challenge, because potential recruits will know that their efforts won't bring a personal financial reward. Sure, a schoolwide bonus would be okay if you could turn over the whole staff. But there's no way to kick-start the process. So even though the principal is trying to reinvigorate the whole school, she will need the ability to single out individual rewards. A small school might be different. A school of two hundred teachers should go lightly on awards that require all two hundred to pull together.

Rough Rule for Sharing 4

> Both politics and psychology lean toward sharing. Always this needs to be respected; sometimes it needs to be resisted.

If teachers were robots, getting a rational compensation scheme up and running wouldn't meet with much resistance. Teachers being much like the rest of us, issues of politics and psychology do come up, and they come up in ways that tend to push toward schoolwide sharing.

One such element is quite rational. Student outcome measures average out more accurately for larger groups of students than for smaller ones, so schoolwide scores are less error-prone than are the scores for any particular teacher. Quite understandably, this pushes risk-averse teachers toward preferring a heavy weight on measures of schoolwide outcomes. If one wants to counterbalance this, local plans might allow more experienced teachers to bank part of their effectiveness pay from year to year.

Most of us dislike being judged, and while this may not be rational, it's very real. That's how egos work. One way to escape ego damage is to be evaluated as part of a group. Despite the suggestion in earlier chapters that under *Profit* the vast majority of teachers will find themselves earning substantial effectiveness pay, fear about being singled out as a bad performer matters. This source of pressure is probably best resisted.

Finally, there's an issue that's partially rational and partially not. Schools can be intensely political places, prone to cliques and in-groups and out-groups. So any system of individually differential effectiveness pay raises legitimate concerns about fairness. A share-and-share alike system eliminates concerns about unfair evaluations. Unfortunately, it also eliminates the fairness element of rewarding hard work. I'll close the chapter with an example in which a school administration and union came together to reach a balance between these two concerns.

UNION AND DISTRICT PULLING TOGETHER

The United Federation of Teachers (UFT), the New York City teachers' union, and the New York City school system have reached an interesting experimental agreement that provides schoolwide bonus pools to select schools. Part of what makes this such an interesting example is that the UFT and the NYC school administration regularly go to war with one another. But they seem to have come up with a compromise that moves everyone forward.

Here are a few elements I've excerpted from the district/union agreement:[3]

- **How is the total amount in the bonus pool determined?** The [school] Compensation Committee will receive an initial pool that is equivalent to $3,000 per full-time UFT-represented member. If the school then meets or exceeds its target it qualifies for the *full* bonus. If the school meets at least 75% of its target, members will receive *half* the amount the Compensation Committee indicated. (All bonus amounts entered will simply be cut to 50%.) If the school does not meet at least 75% of its target, no one will receive a bonus.
- **Is the Compensation Committee required to give every member . . . the same amount?** No. The Compensation Committee can designate any employee to receive any amount it wishes that employee to receive.
- **In summary, can the Compensation Committee choose to distribute the award in *any* way it deems appropriate?** No, the Compensation Committee may not distribute the award based on seniority. Compensation Committees may elect to award each member equally, to differentiate by title, or to differentiate by individual, as long as all the recipients are UFT-represented employees.
- **Will Principals and Assistant Principals receive a bonus if the school meets or exceeds its target?** Yes. If UFT-represented members qualify for the bonus due to the school meeting or exceeding its target, Principals and Assistant Principals will also receive a bonus. However, the Compensation Committee will not be involved in determining the amount of this bonus, which is instead determined by the DOE in consultation with the CSA [the NYC school administrators union].

A lot of thought went into making this fair, and also making it work. Here's an excerpt from the actual "Memorandum of Agreement" about the design and operation of the compensation committee:[4]

> Each Participant School will form a compensation committee composed of the principal and a principal's designee (e.g., an

assistant principal) and two UFT-represented staff members elected in a Chapter supervised election by the UFT-represented staff on an annual basis from among volunteers. The compensation committee will determine, **by consensus**, matters related to both eligibility for and the size of individual awards to UFT-represented staff members. However the compensation committee shall presume that all UFT-represented staff employed at a school that meets the targets for the bonus have contributed to the school's achievement to some extent and therefore should share in the bonus. **If there is no consensus the pool of money will not be distributed to the school.**

9

Compensation: Keeping Your Eye on the Ball

We've talked about paying for success from the heights of thirty thousand feet and then zoomed in for several chapters' worth of details. Now I'd like to take a look from ground level. I'll discuss some of the issues in reaching agreement on a *Profit*-oriented compensation system that you should keep an eye out for. I want to emphasize that the guidelines here deserve attention in designing a system, but they are not intended to be prescriptive.

The material here is intended to be of more than philosophical interest. I hope you'll get involved in moving your local school system toward success. Remember that while moving to a *Profit* system requires being tough-minded, it'll be a win-win-win situation for teachers, student, and America.

In fact, I've made you a little cheat sheet at the end of this chapter. Copy it and use it.[1] Parents, give copies to teachers. Teachers, give copies to parents. Use it as a conversation starter.

WHAT'S NEGOTIABLE AND WHAT ISN'T

I'm going to go through a bunch of details. The importance of a particular detail will vary from one local situation to another. But there are two issues—Mechanism I and local involvement—that matter everywhere. Raising teacher salaries to attract and retain the best simply isn't negotiable. Without higher teacher pay, all other reform efforts are simply fiddling around the edges. Local involvement is also critical, both to get local buy in and to make sure plans fit local needs, but guidelines are likely to evolve from state-level and even national discussions.

If someone tries to sell you teacher compensation restructuring that doesn't include a big raise, walk away. If someone tries to sell you a rigid, top-down plan you might want to listen, but you should be very nervous. So I'll talk about Mechanism I and local involvement first. Past these two, there's a lot more room for negotiation and compromise.

Mechanism I and 40 percent. Remember that to attract and retain a great teacher corps we need to get wages up, about 40 percent on average. We can all discuss whether we want to increase total educational spending or transfer funds from other areas of current spending, but one way or another, teacher salaries have to go up for this to work. Since it'll take a few years for student achievement to rise sufficiently to earn out the whole 40 percent, the starting bill may be a little lower. But the money must be there when teachers deliver on their end. The U.S. has seen too many instances of asking teachers to go through wrenching changes for very little reward. There is a long history of initiating a schooling reform, including talk of modestly higher teacher pay, only to abandon ship after only a few years. A *credible* offer of a real raise gives teachers an enormous reason to join hands with others to make *Profit* to succeed.

Notice we're talking here about something more than the numbers of the 40 percent raise to attract and retain. We also have to get the all the stakeholders to reach agreement. We're asking teachers to change how they do business, with the offer that they'll be rewarded for it. There's a flip side to this. Teachers aren't the only stakeholders. In particular, we have to get public buy in, most particularly taxpayer buy in. It's going to be absolutely necessary to overcome public reluctance to throw more money after yet another reform.

School spending has risen steadily for decades, demonstrating taxpayer willingness to pay for education. Since we're talking about massive and fairly quick infusions of yet more money, taxpayers deserve reassurance that the money will be well spent. We do this by linking spending to results: no results, no increased spending. Careful attention to Mechanism II pretty much guarantees this linkage. Remind people of this, as necessary.

> Performance incentives that reward [teachers and other local decision-makers] for progress toward the goals of the school—while recognizing their freedom to determine how that progress is best achieved—are the best way to focus teachers, principals, and other school personnel on improving education.
>
> *Eric Hanushek*[2]

Involvement of local stakeholders in design. Participation of teachers, administrators, unions, and others with a local stake is absolutely critical in designing a compensation system. There are two quite different reasons for insisting on local design: (1) varying plans for varying needs, and (2) building a foundation of trust for a difficult transition.

Government programs often have the unfortunate habit of imposing uniformity through a one-size-fits-all program. Schooling in America has always emphasized local and state control, resulting in considerable diversity. While some reformers have called for centralized, national policy (as exists in many other countries), we Americans seem to like our messy, jumbled system. With a big change such as differential pay, allowing tailoring to local conditions and encouraging innovation is important. One-size-fits-all is the enemy of flexibility both across place and across time. We need rules that allow for much local and state-by-state flexibility, just so long as "flexibility" doesn't become a codeword for "anything goes." So, for example, a state might vet a variety of test banks and let districts choose from among them. Or the federal government might put up part of the funds for teacher raises and insist the new money be used for differential pay while allowing states and localities decide on the details of how differential pay is to be awarded.

> When Minnesota implemented its Q Comp compensation experiment (described in more detail in Chapter 10, Some (Recent) History Lessons) part of the deal was that each district could develop a local plan which would then be submitted to the state department of education for final approval.

The need to build a foundation of trust cannot be overemphasized. We need to remember that a partial linkage of pay to results is an enormous shock to the system. Even though differential pay is the vehicle for delivering a major raise, it's still scary to teachers accustomed to lockstep compensation. An emphasis on measuring student outcomes is at least potentially scary for parents, too. There's no way to prove in advance that a plan will be perfect. (After all, it won't be perfect.) When different stakeholders come together to build the plan, they're enormously more likely to be willing to ride out the inevitable implementation bumps and ripples together.

NUTS AND BOLTS

Let's go through some of the nuts and bolts. My hope is that outlining some of the issues that will arise during discussions will facilitate keeping such discussions on a positive track. Remember, these suggestions are guidelines, not prescriptions.

Transparency about expectations and rewards. If you want people to buy into a new way of doing business, they need to understand what's expected of them. That argues for transparency. Attempts at merit pay plans two decades back failed on this issue. Dick Murnane and coauthors put it this way in widely cited research, "[M]ost merit pay plans died because administrators could not provide convincing answers to two questions from teachers: Why did my colleagues get merit pay, and I did not? And What can I do to get merit pay?"[3] Let me take Murnane and coauthors' point a little further. Teachers aren't the only stakeholders. Taxpayers should know not only a school district's goals, but how the school is going to measure progress toward those goals. Parents should be provided information on how their kids are stacking up on external metrics as well as the usual teacher-generated report cards.

Underlying calls for transparency is the need for trust. Participants need to understand the basic rules of the game if they're to respond to incentives. A little slippage on understanding exact formulas or complex statistical techniques is okay, so long as the details are vouched for by someone trustworthy. Who that trustworthy party is will vary. Interestingly, while we don't usually think of it this way, one perspective is that workers hire unions to be their agent in handling complex negotiations. So where teachers trust their local to stand up for them, they may have more tolerance for complex arrangements because they can count on the union to protect them from later perceived shenanigans. In other places, the PTA or ad hoc community groups may be able to play the honest broker role.

Wharton School emeritus professor Anita Summers offers this analogy on transparency and trust, "[I don't] require a transparent understanding of the operating characteristics of my car; I trust the experts on the techniques. So must it be in educational evaluation."[4]

Transparency is important. If stakeholders trust the system design, they don't always need to understand every detail. If stakeholders don't trust the system, no amount of transparency is going to make it work.

Differential pay is an add-on, on top of traditional base pay. Differential pay is important, but base pay doesn't go away. Businesses use some differential pay, but for most people the majority of compensation comes in the form of base pay. Annual raises and job promotions are important extras; they're more than icing, but not the whole cake. Differential pay for teachers is a vital element in reinvigoration. Differential pay is what puts teeth in Mechanism II. But let's not go nuts about it.

Existing pay promises are grandfathered in. Even though extra pay for graduate degrees and more experience is largely unwarranted, we can't go breaking faith with millions of existing teachers. While adding differential pay, most programs will grandfather in current teachers while offering a different base pay system for new teachers. Current teachers could even be offered a choice: keep your old arrangement, or participate in the new system and become eligible for the new pay boosts. If we don't keep our old promises, why should anyone believe our new ones?

Almost all teachers earn some differential pay and most teachers regularly earn substantial differential pay. We're not trying to single out a handful of top performers; we're going to move the whole spectrum. Our goal is to make the average teacher do as well as the current pretty good teacher. In the new regime, we expect the average teacher to be picking up that additional 40 percent. Some won't make that much, and a few won't get any differential pay. A small number should be earning a lot more than the 40 percent for truly outstanding performance. Across-the-board standard pay increases would defeat the purpose, but spreading around the benefits with a fair amount of variation, so that most people get something, is fair and means that there's something in it for most everyone.

Differential pay should include both schoolwide and individual teacher components. There are at least two reasons for having a significant schoolwide component to differential pay. Remember that part of Mechanism II is the incentive to step up to difficult conversations. To get the difficult conversation part working, we want teachers to have skin in the game for more than just what happens within the walls of their own classroom. To phrase the issue in a more positive way, we want to create an incentive for teamwork. The second issue is practical. Teachers (and teacher unions) are far more receptive to differential pay when it's distributed schoolwide.

Going further down this road, appreciating flexibility in pay systems means school districts should be allowed more choices than just individual teacher versus schoolwide. Why not base some components of pay on the success of small teaching teams? Why not an entire school district? Different arrangements will make sense for different situations.

Multiple paths to differential pay. Schools have a variety of tasks that need to be done well. Some teachers will offer a balanced portfolio of tasks that they do well. Others will do acceptably in most things and really excel in one aspect. As long as the needs of the students are met by the school working together, different contributions by different teachers should be honored and rewarded.

Differential pay is *not* merit pay. Differential pay is not intended to be a measure of someone's intrinsic worth. People have all sorts of legitimate reasons for seeking out higher- or lower-paying career paths. So long as those choices do include doing a top-notch job with your students, different paths should all be honored, even if they don't pay the same amounts.

It should be considered perfectly acceptable for teachers to make choices that lead to low differential payments. Some perfectly meritorious choices that teachers can make that would lead to low differential pay might include

- Teaching smaller numbers of students, but teaching them well
- Limiting participation in out-of-classroom activities
- Choosing to focus on easy-to-teach students

Administrators need to have skin in the game too. The folks picking teachers and leading schools should have pay linked in part to how well those teachers do. Two prominent researchers put it this way, "Of particular importance to the success of such pay programs, and to school effectiveness more generally, is the accountability of administrators. Unless those who make personnel decisions have a strong incentive, they are unlikely to make difficult, high-stakes choices regarding teacher pay, promotion, and employment."[5] Administrators should be motivated to work toward the same goals as teachers, encouraging them to support and their staff in ways that will help everyone win. Pay systems should set up teachers and administrators as team members, not strangers or adversaries.

Use multiple measurements. Attempts to measure teacher output have too often focused on a single high-stakes test. If we're appropriately humble about the difficulty of measurement, we'll eschew the idea that one afternoon with a number 2 pencil can adequately measure what a student has learned or what a teacher has taught. Differential pay should be linked to multiple measurements: lots of small tests, class visits from external evaluators, qualifications like the NBCT, rewards for training and graduate education that have themselves been vetted.

Use value-added measures: reward progress. I talked about value-added measures (VAM) in Chapter 7, Effectiveness Pay. The idea is that teachers get rewarded for the progress their students make. If a student starts out two years behind and makes one-and-a-half-year's progress, that's pretty good. If a student starts out two years ahead and makes half-a-year progress, that's not so good. Taking students as they come and being expected to move them all forward gives teachers and schools the right incentives. Plus, it's fair to all.

Use objective measurements. In return for higher pay, we're going to insist on serious, objective evidence of improved results. The problem with a single high-stakes test isn't with the word "test," it's with the phrase "single high-stakes." Tests and other nonsubjective yardsticks should make up the core of results measurement. Some amount of subjectivity is inevitable, but objectivity should be the core.

Use nonmanipulable measurements. Bluntly, it should be hard to teach to the test without helping students really learn the underlying material. When money gets linked to measurements, pressure will build to tinker with those measurements. You wouldn't want to link teacher pay to grades assigned by the teacher—you'd mysteriously end up with entire schools full of straight-A students. Similarly, rewarding a school for increased graduation rates works a lot better if there is an external proficiency standard for the diploma than if the school can decide on its own who graduates.

SAMPLES

You can see that there are lots of different issues at play in setting up a *Profit* compensation plan. Of course, at a given school some of the issues will matter and others won't. To help kick-start thinking, here are three plans that might be chosen in three fictional situations:

March to a Different Drummer Elementary. MDDE is a three hundred-fifty student K–5 elementary. The school focuses on the whole child. It's the kind of place where kids address their teachers by their first names and everyone spends a lot of time sitting in circles on the floor. Teachers tend to stay at the school for many years and form a tight group which includes the principal, himself a former MDDE teacher. The clientele is mostly middle class, there is a long waiting list to get into the school, and a large majority of students attend for their entire elementary school experience. Parental support for the school's mission and for the teachers is very strong, although there is mild concern about the adequacy of math and science instruction. Teachers are uniformly opposed to standardized testing. On district-mandated standardized tests, students typically perform well, although given the student body's relatively high socioeconomic background, scores are not outstanding. Despite its popularity with the community, the school and the district administration are frequently in conflict since MDDE doesn't fit neatly into any of the administration's pigeonholes.

FICTIONAL MDDE BONUS PLAN

1. MDDE teachers agree to pick from the menu of nationally vetted, grade-level appropriate tests a reading test, a math test, and two other subject matter tests. Tests will be chosen each spring for use the following year.
2. Kindergarteners are not tested. First and second graders are tested twice a year; third, fourth, and fifth graders are tested four times a year. Average scores are reported relative to the national average for non–free-or-reduced lunch students in the same grade (with an adjustment for tests given part way through the year).
3. Points are awarded according to the number of "weeks" by which students in each grade beat the national average.

Grade	**Weeks ahead**	**Goal**	**Column 2 divided by column 3**	**Weight**	**Column 4 times column 5**
1		4		2	
2		8		2	
3		12		6	
4		16		15	
5		20		15 Total	

4. The school bonus pool equals the base salaries of the teachers and principal, multiplied by the total number of points divided by 100. (If goals are met exactly, that would equal 40 percent of base salaries.)
5. The school bonus pool is split evenly among teachers and principal.
6. One teacher chosen by the principal can earn an extra 5 percent for attending a one-week summer training session and sharing the results with the entire staff. When a new teacher joins the staff, one experienced teacher will receive a 10 percent salary supplement for working five extra hours a week as a mentor to the new teacher.

The MDDE plan doesn't match up with all of our design principles. Notably, bonuses are essentially entirely team-based with no individual component. But the teachers are a tight-knit team and they really want it that way. The teachers believe that their "whole child" approach builds the foundations of academic success in the early years. They prefer to weight objective measures more heavily in later years. Note that while value-added measures aren't used formally, much of the same effect is achieved by using a national norm that excludes free-or-reduced lunch students. Adding on to this, the teachers have agreed to improve student performance by four weeks each school year, as compared to *Profit* goal of three.

Dual Population High School. DPHS is a medium-sized, urban, academic high school that for historical reasons draws from two populations: neighborhood kids from a variety of income levels, almost all of whom are African American, and kids from the citywide accelerated program who are funneled into DPHS for high school, almost all of whom are white or Asian American and typically come from high-income families. Academic performance among the neighborhood kids ranges from excellent to disastrous, and dropout rates are high. In contrast, nearly all the kids from the accelerated program will attend college, many going to Ivy League schools or their equivalent. The two groups of students get along surprisingly well, although there isn't a lot of joint socializing outside school. The corresponding two parent groups, on the other hand, are often at each other's throat, each feeling that the other set of kids gets an unfair share of resources. As a result, the school finds it very difficult to implement positive changes. Some teachers in the school are teaching-award winners. A few teachers are clearly incompetent.

The DPHS plan balances individual and team incentives. It's designed so that teachers have an incentive to value growth by both groups of students. This is a good idea, and it also serves to placate both groups of parents. Note that the Advanced Placement bonuses aren't based on value-added; of course, students in these courses are all good students. The per pupil payments are rigged to give teachers the incentive to attract students into AP classes who might not ordinarily think of taking one. At the same time, tying payments to scores makes it unlikely that a teacher will water down a class.

Big City School System. BCSS is the municipal school system for a large east coast city. While the school system has many bright lights, on

FICTIONAL DPHS BONUS PLAN

1. Four nationally vetted tests are used for each subject, two picked by the teachers in the relevant department at DPHS and two picked by the school district. (Teachers may also use the test results in computing term grades, if they wish.) However, in the school's numerous Advanced Placement classes, results of AP tests are used instead. For one innovative science class for which no national tests are available, the school contracts with faculty at a local college to evaluate student portfolios. Similarly, the school's well-regarded music programs are "graded" by outside adjudicators, professional musicians—most members of the city's symphony orchestra.
2. Each teacher receives a bonus based on a value-added measure of her students' test results. The bonus is zero for one year growth, 20 percent for 1 year plus three weeks, and 40 percent for 1 year plus six weeks. The exception is AP classes, where teachers receive a $350 for each student grade of 5 on the AP test (that's the highest grade given); $200 for each grade of 4; and $100 for each grade of 3. (Most colleges don't give credit for scores below 3.)
3. NBCT's receive a 10 percent bonus. Teachers who have gone through a certified training program for teaching advanced placement courses receive a five percent bonus.
4. All teachers in the school receive a one percent bonus for each point by which the school's four-year graduation rate exceeds 90 percent. (Students have to pass a state proficiency requirement to be eligible for a diploma.) All teachers receive a one percent bonus for each point by which the fraction of juniors and seniors who take the SAT *and* score above 1700. However, a teacher who has not received an individual bonus for two consecutive years is ineligible for the school-wide bonus.
5. The principal receives a bonus equal to 1.5 times the average teacher bonus. Assistant principals receive a bonus equal to the average teacher bonus.

average it's a disaster. Student performance averages nearly two grade levels below national norms, despite per pupil spending levels that are among the highest in the country. Teacher salaries are high by national standards, but not when compared to the high incomes of other city residents. The new, reform-minded superintendent and the teachers' union are at loggerheads over the issue of removing incompetent teachers.

In some ways the fictional BCSS plan looks standard. Note though, that the plan also provides paths for unjamming the union/district relationship. The district offers much more attractive pay in return for better student outcomes and labor peace. Teachers get extra protection from unfair disciplinary issues and get more of a say in

---

FICTIONAL BCSS BONUS PLAN

1. Teachers in each school can decide whether to opt-in to a *Profit* plan. Opting in requires agreement of 75 percent of the teachers in a school. In opt-in schools, no teacher will be fired for the first two years of the program, except for moral turpitude. In opt-out schools, the union agrees to an expedited disciplinary procedure for teachers charged with gross incompetence.
2. Teachers in opt-out schools remain on the existing salary schedule. BCSS and the district agree to a five-year contract in which steps on the existing schedule will increase 1 percent a year. Teachers in opt-out schools wishing to transfer stand first in line for vacancies in opt-in schools.
3. Opt-in schools measure success using value-added measures on nationally vetted tests. BCSS chooses a standard set of tests for each grade level, but each school can add tests. Each teacher receives a bonus based on a value-added measure of her students' test results. The bonus is zero for one year growth, 20 percent for 1 year plus three weeks, and 40 percent for 1 year plus six weeks.
4. An amount equal to the sum of the individual teacher bonuses in an opt-in school goes into a school-wide fund. This fund is distributed by a two-teacher/two-administrator committee in anyway the committee thinks best, but unanimous agreement is required.
5. Principals receive 1.5 teacher shares, other administrators one teacher share. However, for the first five years of the program, administrators in schools with historical results more than one year behind the national average receive double bonuses.
6. NBCTs receive a 10 percent bonus in all schools.
7. BCSS and the union agree to run a one month "master teacher academy" each summer. Graduates receive 10 percent bonuses

in all schools; the program—and continuation of the bonuses—to be reviewed in five years.

8. BCSS and the union agree to run a one month "skills improvement" academy each summer. Teachers in opt-in schools who receive less than five percent bonuses are eligible to attend (once) and receive a month's salary for so doing.

---

distributing rewards. The union has arranged for less successful teachers to have a way to turn around their careers.

You'll understand that these little one-page snippets oversimplify the real world. So ask how you'd design your plan differently for *your* local needs!

Finally, if you don't mind me saying "conversation starter" and "guideline, not prescription" one more time, I'll point you to the ready-for-you-to-copy checklist on the next page.

CHECKLIST FOR A DIFFERENTIAL PAY SYSTEM
FROM *PROFIT OF EDUCATION*

☐ **Mechanism II, sufficient funds for a 40 percent raise**
☐ **Involvement of local stakeholders in design.**

☐ Transparency about expectations and rewards.
☐ Differential pay is an add-on, on top of traditional base pay. Differential pay is important, but base pay doesn't go away.
☐ Existing pay promises are grandfathered in.
☐ Almost all teachers earn some differential pay and most teachers regularly earn substantial differential pay.
☐ Includes both schoolwide and individual teacher components.
☐ Multiple paths to differential pay.
☐ Differential pay is *not* merit pay.
☐ Administrators have skin in the game too.
☐ Use multiple measurements.
☐ Use value-added measures; reward progress.
☐ Use objective measurements.
☐ Use nonmanipulable measurements.

10

Some (Recent) History Lessons

It's good to set details aside for a moment and remind ourselves that the big picture solution I'm suggesting is quite routine. I'm arguing that we should take the everyday, commonplace method of compensation in the American economy and apply it to the way we pay our teachers. Most of us agree that a first-rate education for the nation's children is something we want. We know where the key leverage point is to make our investment, and how much money it's going to take. (It's the teachers who make the difference, and it's going to take a ballpark 40 percent raise.) We'll make sure that the money spent can be tracked to the desired results. (That's why *Profit* links pay increases to student success instead of simply dumping funds into the pot.) The American economy isn't perfect (nor will *Profit* be), but it's the envy of most of the world. America's schools should also become the envy of the world, or put better, they should *once again* become the envy of the world.

Let's run schools on tried-and-true American principles, displacing the tried-and-failed practices now in use. I'm hardly the first one to say this.[1] More importantly, boots-on-the-ground reformers have already taken some solid first steps toward a complete *Profit* reinvigoration. The ideas I'm advocating are no longer revolutionary, even if the scale of change called for is much bigger than what we've seen to date. Let's look at several at several up-and-running programs. There are interesting details in these leading-edge attempts, but the most important lesson is simply that the political barriers to adopting *Profit* are demonstrably surmountable. It has been done, and for the first time there is real federal support for overcoming such barriers.

NO LONGER REVOLUTIONARY

We talked in the last few chapters about *Profit* working through Mechanism I (recruit and retain the best) and Mechanism II (skin in the game). Nearly all the existing steps in *Profit's* direction have been Mechanism II deals that arrange some kind of performance incentive, albeit often small ones, for teachers. The absence of Mechanism I steps, making teaching a financially attractive career choice, seems a little odd, given that: (1) the rhetoric about raising teacher pay has gone on for decades, and (2) over those decades we've supported greatly increased spending on schools—just not for teacher salaries. In a way, the purpose of this book is to make clear that since it's the teachers who matter, that's where the money needs to be spent (but spent in the right way).

Nonetheless, there is one Mechanism I example that you already know about. Wealthy school districts often pay top salaries to attract the very best teachers.[2] I offer the example of Scarsdale, NY, a smallish, very wealthy town about ten miles north of the New York City border. (I grew up and attended school in a not-so-wealthy town next door to Scarsdale.)

In Scarsdale, 99 percent of students go to college. On a recent international science reasoning test, Scarsdale students outperformed the foreign country with the world's highest scores (Finland).[3] Scarsdale may have the highest per capita income among all New York State school districts,[4] and it's a bedroom community in which school quality is very important both in terms of the community's goals and in terms of keeping up property values. Like most school districts in New York State (outside of incorporated cities), Scarsdale taxpayers vote on the school budget every year. When given the option, does the school, and do the taxpayers, put their money into teacher salaries?

Yes. The median Scarsdale teacher earns $116,000![5] I'm arguing for a 40 percent increase, while Scarsdale is already paying 157 percent above the national median. Scarsdale is an extreme example, but it shows that people who have money do put it into paying to attract the very best teachers.

Let's turn to Mechanism II efforts. There are a lot of them. We're well past the point where anyone can argue that that incentive schemes are politically infeasible. The National Center on Performance Incentives reports incentive programs underway in twenty-four states plus the District of Columbia, identifying fifty-eight separate efforts.[6] But I don't want to mislead you. While political acceptability seems to have been established, these are mostly pretty small programs. Although in a couple of cases top-end bonuses can be 10 to 20 percent of salary, most of these programs don't raise average teacher salaries more than a few percentage points.

Many of these local efforts have been supported by the federal Department of Education's Teacher Incentive Fund, which states its purpose is "to support programs that develop and implement performance-based teacher and principal compensation systems, based primarily on increases in student achievement, in high-need schools."[7] Unfortunately the federal effort has been of the on-again/off-again genre that plagues school reform. The program was funded in 2006, not funded in 2007, and funded again in 2008. Just so you'll understand the scale, the highest funding level could have supplemented yearly pay for every American teacher—by all of $33.

THE OBAMA ADMINISTRATION

The Obama administration and Secretary of Education Arne Duncan have started a vigorous effort to bring public education up to snuff for all our children. As evidence, I offer the fact that one of the first changes made by the new administration was to increase the Teacher Incentive Fund by a factor of five. While the administration advocates on several fronts that wouldn't be part of a *Profit* plan, calling for more national curricular standards and longer school days for example, much of their drive lines up well with the ideas we have been looking at. Let me talk about some of what's being done, mostly by quoting the eloquent words of Arne Duncan. You'll see that these are largely Mechanism II items. Then let's see about the missing—fatally missing—Mechanism I piece:

> Nothing is more important than getting great teachers into our classrooms and great principals into our schools. And there are millions of hard-working, dedicated teachers in schools all across America.
>
> [on teachers making the difference[8]]

> I am big believer in [the NBPTS] program, but let's also be honest: school systems pay teachers billions of dollars more each year for earning PD [professional development] credentials that do very little to improve the quality of teaching.

At the same time, many schools give nothing at all to the teachers who go the extra mile and make all the difference in students' lives. Excellence matters and we should honor it—fairly, transparently, and on terms teachers can embrace.

[on Qualification Measures[9]]

Now I absolutely respect the concerns of teachers that test scores alone, they should never be used solely to determine salaries. I absolutely agree with that sentiment. I also appreciate that growth models as they exist today are far less than perfect. We have a lot of work still ahead of us.

But to somehow suggest that we should not link student achievement and teacher effectiveness, it's like suggesting we judge a sports team without looking at the box score.

[on Effectiveness Measures[10]]

We need tests that measure whether students are mastering complex materials and can apply their knowledge in ways that show that they are ready for college and careers.

We need tests that go beyond multiple choice—and we know that these kinds of tests are expensive to develop. It will cost way too much if each state is doing this on its own.

Collaboration makes it possible for this to happen quickly and affordably.

[on tests[11]]

We will ask millions of teachers to use student achievement and annual growth to drive instruction and evaluation. . . . Data may not tell us the whole truth, but it certainly doesn't lie. . . . Our best teachers today are using real time data in ways that would have been unimaginable just five years ago.

We will also ask whether the data around student achievement is linked to teacher effectiveness. Believe it or not, several states including New York, Wisconsin, and California, have laws, they have laws that create a firewall between students and teacher data. Think about that, laws that prohibit us from connecting children to the adults who teach them. . . .

[on using data[12]]

Does this sound familiar? The key to reinvigoration is the teachers. It's good to pay for the right qualifications. We need to measure effectiveness, and that does mean student tests. Data and data systems are needed to making this all work. Basically, these are all Mechanism II reforms—which is great news because Mechanism II is typically the controversial piece.

What's missing? Mechanism I. To be blunt, using the proposed reforms to reshuffle pay among current teachers won't do the trick. The administration has not yet stepped up to the plate when it comes to raising teacher pay.[13] Let me quote Arne Duncan once more, this time speaking to the National Education Association, "I've seen how much these educators want to be valued for their work and honored for what they are: dedicated, professional, compassionate, serious and responsible."[14] While focusing on this single quote is probably unfair, please, hold the talk about "valued" and "honored" until after we've come up with cash-on-the-barrelhead.

We're *this close.* The Obama administration and Congress have anted up $100 billion for education as part of the 2009 emergency stimulus package. While a hunk of that will go to higher teacher salaries, most of the spending will replace state spending to keep teachers from being laid off, and for other items. More importantly, the massive increase in federal education money is temporary. It goes away when the stimulus is no longer needed. So a college student thinking about a teaching career has little more financial incentive in that direction today than was true last year, or a decade ago. Now, if we could turn the education stimulus money into permanent funding, spent in a *Profitable* way—wouldn't that be something! We'll return to this issue of federal contributions in Chapter 13, Getting There.

LESSONS FROM WHAT'S WORKED

You know how a kid gets a problem label early in life, and that label sticks long after the problem has disappeared? Sometimes it feels as if education reform has the same problem, getting little credit when it does good. The fact is that there have been a number of positive reform efforts underway for several years that have been important on the local scale, although they haven't yet changed the national picture. There's a lot to be learned from these programs about how to bring people together and get some Mechanism II reforms in place.

The important lesson is that these efforts have effected change, proving that the position that *Profit* can't happen is no longer tenable. We've seen changes happen. Let's talk about a particular model responsible for inspiring a number of programs that are up and running.

Teacher Advancement Program: TAP

The Milken Foundation's Teacher Advancement Program (TAP) advocates a mix of multiple career paths and teacher bonuses based on student achievement, much like the qualifications and effectiveness models I've described.[15] The program now operates in over 130 schools and has become a national model for reform. Early reports provide evidence supporting the effectiveness of TAP's use of teacher incentives. One study, by Eric Hanushek, suggests that TAP programs are very cost-effective, estimating that the program incentives pay for themselves twice over in terms of gains to the students.[16] (In Chapter 12, Payback!, I'll take a similar look at the cost effectiveness of *Profit.)* In a second study, Lewis Solmon and colleagues ranked teachers according to student test performance and then compared rankings of TAP and non-TAP teachers. TAP teachers were more likely than others to be "way above" and less likely to be "way below."[17] A third study, by Matt Springer and colleagues, is particularly notable because the authors used a different test to measure student results than the test used for determining teacher bonuses, in this way guaranteeing that the results are not the result of teaching to the test. TAP students again outperformed students of non-TAP teachers.[18]

But in terms of getting reform in motion, there's a lesson on top of simply saying that incentives work; after all, incentives working is not that surprising. Solmon and colleagues surveyed teachers about attitudes about TAP, finding

> contrary to popular belief, performance pay has neither led to competition nor susceptibility to principal bias in TAP schools. Clearly, as TAP shows, collaboration can remain strong despite the implementation of performance pay, and principal bias need not distort performance pay decisions. This is in sharp contrast to teachers who have not experienced TAP. Overall, we find that TAP teachers compared to non-TAP teachers experience higher quality professional development as well as more opportunities for collaboration and collegiality, and ways to improve their effectiveness in the classroom.[19]

WHAT TAP SAYS

As a result of TAP, talented teachers can advance professionally and earn higher salaries, just as in other careers. And they can do so without leaving the classroom, where they are needed most.

TAP brochure[20]

WHAT A UNION PRESIDENT SAYS

There are things happening at TAP schools that should be happening at all schools. Teacher incentives and evaluations are provided in a fair manner, based on teaching skills and academic gains.

Rhonda Johnson, President, Columbus Education Association[21]

As a model program, TAP has become a jumping-off point for efforts across the nation. Chicago's pilot TAP program is especially notable and has a specific focus on schools with low-income students.[22] Among the attributes of the program are success-based bonuses averaging $4,000 a teacher, as well as opportunities to become a Lead Teacher with a $15,000 bonus or a Mentor Teacher with a $7,000 bonus. Administrators are also eligible for bonuses based on schoolwide performance.

Chicago TAP is a joint program between the Chicago schools and the Chicago Teachers Union. In fact, the formal Memorandum of Understanding between the district and the union established a joint

FROM THE CHICAGO TAP FAQ

Chicago TAP is based on the premise that all children can learn, regardless of external factors and socioeconomic conditions. That is why classroom gains are measured through "value-added" growth, rather than reaching a specific attainment level. This means that regardless of where their students start the year academically, teachers are evaluated and rewarded based upon how much their students improve, not by the percentage of students that "meet" or "exceed" on standardized tests.[23]

district/union committee to get the program off the ground. For a school to join the program, 75 percent of teachers in that school have to agree.

Two TAP takeaway lessons: (1) financial incentives work in practice, and (2) district/union/teacher joint efforts can happen and leave teachers happier as well as financially rewarded.

Minnesota: Q Comp

Districts in Minnesota can opt into Q Comp, Minnesota's Quality Compensation for Teachers program. As of January 2009, nearly one-third of the state's students were in participating districts.[24] (Most were concentrated in a relatively small number of large districts.) Q Comp provides roughly two hundred dollars per student in extra state funding, amounting to an increase of about 3 percent of the instructional budget for state schools. Inspired in part by the TAP program, Q Comp is designed around five components:

- Career ladder/advancement options
- Job-embedded professional development
- Teacher evaluation
- Performance pay
- Alternative salary schedule

Several aspects are particularly notable. Teacher evaluations must be made by more than one evaluator. At least 60 percent of bonus compensation must be based on performance pay. The plan is intended to be permanent, not a temporary grant. Both the superintendent of schools and the head of a district's teacher's union have to sign off on a district's plan.

It's early to find much evidence of how Q Comp is working out, although the one available study is positive, finding that, "There is a significant and positive relationship between the number of years a school has been implementing Q Comp and student achievement."[25]

Minnesota's legislative auditor has reviewed Q Comp and raised questions about how successful the implementation has been.[26] While many of these are issues about how the program has been administered, the auditor also has some interesting findings about teacher attitudes.

First the good news. The majority of Q Comp teachers agreed with the survey questions, "The Q Comp program has improved teacher professional development" and "The Q Comp program has improved professional relationships among teachers."[27]

Now the not-quite-so-good-news. Teachers in Minnesota don't like effectiveness pay. In a minute I'll suggest this is exactly what we should expect and that it contains an important lesson. The facts first. Just over half of Q Comp teachers feel negatively about the effect of linking teacher pay to student test scores, although this is less that the three-quarters of non–Q Comp teachers who feel negatively about it. Q Comp teachers are about neutral on using performance evaluations, while non–Q Comp teachers are again more negative.[28]

Since Q Comp programs are locally designed, different schools allocate Q Comp pay differently. The sample pay allocation presented by the legislative auditor assigns one-fourth of performance pay to schoolwide student test score gains, one-fourth to a teacher's own students' student test score gains, and half of performance pay to teacher evaluations. In the auditor's example, the maximum total award is two thousand dollars.[29]

So why are many Q Comp teachers turned off by linking pay to student achievement? Perhaps because the reward is only a few percent of their salaries? (If half of the Q Comp bonus is linked to student results, as in the auditor's example, that comes to about 2 percent of the average Minnesota teacher salary.) So the lesson we can learn from Q Comp is that large disruptions in compensation for a small amount of money are, unsurprisingly, unpopular.

LESSONS

Mechanism II changes are up and running across the nation. It's far too late for antireformers to argue that the changes won't be accepted—they already have been in many places. As for Mechanism I, so far, not so much.

11

The Money Trail

Some people think the education sector is starved for money, others think it's overfed. My view is that the issue isn't too little or too much; our goal ought to be to spend money where it gets results. Most of *Profit* is devoted to the idea that raising teacher salaries is the key to reinvigorating education. Because raising teacher pay won't be cheap (although it *will* be worth every penny), people are going to ask where the money's going to come from. People *ought* to ask where the money's going to come from. There are only two choices: either we increase total education spending or we redirect part of the existing stream of education spending into teacher salaries. I firmly believe that the former is the right answer. Higher teacher salaries should be thought of as an investment, and I'll present evidence later in the book that this is an investment with a high return. Nonetheless, in some districts the economic or political situation may require that part of the funding for better teacher salaries be scraped out of other school spending.[1]

In order to make sensible spending decisions going forward, we need to understand the spending patterns we have now. Here are two facts to frame the discussion. Between the 1965–66 school year and the 2005–06 school year, real expenditure per student almost tripled, rising 2.6 percent a year.[2,3] Over those same forty years, the annual salary of classroom teachers rose only 21 percent, or half a percent per year. In other words we do spend much more per student than we used to, but almost all the money has gone for purchases other than higher teacher salaries.

WHERE HAS THE MONEY GONE?

If we've not put money into higher teacher salaries, where did it go? The increased dollars have gone into four major areas: (1) noninstructional personnel, supplies, fuel, and all the things that a school uses, excluding the cost of people directly engaged in teaching; (2) teacher aides; (3) special education; and (4) a drastic drop in the student/teacher ratio.

As we get started looking at the numbers, I need to give a practical warning. There's a good deal of slippage in putting together school spending data because the thousands of American school districts use incompatible budgeting systems. The incompatibilities were even greater in the past, making historical comparisons even more dicey. Nonetheless, researchers have pieced together a reasonably clear set of facts. So the gist of the numbers that follow is correct even though the data is imperfect.

Unfortunately, the scientific evidence on the efficient allocation of education dollars is far less definitive. (With the exception described in Chapter 1, Teachers Make the Difference—that one is dead solid.) I'll tell you where the money is going, but I won't tell you that a given category is a particularly attractive or particularly unattractive target for cutting spending. At a national level, firm evidence just isn't there. Where there is useful evidence I'll share it with you.

We Spend More on Everything Other Than People Instructing Students

In a study by the National Research Council, Eric Hanushek found that "Between 1960 and 1990, instructional staff expenditures fell from 61 percent to 46 percent of total current expenditures."[4] Since the fraction spent on instructional staff fell, we know that the fraction spent on everything else rose. That "everything else" includes maintenance, energy for heating and cooling, administrative staff, student transportation, and all the other things that keep a school up and running. It also includes classroom supplies, books, and computers.[5] There isn't direct evidence on whether this shift in spending away from instructional personnel was a good idea or bad, but we do know that it was expensive. According to Hanushek's calculations, if spending growth for this "other than instructional personnel" catchall had been held down to the same rate as spending growth on instructional personnel, education today would be 25 percent cheaper. That

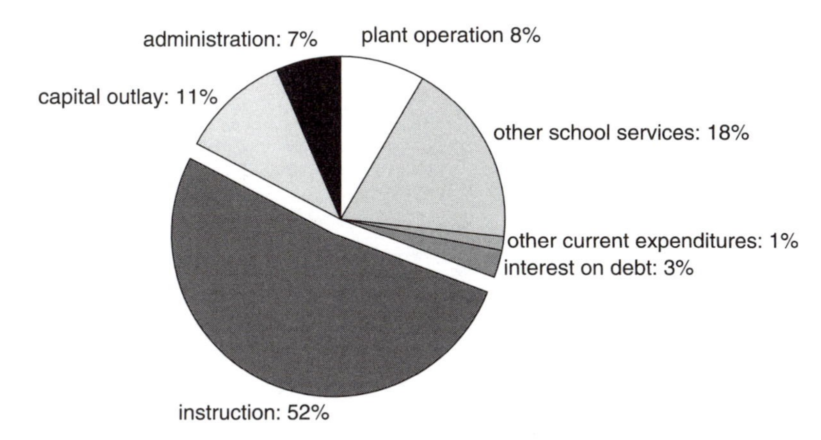

Figure 13 Spending on Public Education

25 percent would, by the way, be about the right amount to pay the entire bill for *Profit*.

Where that leaves us, as you'll see in Figure 13, is with instruction being about half of school spending.[6] Almost all the instruction money goes to salaries or benefits. I'll dive now into the pie slice that goes directly for instruction.

Teacher Aides

There are six million women and men employed in public schools. As you can see in Figure 14, teachers, teacher aides, and the support staff comprise 90 percent of school employees; the remaining 10 percent include district and school administrators, instructional coordinators, librarians, and guidance counselors.[7]

The group that has really grown in size is aides. Between 1990 and 2006 the number of instructional aides rose 78 percent, which was much faster than the 33 percent increase in the number of teachers.[8] In the most recent survey available, one-third of teachers report assistance from a teacher aide.[9] Aides assist with instruction, help maintain the classroom environment, supervise lunchrooms, and carry out secretarial tasks.[10]

The U.S. is somewhat peculiar among the industrialized countries in the use of teacher aides, using nearly triple the number of aides when compared to other countries. Table 4 shows that the combined number of teachers plus teacher aides per thousand students is about

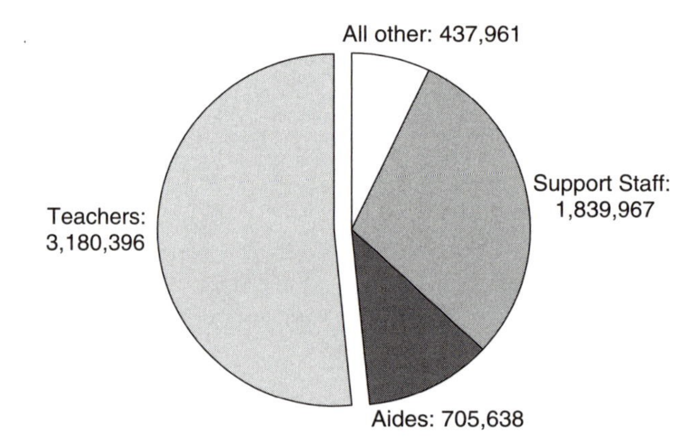

Figure 14 Public School Employees—6 Million Strong

Table 4 Staffing in the U.S. and Other Industrialized Economies

Staff per 1,000 students	U.S.	OECD average
Classroom teachers, academic staff, and other teachers	62.1	71.4
Teacher aides and teaching/research assistants	11.5	3.4

the same in the U.S. and abroad. But we split it differently, using fewer teachers and more teacher aides.[11]

Little scientific evidence exists on whether the routine deployment of teacher aides leads to better student outcomes. The main lead we have comes from the Tennessee STAR experiment, which randomly assigned some students to classes with a full-time aide and other students to similar sized classes without a full-time aide (although some may have had part-time aides). Evaluating the results of the experiment, Alan Krueger found that having a full-time aide made at most a very modest difference.[12] While there are surely specific cases where a classroom aide is invaluable, one can't help but wonder if we haven't overdone it.

Special Education

The cost of special education is largely irrelevant when looking for dollars to fund *Profit*. That may sound startling since it is widely believed that growth in special education is responsible for the increased cost of education. The truth is that while special education is responsible for a piece of rising costs, it's not that big a piece. Let's spend a minute nailing this one down, just so that no one uses special education as an excuse for why we can't do *Profit*. (It should go without saying that special ed kids will benefit from a reinvigorated teacher corps just like everyone else.)

Special ed kids require more individual attention. So there are fewer students assigned to each teacher, and in some cases there are other added costs. But special ed students form a small minority. Eric Hanushek sums up the budget implications, saying, "despite significant growth in special education, new programs for the handicapped appear in fact to have played a relatively minor role in both the growth in spending and the decline in pupil-teacher ratios."[13]

Here are some raw facts. It costs us nearly twice as much to educate a special education student as it does to educate a regular education student. About 13 percent of students receive special education services, up from 8 percent at the end of the 1970s.[14] In 1999–2000, the cost of special ed—on top of what it would have cost to provide regular educational services to special ed students—was 14 percent of school spending. While special education spending has risen, the increase comes from the increased number of students receiving special ed, rather from an increase in the cost per student. (The cost per student has fallen slightly when compared to the cost of regular education.[15])

In other words, while spending on special education matters, it's not the explanation for why per pupil spending has nearly tripled.

THE GREAT INTENSIFICATION

Figure 15 shows the fundamental story of increased school spending: fewer students per teacher. In what has been called "the great intensification,"[16] we've almost cut in half the number of students for each teacher.[17] If teachers taught anywhere near the number of students as in the old days, there'd be plenty of money for *Profit* and quite a bit left over. Shouldn't we just raise class size to raise teacher salaries? The answer is "not so fast." Let's talk about this surprisingly complicated story.

The first key point is that the public loves—loves, loves, loves—the idea of smaller classes.[18] One recent survey found that 77 percent of

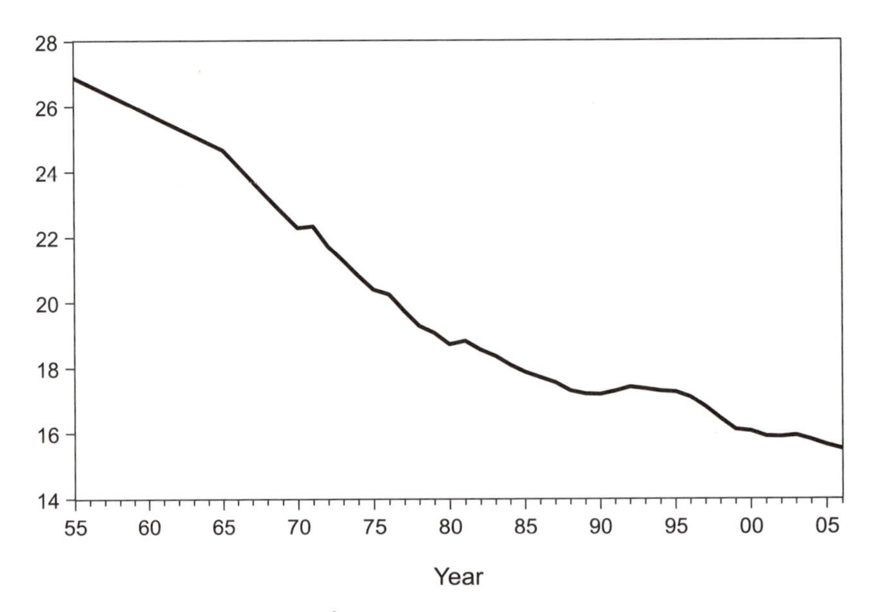

Figure 15 Students Per Teacher

Americans prefer lower class size to higher teacher salaries.[19] The issue is not whether smaller classes improve student learning (they do), but whether the improvement is worth the enormous expense. Unlike some expenditures, class size reduction has received quite a bit of scientific attention. The scientific consensus has shifted over time from the position that reducing student/teacher ratios does nothing, to the idea that lower ratios help, but not very much. Economist Eric Hanushek summarized much of the early research:[20]

> Studies show that reducing class size usually has no general effect on student performance, but because teacher compensation is already the schools' biggest single expense, smaller classes and commensurately more teachers raise costs dramatically.

More recent research by Hanushek and colleagues in Dallas finds that smaller classes do help a little.[21] Alan Krueger's research on the Tennessee STAR experiment finds larger improvements from smaller class sizes.[22] While the public at large, parents of school children, and teachers, all think small classes are wonderful, current research results are somewhere between "the evidence is unclear" and "small classes

NEW YORK MAYOR MICHAEL BLOOMBERG QUOTED IN THE *NY TIMES* ON CLASS SIZE VERSUS BETTER TEACHERS

"If you're going to spend an extra dollar, personally, I would always rather spend it on the people that deliver the service," Mr. Bloomberg said . . . calling class size "an interesting number."

"It's the teacher looking a child in the eye, and teachers can look lots of children in the eye," he added. "If you have to have smaller class size or better teachers, go with the better teachers every time."

New York Times, February 21, 2009[23]

are not worth their cost." Doug Harris sums up what we know, saying, "The apparent conclusion is that broad-based class-size reduction would be inefficient, even in the elementary grades where the evidence of benefits is strongest."[24,25]

There's another way to look at all this.

We have seen a massive, sustained drop in the student/teacher ratio over five decades. If small classes were the solution, then schools should already be top performers—which isn't the case. One possibility is that having fewer students per teacher isn't quite the same thing as having smaller classes. While public schools have about fifteen students per teacher, the average elementary school class size is twenty and the average secondary school class size is twenty-five.[26]

A little bit of the discrepancy is due the exclusion of special education from class size counts but not from calculation of student/teacher ratios, but most of the discrepancy appears to be real rather than accounting differences. (Special education teachers comprise less than 15 percent of the teacher corps, not enough to explain the class size discrepancy.[27]) National Education Association data suggests that elementary school class sizes are smaller than in the past, while secondary school class sizes are not.[28] Anecdotally, there also appears to have been an increase in math and reading specialists, teachers who float from one classroom to another. At the secondary school level teachers do meet far fewer students per day than they did in the past, the average falling from 135 in 1971 to 86 in 2001.[29] A portion of this is due to a drop in the average number of class periods from 7 a day to 6.[30]

The average secondary school class size ranges from nineteen in Vermont to thirty in California.[31]

If we're looking to get money back from current spending to boost teacher salaries, increasing the student/teacher ratio makes an attractive target. Without wanting to sound *too* mercenary about it, the fact is that if a teacher can handle more students successfully then we can more easily afford to raise her pay. Nonetheless, we can't get started this way. Remember that Mechanism I works in part through drawing new recruits into teaching. If we start off by slicing out teaching slots, there won't be anywhere for the new recruits to teach. If we were to finance a 40 percent raise simply by cutting out teachers, we'd have to cut out all hiring for five to ten years—which would be a pretty dumb way to start a reinvigoration of the teacher corps.

So it's possible that we might have fewer teachers several decades from now, but it's not the way to get started.

Before we leave the questions of where the money's gone and whether we can get some of it back, I want to raise one more political, or perhaps psychological, issue.

Because schools have not been terribly results-oriented, many of the public discussions about increasing spending in some particular direction have taken place in a vacuum. So we ask whether having more aides or smaller classes would be nice, and everyone (correctly) answers in the affirmative. In particular, teachers and teacher unions push hard for nicer, albeit more expensive, working conditions.

One charter school, The Equity Project (TEP) in New York City, plans to raise *base* teacher salaries to $125,000 *plus $25,000 bonuses—all without increasing spending one dime.* How? A combination of two changes. First, teachers will work much longer hours in the school building, taking on the jobs performed elsewhere by assistant principals and other staff, thus increasing the size of the teacher salary pool. Second, class sizes will increase from twenty-six to thirty, reducing the number of teachers who need to be funded out of the available salary pool.[32]

Table 5 Teacher Preferences for Annual Pay Increases Versus Workplace Changes

Choice	Percent who preferred a $5,000 salary increase instead of the stated alternative
Two fewer students in all of the classes you teach	83%
A new full-time teacher's aide who splits time between your class and four other teachers at your school	88%
3.5 more hours of prep time each week	69%

In part, I suspect this is due to negotiators never having been faced with the choice of higher teacher salaries instead. When actually faced with that choice, teachers do opt for higher salaries.

Two researchers, Michael DeArmond and Dan Goldhaber, asked the question the right way by offering teachers equal-cost choices. The pair surveyed thousands of teachers and asked about a $5,000 pay boost versus three improvements in working conditions that would cost about the same amount. As you can see in Table 5, when the choice is put on a level playing field, a strong majority of teachers decide a higher salary looks awfully attractive.[33]

DOLLARS AND CENTS

Let's get down to brass tacks; just how much money do we need to raise? Using the latest available teacher salary data, a 40 percent raise adds about twenty thousand dollars to the average salary. There are slightly over three million teachers. Twenty thousand dollars times three million teachers comes to sixty billion dollars. Increases in fringe benefits have to be added to the cost of higher salaries. Some money also needs to be provided for administrators and others. And because the latest data is several years old, something has to be added for intervening inflation. All in all, my calculations bring it up to $88.5 billion.[34] Since I'd rather overestimate costs and reduce the chance of unpleasant surprises later, let's round this up to $90 billion.

Is $90 billion a lot of money? Well of course it is! But what does it mean in perspective?

- A $90 billion increase would absorb 65 cents from every $100 the nation produces
- A $90 billion increase would raise total spending on public education by about 15 percent
- A 15 percent increase is small compared to existing statewide spending differences[35]
  - The difference between the highest (New Jersey) and lowest (Utah) per student spending is 250 percent.
  - Adding 15 percent to the spending of the middle-ranked state (Colorado) would only move it from position 26 to position 15
- $90 billion is about two-thirds the expected federal cost of the wars in Iraq and Afghanistan in fiscal 2009
- $90 billion is less than the federal government committed to education in the 2009 stimulus package

Traditionally, education has been financed mostly at the state and local level. Today (other than the stimulus package) federal spending accounts for 9 or 10 percent of costs, with the rest split roughly equally between state and local governments.[36] Interestingly, public opinion has shifted in the last decade toward federal financing and away from the use of local taxes. Responses to the 40th annual Phi Delta Kappa/Gallup Poll in Table 6 show that Americans now view education funding as a shared local/state/federal responsibility.[37]

Profit, too, should be a shared local/state/federal responsibility.

We don't need $90 billion on Day 1. We're paying for results and it's going to take a few years for all schools to ramp up to meet the challenge—and earn the money. We do, however, need a credible promise that the money will be there when it has been earned. The federal government is probably better than other governmental levels

Table 6 Responses to "Which do you think is the best way to finance the public schools?"

	1997	2008
Local taxes	27%	20%
State taxes	34	35
Federal taxes	30	37

at making this sort of promise credible. As it happens, the federal government is in a position to ramp down its education stimulus spending just as *Profit* spending will be coming online. The additional reason that the federal government should put up much of the cash is that it's the federal government that will earn most of it back in increased tax revenues.

QUICK MONEY SUMMARY

We are spending a lot more money on education than we used to, but we're not spending it on higher teacher salaries where it would get solid results. Is there education money that should be transferred out of other categories? Quite possibly, but we're short on evidence at the national level. Funding allocation is done at the state and local level, and it's probably best if decisions about cutting out other items are made by those closest to the particular situation. I do argue that the federal government is in a good position to fund an increase, and certainly such an increase should be designated for higher teacher pay rather than being thrown into the general funding pot. In the next chapter, I'll argue that a $90 billion increase isn't a cost at all. Rather, it's an investment that will pay for itself in hard cash!

12

Payback!

> The conclusion of the cost considerations is simple. The benefits from quality improvements are very large. Thus, they can support incentive programs that are quite large and expansive *if the programs work.*
>
> *Eric Hanushek*[1]

Ninety billion dollars a year sounds like a lot of money because, well, it *is* a lot of money. Of course, straightening out our education system will prepare a better life for our children and grandchildren, reduce poverty, lower crime, and, doubtless, lead to an all around better society.

But is it *Profit*able?

Yes.

Profit pays for itself. While talking about "investing in education" is almost a cliché, *Profit* is an investment in the real sense. Education has such a high economic return that higher productivity among future generations of workers will, down the road, overwhelm the costs of higher teacher salaries today. In fact, the return to education is so great that increased tax revenues generated by these productivity gains will more than repay the cost of *Profit.* In the long run, *Profit* will reduce the government deficit in the same way that a wise private investment helps out the family budget. And reassuringly, calculations show the economic advantage of *Profit* is so large as to leave a considerable margin for error. Because the return on education is so high, *Profit* comes with a very healthy cushion against the kinds of problems that inevitably accompany something new.

In this chapter I want to discuss both the economic return and the "better society" aspects. The details of the economic return calculations get fairly wonkish. So I'm going to give you a very quick first pass at the economic calculation, then discuss the broader social issues, and then return to a more detailed examination of the economics. What you'll see in that first-pass calculation is that, even if all you care about is the value of increased productivity, the benefits of *Profit* far outweigh the costs. The more detailed calculations account for several issues that revolve around the timing of benefits versus costs, but it turns out that the first-pass calculation is essentially accurate.

Most of us think that education has lots of very real value in addition to the economic value of making workers more productive. I certainly think so. These nonpecuniary values are hard to measure, so in my calculations I'm going to pretend that they're not there at all. *Profit* passes the benefit-cost test analysis without them.

EDUCATION AS AN INVESTMENT: A QUICK CALCULATION

The goal of *Profit* is an increase in educational achievement equivalent to one additional year of schooling. *Profit's* economic power stems directly from the link between education and lifetime earnings: an additional year of education raises earnings by an average of 10 percent.

People are a modern economy's most important economic asset. While capital and natural resources matter, people are responsible for about two-thirds of economic output.

Not surprisingly, economists have devoted great effort to estimating the effect of education on productivity. Making such estimates is harder than one might think because it can be difficult to distinguish between more education making people more productive, and the alternative possibility that people who are more productive often decide to get more education (both are true to some extent). After an incredible amount of careful statistical work to untangle the direction of causality, the bottom line is the one given above: an additional year of education raises worker productivity by 10 percent.[2]

Compensation (pay plus benefits) in the United States is $8,000 billion a year (or $8 trillion).[3] Ten percent of this is $800 billion a year. An $800 billion annual payback swamps the cost of a $90 billion annual investment. Nine-to-one—now that's a *Profit*able investment![4]

It's socially profitable for the government to increase education spending when the benefit to the population is more than the cost of the spending. In other words, "we"—in the form of our government—ought to invest when the benefit to "us"—the nation's people, outweighs the cost. But in our imperfect political system we sometimes worry about government budget balances. So let's ask the politically relevant question about what *Profit* will do to the long-run budget deficit.

> Each additional year of schooling appears to raise earnings by about 10 percent in the United States.
> *Alan Krueger and Mikael Lindahl*[5]

Federal, state, and local governments take in about thirty cents on the dollar of the nation's production, about three-fifths being federal and the rest state and local.[6] Thirty cents out of each $800 billion comes to $240 billion a year. In other words, *Profit* will pay for itself in tax dollars more than twice over. So in the long run, *Profit* will be a major step toward eliminating the budget deficit. Whether looked at from the viewpoint of all Americans or from the more limited perspective of the government, the purely financial returns to *Profit* far outweigh its cost.

MONEY ISN'T EVERYTHING

Reinvigorating education will make the economy grow. It's nice to know that the reinvigoration will pay for itself, but being a wealthier society isn't the only thing I care about, nor, I suspect, is it the only thing you care about. As all parents know in their gut, a good education is a key to a child having a happy life as well a productive one. A good education is also a key to a happy society. In particular, there are three social issues I want to call attention to: (1) nonpecuniary benefits such as better health and lower crime, (2) narrowing the inequality gap, and (3) restoring our international competitive position.

Nonpecuniary Benefits

Education makes for a better life in a long list of ways. You can probably think of quite a few. I'll mention a few here based on a list put together by sociologist Robert Haveman and economist Barbara Wolfe.[7]

- More-educated people are healthier and live longer lives
- More-educated people have healthier spouses

- More parent education leads to better child outcomes: better health, better cognitive development, and higher earnings when the child becomes an adult
- More-educated couples do a better job at attaining desired family size. In other words they're more likely to end up with the number of children they'd like to have
- More education leads to jobs with nicer working conditions and better fringe benefits[8]
- More-educated consumers make more efficient purchasing decisions
- More education leads to greater charitable contributions, including greater contributions of time, as well as money[9]

Education does much more than simply raise income—although the increase in income is the part that's most easily measurable. We'd all agree that keeping our family healthy is valuable even though putting a price tag on health is tough. Haveman and Wolfe ballpark dollar values of the nonincome items listed above. Their calculations suggest that these nonpecuniary benefits are valued at an amount roughly equal to the direct increase in higher income.[10] Even leaving aside impossible-to-measure values such as richer intellectual lives, the results suggest that the total benefits of more education are twice those of the productivity-oriented measure that I'm using.

I want to add one more item to our nonpecuniary list. Education lowers crime.[11] Research by Lochner and Moretti finds that one additional year of schooling decreases the percentage of men who are incarcerated by 15 to 20 percent.[12] Further, high school graduates are about 30 percent less likely than dropouts (controlling for similarity of background) to earn any income from crime, and 80 percent less likely to do something that lands them in jail. The researchers show that this is really due to less crime, not just perps being smarter at getting away with it.[13] Further, Lochner and Moretti add up the harm done to crime victims and the cost of locking up criminals. Their computations suggest that the value to society of reduced crime from more high school graduation may add as much as 25 percent to the private value of higher income received by the student.[14]

Inequality

To many, the biggest problem with our current education system is that some children get what they need and some don't. In my view, the goal of *Profit* is a better education for all children. Nonetheless, the achievement gap concerns everyone.

Education is becoming increasingly important in reducing inequality because the pay gap between skilled and unskilled work is growing. The Harvard team of Goldin and Katz say it well. "The first reason . . . [for] the sharp rise in wage differentials [is an increase] in the rate of growth of the . . . demand for highly educated and more-skilled workers [relative to the demand for the less skilled.]"[15] Increasingly, skilled jobs bring good incomes to many, but our weak educational system leaves out many more.

We've already discussed, in Chapter 1, Teachers make the Difference, some of the evidence that good teachers are especially important for at-risk students. Let's talk a little about the softer side of the story.

Students need support, guidance, and advocacy from parents, teachers, and community. Well-educated, well-off parents can pick up some of the slack when good teachers are MIA. Well-off parents are generally good advocates for their children's needs. Of course, the same is sometimes true of not-so-well-educated parents, but not nearly so often. Less-educated parents have fewer resources, less familiarity in working the school system, and, often, a lesser sense of entitlement for their kids. Good teachers are even more important for at-risk students because, on average, at-risk students don't have as strong a parental safety net.

I'll share an anecdote about my younger daughter's school experience that helps illustrate the advantage of having school-savvy parents. The short version of the story is that one year my daughter was assigned to a truly awful math teacher. (As it happens, he was a novice teacher who was both sincere and dedicated, but who just wasn't cut out for the job.) The first part of the anecdote is that my wife and I ended up spending a lot of time that year helping our daughter with her math. We didn't do nearly as good a job as some of the truly splendid math teachers my daughter had in other years, but we could mitigate most of the damage. We had the time, knowledge, and resources to do this. Not all parents do. An unsuccessful teacher was bad for our daughter, but it wasn't nearly so bad as it would have been for a kid whose parents couldn't play catch-up at home.

Let me put this another way. A great kindergarten teacher is important for every child. A great kindergarten teacher is a lot more important for a kid from a bookless home than for a kid who's been read a bedtime story every night since birth. For a kid from a family in poverty the odds of having that bedtime story are a lot lower.

> Teacher quality matters—a lot. Teachers' knowledge and skills are the most vital in-school factors influencing children's learning. And, for children from disadvantaged backgrounds or troubled home environments, quality teaching is even more important.
>
> *Andrew Leigh and Sara Mead*[16]

That's not where the anecdote ends though. My daughter's school promised us a particularly good math teacher the next school year as a form of recompense. As happens with schools all too frequently, somehow no one ever followed through on the promise. After a few calls without results, my wife left a message on the school's answering machine politely explaining that she understood how busy everyone was and that we didn't want to be disruptive, so she would be in the guidance counselor's office at 9 o'clock the next morning and would simply sit there—all day, every day—until the school was able to fix things. You guessed it; my daughter was instantly assigned to the promised teacher.

Upper-middle class parents frequently make effective advocates for their kids. On average, families in poverty are less effective. After all, my wife was in a position to miss work as long as was necessary to get what she wanted. Many parents aren't. Good teachers, of course, are themselves advocates for "their kids," partially substituting for parents who can't or don't play that role.[17] Under *Profit,* teachers have a financial incentive to advocate for *all* kids, but I'm willing to bet that it's poor kids who are the most in need of that extra advocacy.

Our International Competitive Position

Depending on the education measure you look at, the United States is kind of an average industrialized country or maybe somewhat below average. Among the OECD countries, our main industrialized competition, we're below average in math and science.[18] Of course, math and science aren't everything—we do break into the top half in reading.[19] We also nearly break into the top half in terms of college degrees granted.[20] Let's be fair. Someone has to have a mediocre ranking; why not us?

Assuming you're an American reader, I imagine that your blood pressure rose with that last sentence.[21] We don't like to think of mediocrity as our goal.

There's a good argument to be made that America's dominance in the twentieth century was a direct result of our provision of a broad-based, high-quality education.[22] In the first half to three-quarters of the last century, the U.S. clearly had a better education system than our competitors. That hasn't been true in a long time. The rest of the industrialized world has caught up with us and passed us by in education. We've been coasting on our earlier educational lead. Goldin and Katz are depressingly clear on this point:

> Not long ago the United States led the world in education and had done so for quite some time. . . . the long-standing U.S. lead in education has disappeared. The United States is no longer the first in the world in high school and college graduation rates and lags considerably in K–12 quality indicators. . . . by the early 2000s the United States . . . had an upper secondary graduation rate that put it in the bottom third of the 26 OECD nations.[23]

The consequences of dropping behind in education are accelerating because the importance of skills is increasing. Murnane and Steele put it well:

> The problem is that technological advances have routinized manufacturing and clerical jobs and facilitated international competition, thereby increasing the demand for cognitive skills, especially problem-solving and communication skills. The nation's educational problem, in other words, is that an education that was good enough to allow Americans to earn a decent living in the economy of 1973 is not good enough to enable them to earn a decent living today.[24]

International tests of reading show the U.S. to be a middle-of-the-pack performer. In the most recent (2003) Program for International Student Assessment (PISA), reading scores, American fifteen-year-olds ranked at the OECD average.[25] In contrast, in the most recent (2006) comparison of science learning among industrialized countries, American fifteen-year-olds fell below the OECD average. We were beaten by sixteen OECD countries, tied eight, and we passed five.[26] In math, twenty-three OECD countries beat us; we tied two and beat four.[27]

America doesn't like to think of itself as a somewhat below-average place. We do like a challenge. And we know how to win this one.

EDUCATION AS AN INVESTMENT: A MORE THOROUGH CALCULATION

Let's return to the purely dollars and cents side of *Profit*. I'm going to expand on the calculations earlier in the chapter, filling in details, but the bottom line won't change.

Education makes people work smarter and therefore more productively. About two-thirds of output is attributable to labor. Total output in the United States, our Gross Domestic Product (GDP), is $14 trillion a year. That's $14,000 billion. Two-thirds of $14,000 billion comes to $9,333 billion a year. Since *Profit* will increase labor productivity 10 percent, output will rise about $933 billion. That's a bit higher than the quick estimate earlier in the chapter, which left out non–compensation-related returns to labor, such as the earnings of the self-employed.

So we're roughly talking about a ten to one payoff. Close to $1 trillion a year down the line.

Invest Today for Tomorrow's Return

Of course, payoffs down the line are not the same thing as big costs today. Education is a long-term investment where we put the money in upfront for a large payback down the road. With most private investments, we expect the investment not only to pay off, but to pay off with interest. The longer we hold the investment, the more interest we expect to accumulate. Economists work this problem backwards, computing what we call the "net present value" of an investment. For example, when interest rates on U.S. treasury bonds are 2 percent, then a bond that pays $100 one year from now is worth $98 dollars today, and a bond that pays the same $100 two years from now is worth (about) $96 today.[28] In other words, a $1 trillion annual payback decades in the future is worth considerably less than $1 trillion today.

Well, maybe. Getting the calculation right depends on two factors: the appropriate interest rate and the growth in labor productivity. The appropriate interest rate to be used for this sort of calculation is what's called the "social rate of discount." Economists argue on both philosophical and technical grounds about the appropriate number, estimates generally being in the 0 to 3 percent range. At 0 percent, $1 trillion in the future is the same as $1 trillion today. At 3 percent, it's considerably less. Interestingly, the interest rate on ten-year, inflation-adjusted U.S. government bonds (a good measure of what it costs the government to borrow) is generally in the 2 to 3 percent range.

The second time-adjustment factor arises from growth in labor productivity. As an example, suppose that the average worker produced $1,000 worth of goods and services this year and that productivity rises by 2 percent per year. In this case, the average worker will produce $1,020 next year, $1,040 the year after, and so forth. A 10 percent *Profit*-generated increase will be $100, then $102, then $104.[29] So productivity growth increases *Profit* returns.

However, there are other factors that lower *Profit* returns. First, if we want Mechanism II to stay effective, teacher salary raises will have to rise at roughly the rate of productivity growth. That will increase the cost of *Profit* over time. Second, the first students graduating under *Profit* will have had the benefit of a reinvigorated teacher corps for only part of their schooling and so won't get the full benefit. In the long run this doesn't matter, but it does decrease the initial productivity gain. Third, it will take time for better-educated students to become a large fraction of the workforce. Newly graduated students entering the workforce replace existing workers at a rate of about 2.1 percent per year.[30]

Finally there is good, but not conclusive, evidence that education increases not just the level of labor productivity, but the ongoing rate of growth of the economy.[31] Hanushek and coauthors write "each additional year of average schooling in a country increased the average 40-year growth rate in GDP by about 0.37 percentage points."[32] Similarly, Bils and Klenow estimate that an additional year of schooling adds 0.3 percent to annual growth.[33] The scientific literature on this is unsettled, and the overall evidence has been called "fragile."[34] So while this effect is likely important, I'll leave it out of the calculations in order to be conservative.

I've put all these considerations together in a small computer simulation model. As it turns out, the rough calculation earlier in the chapter of a nine-to-one payback from *Profit* is pretty accurate. Doing the calculations right does serve to emphasize that *Profit* is an investment that pays off (in the pure economic sense) down the road. The first several years of the program will cost us money for a big positive return a little later. (This is true of any K–12 investment.) Because taxes recapture only a fraction of increased productivity, it takes longer for the government than for the economy to get into the black.[35]

Figure 16 shows the year-by-year net flows from the first fifty years of *Profit*. For the first eight or nine years costs outweigh benefits while we wait for better educated students to flow into the workforce. Eventually, productivity-driven benefits swamp costs.

Because Figure 16 shows annual benefits less annual costs, it doesn't account for the fact that the costs come earlier than the benefits. To get the accounting right, we want to discount later benefits. I've done this in Figure 17. After discounting for the time it takes for benefits to kick in, I find cumulative costs and benefits balance in year fifteen. Everything after that is pure gravy.

In addition to looking year by year, we can total the discounted costs and benefits over the first fifty years to find *Profit's* net present value. The net present value comes to $18 trillion—which is like getting an extra year's worth of goods and services for the entire U.S. economy (plus a little more).

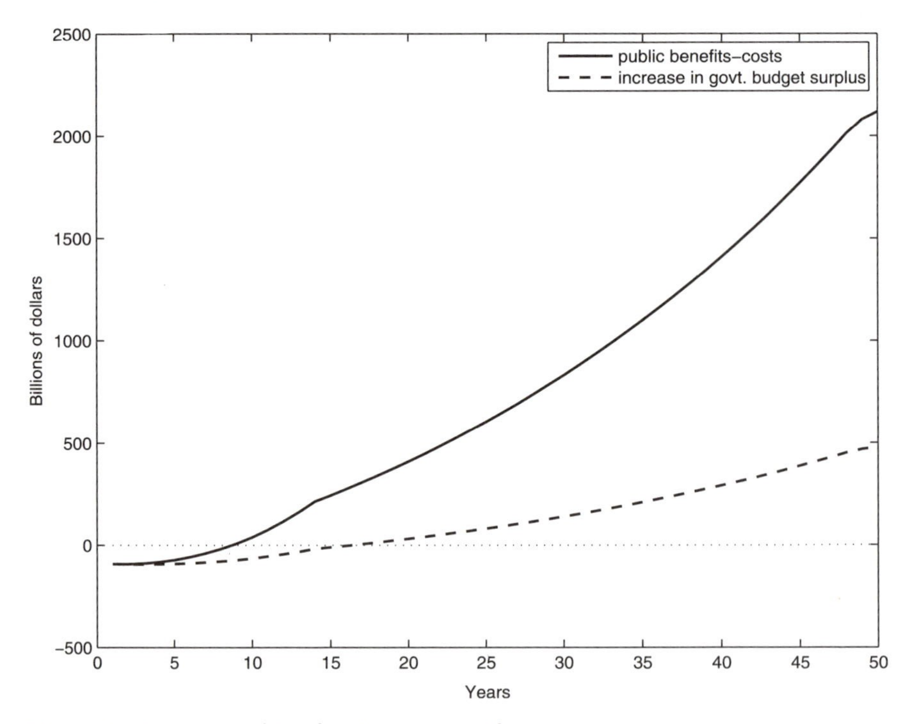

Figure 16 50 years of *Profit*—Base Case Flows

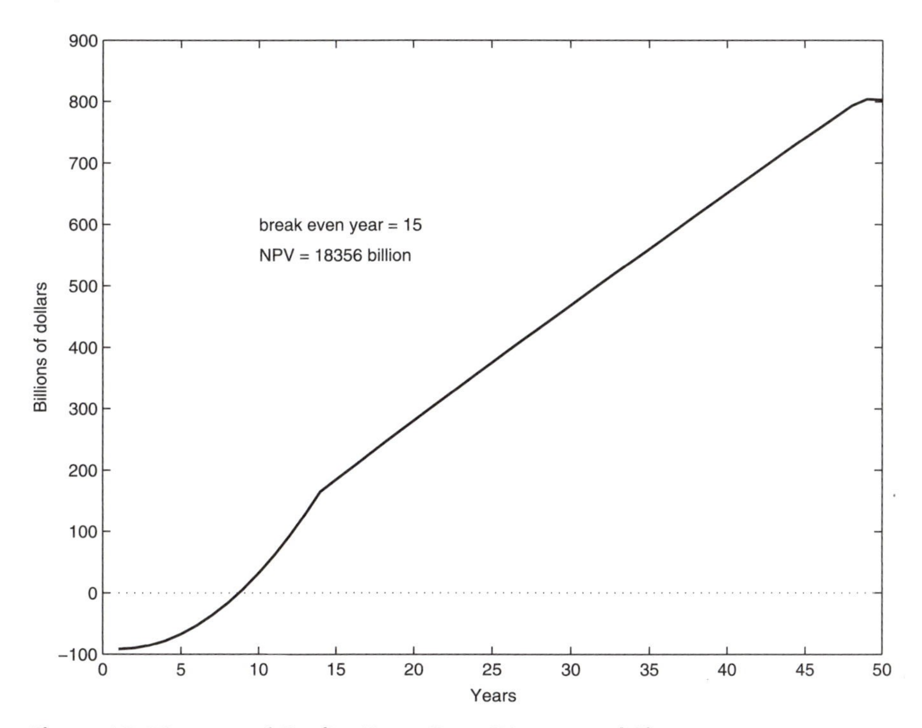

Figure 17 50 years of *Profit*—Base Case Discounted Flows

A sensible government increases education spending when the benefit to the population is more than the cost of the spending (as in Figure 17), although a calculation of benefit should include the nonpecuniary returns that I've omitted in an effort to be extra conservative. So as earlier in the chapter, let's ask the political question about what will happen to the government's debt. In Figure 18 I've computed the effect of *Profit* on the *future value* of the accumulated government debt. You can see that the government debt grows for 30+ years, reflecting both upfront costs and the interest that accumulates on those costs. However in the long run, as better educated students fill out the workforce, *Profit* greatly reduces the government debt.

> IF YOU WANT TO BE DRAMATIC ABOUT IT . . .
>
> *Profit* will wipe out half the national debt.[36]

Where does all this put us compared to the quick calculation early in the chapter? The early calculation turns out to be about right, although it takes a while for enough students to graduate

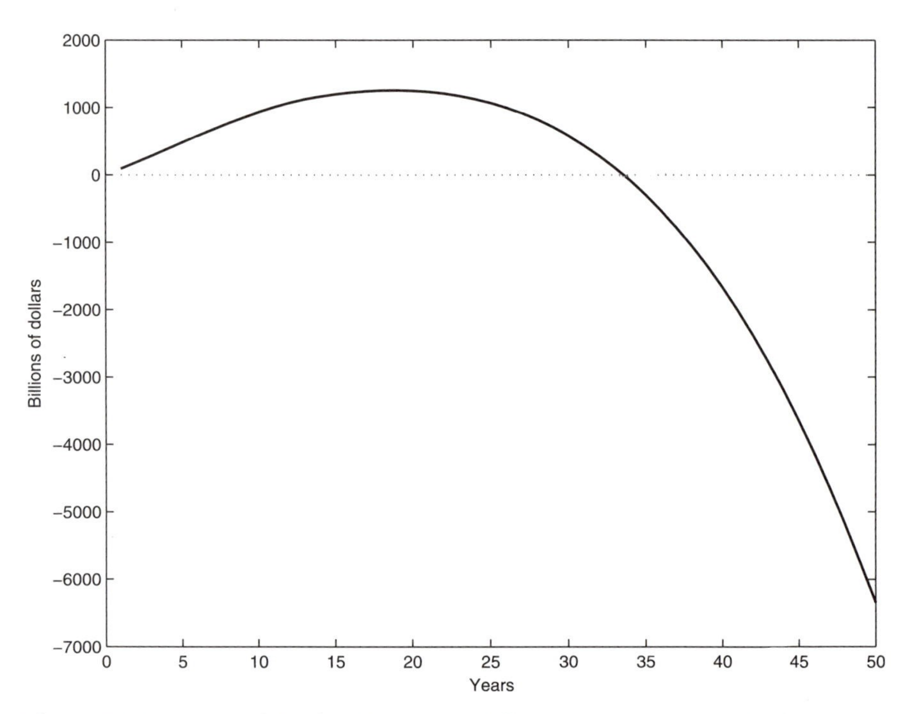

Figure 18 50 years of *Profit*—Base Case Effect on Government Debt

for the full benefits to come online. In fact, the quick opening calculation underestimated the long-run benefit cost ratio, which turns out to be ten to one![37]

Economists debate the right numbers to use for discount rates and for growth rates, so I've recalculated the effects of *Profit* for optimistic and pessimistic assumptions and show the results in Table 7. Just to be clear, all the cases share the same calculations about the costs and results of *Profit*. The differences show the effects of different assumptions about the economy. Most particularly, none of the cases factor in any of the nonpecuniary or growth effects mentioned in this chapter. Only additions to labor productivity get counted.

A FINAL THOUGHT ON PAYBACK

I believe in investing in children. The really important return is having happy, successful, children who will lead a good life. The dollars-

Table 7 Effect of Alternative Assumptions on Payback Projections

	Discount rate	**Growth rate**	**NPV (billions)**	**Breakeven year annual benefit-cost**	**Breakeven year cumulative, discounted benefit-cost**
Optimistic case	0.01	0.0206	$28,780	9	14
Base case	0.02	0.0186	$18,356	9	15
Pessimistic case	0.04	0.0186	$9,316	9	15

and-cents part of that investment matters, but to me it's not primary. Perhaps unfortunately, money is the part of the return that we can measure best. Whether you share my belief in the primacy of some of the softer values or not, it's reassuring to know that *Profit* will pay for itself as a straight economic investment.

13

Getting There

> The truth is that, after two decades of well-publicized effort, public school systems in the United States remain about where they were in 1983.
>
> *Paul T. Hill and James Harvey*[1]

I hope you are convinced that rewarding successful teachers will reenergize our educational system. A fairly big investment today will provide a *very* big downstream return. The education research is clear. The economics is clear. All that's required is the will to step out of our comfort zone and move forward.

That's the big picture. This chapter focuses on getting past barriers to renewal. While I'll talk a little bit about some technical issues, most of the chapter is about overcoming inertia. Since we're talking about a big step, I want to highlight why we need a *big* step rather than a series of small steps. Then I'll talk about why there's a special role for the federal government to play in paying for *Profit.*

GREAT LEAPS VERSUS INCREMENTALISM

After many, many years, I'm finally having the basement bathroom remodeled. As I'm writing this paragraph, our carpenter is downstairs breaking out old concrete. Very loud hammer rings tell me he's hitting that concrete really hard. It's not a job that calls for a series of love taps. We've been talking about creating a fundamental change in our education system. Could we give the system a small tap instead, just to get a small result? Maybe just to get started? After all, a small change is surely an easier sell. Let me start off saying no to incrementalism as a general rule and then discuss a few ways in which incrementalism could be okay.

Our current teacher pay setup is like concrete in two ways. First, most teachers think that getting evaluated for student results will be wrenching. To get them to sign on, the reward has to outweigh the perceived pain. (My forecast is that down the road, well-thought-out evaluations will turn out to be not so painful, but upfront perceptions are what matter here.) If we offer a small reward just to get started, we'll never get started at all. Second, the decision to start/stay in/return to teaching is a big step for an individual. I suspect that a dramatic change in the attractiveness of a teaching career will have a disproportionately large effect on those decisions.

There's one more piece arguing against promising a small raise this year, another one next year, etc. It's the credibility issue. A 40 percent raise offered today is credible; a 5 percent a year raise for the next eight years, less so. If we want teachers and potential teachers to make long-term choices, they have to believe that the rewards are long-term too.

But there is one sense which incrementalism might work. Local school districts can get started without waiting for a national effort. Returning to the concrete metaphor, you have to hit really hard, but you can make progress by hitting really hard just in one spot.

Suppose a single school district were to dramatically raise teacher pay through funding the kinds of bonuses we've talked about. (Or a modest number of districts around the country, each working on its own.) Would the benefits of paying for teacher success come through? When a single district moves forward with *Profit* while those around it stand still, that district can attract the best teachers from the existing teacher pool. The nation as a whole makes the teaching profession more attractive by drawing potential teachers away from alternative careers, but a single district can simply swipe the most successful teachers from neighboring districts. Moving around teachers doesn't do anything for education as a whole, but it sure can help a single district.

Admittedly a single school district, especially a modest-sized district, lacks the economies of scale to develop tests, data systems, and so on. So going to *Profit* without state and national infrastructure support is somewhat daunting. On the other hand, if you live in a district with skyrocketing student outcomes while the districts around you sit on their duffs, . . . well just imagine what'll be happening to property values.

ONE CHARTER SCHOOL TAKES THE BULL BY THE HORNS

The Equity Project (TEP) Charter School believes that teacher quality is the most important factor in achieving educational equity for low income students. Spurred by this belief, TEP reallocates its public funds by making an unprecedented investment in attracting and retaining great teachers.

How? First, all TEP teachers earn a $125,000 salary, plus an annual bonus of up to $25,000.[2]

As a new startup, this single charter middle school attracted six hundred applicants for eight teacher openings![3]

There is also a sense in which even if we start full bore, expenses will be incremental. Suppose we promise every teacher a 40 percent raise if every teacher hits her *Profit* target.

Even in a successful program, they're not all going to hit their target the first year or the second year. So while we have to be credibly prepared to pay the full 40 percent—and while some first-year bonuses will be 40 percent (or more!)—realistically it will be a few years before the costs ramp up to the full 40 percent.

THE STATE AND FEDERAL ROLE

What about *Profit* at the state level? A number of states have made serious moves toward incentive and accountability systems. Unfortunately, much less progress has been made toward raising teacher pay by a significant amount. Can an entire state move to *Profit* without a national change? The argument is somewhat like the argument about a single district switching, but the difference in scale changes the answers a little.[4] States have some advantage over single districts simply because they can share the cost of infrastructure development over the entire state. States are also in a better position to capture the downstream tax revenue increases than are individual districts, and generally have more flexibility in deciding on taxing and spending.

However, stealing great teachers from neighboring districts doesn't work so well at the state level because teachers are far less mobile across states than across districts.

Let me share some useful data about cross-state teacher mobility. No one knows exactly how much teachers move around. In particular, we don't know how often teachers attend college (where they prepare for a career) in one state and then take a job in another state. We do know whether teachers are working in the state in which they themselves were born. It turns out that one half of teachers work in their birth state and one half have moved.[5]

While an isolated school district can grab top teachers from surrounding districts, states have a much more limited ability to do so. Some teacher recruiting goes on across state boundaries, but not that much. So for Mechanism I to come into play, states have to attract the best new entrants into teaching. This means change may come more slowly than for an individual district. On the other hand, to the extent that many of a state's teachers are trained in teacher colleges within the state, the state has the opportunity to work together with those colleges for new training methods in a way that isn't feasible for a single district. There is no doubt that scattered districts or a single state can move to *Profit,* but it will certainly be easier if many areas start pounding away at the same time.

What's the role for the federal government? Education in America has traditionally been the province of state and local governments. We can keep it that way, but there is one area where federal involvement is crucial. *Money.* America's mixed national/state/local fiscal system is much more flexible at the federal level than it is at the state or local level. In practicality, a good chunk of the investment money needs to be federal.

The first part of the practical issue is that states and local districts have restrictions on what kinds of investments they can finance. We know that *Profit* calls for an upfront investment for big downstream return. Economists call making people more productive an investment in *human capital.* States borrow money for physical capital projects, highways, school buildings, and the like. They generally aren't allowed to borrow for human capital investments even if those investments have a great payback. That means that at the state level, taxpayers have to be willing to pay now for educational investments that largely benefit their children rather than themselves. In contrast, the federal government can borrow to finance projects that pay off down the road.

The second state/local versus national financing issue returns to the question of whether the point of *Profit* is to educate our kids or the point is to lower long-run budget deficits. From the national vantage, both happen. In contrast, at the local district level most students end up living somewhere else (and paying taxes somewhere else) as adults. In other words, the federal government is better situated to recoup its investment in purely financial terms than is a local district. If an isolated school uses *Profit* to massively improve student outcomes, it's great for the students, it's probably great for property values, but the district isn't likely to be repaid for a job well done. (On the other hand, the higher property value argument may be fairly persuasive to taxpayers.)

Historically, paying for education has been a state and local responsibility, with the federal government kicking in 9 percent or less. While individual districts and states certainly can step up, my guess is that the federal government will need to pick up more than its historical share. This is exactly what the federal government did to reduce teacher layoffs during the recent recession. For further perspective, suppose that the federal government paid for every cent of *Profit*. Even in this lopsided hypothetical case, state and local financing would still completely dominate; the state and local share of total education costs would be about 78 percent.[6]

BRINGING STAKEHOLDERS TOGETHER

Tony Wagner, in *The Global Achievement Gap*, offers a great phrase, "reform du jour," to describe the fleeting fashions in school and curriculum redesign.[7] Teachers and taxpayers have both been burned before.[8] If we want buy in to *Profit*, we'll have to make a credible case to teachers that the benefits will stick around for a while. We'll have to make a credible case to taxpayers that pay and results are linked.

One source of potential opposition is those who oppose higher pay for teachers because they think it won't do any good. The link-pay-to-results aspect of *Profit* answers that concern. But program design will have to be credible on the point that bonus payments will not gradually degenerate into across-the-boardism. Maintaining credibility that we won't just spread the money around will take some special care, since we expect that most teachers will in fact earn bonuses. There needs to be transparency that bonus payments becoming the norm results only from success becoming the norm.

On the teacher side there will inevitably be suspicion that raises will disappear the first time the economy hits a bump. This is one reason that experiments won't be very welcome unless there is a promise of funding for the medium- or long-term. There are, however, options that local districts may find useful in getting teacher buy in. One way to do this is to give individual teachers a choice of sticking to their existing compensation plan or switching to a *Profit* plan, a grandfather clause of sorts. Research by Carl Nadler and Matt Wiswall on adoption of the Minnesota Q Comp plan shows that some kind of grandfathering plays an important part in acceptance of plans, especially by the most experienced teachers.[9]

Another important set of stakeholders are all the folks who have been active in school reform movements. How does *Profit* mix with existing reform movements, especially vouchers and charter schools? On the surface, *Profit* plans aren't necessarily pro or con with respect to the debate about traditional public schools, charter schools, or vouchers. Teachers and schools that succeed get rewarded no matter how they're organized. The difference under *Profit* is that these reform programs that succeed at producing student achievement will be able to reward their teachers accordingly. My guess is that once the opportunities are offered, charter schools will be quick to jump onto the *Profit* bandwagon.

What about Teach For America, possibly America's best-known effort for reinvigorating the teacher corps? Reservations on the part of some education researchers because TFAers lack formal teacher credentials notwithstanding, TFA attracts remarkably talented college students to become teachers, offering them both a challenge and a chance to give to back to the community. But not very many TFAers keep teaching as a long-term career. After all, these are young people with excellent alternatives. Some get turned on and stay in education, but most move on with their lives. So as it stands, Teach For America is a success but not a solution.[10] Now suppose that a talented TFAer approaching the end of her commitment could look forward to a 40 percent higher salary than at the present. When teacher pay is more like what you can earn in an alternative career, I think we'll see a lot more of this talented group staying for the long haul.

HITTING THE GROUND RUNNING: SOME MISSING PIECES OF INFRASTRUCTURE

Some of the infrastructure needed for *Profit* would be best developed once, so that costs can be spread across many schools, rather than have each school develop tools from scratch. What tools do schools need that they can't easily or cost-effectively supply themselves? In particular, during the start-up phase what services need to be made available to districts? There are at least four components that are critical.

Tests. Making good tests is expensive. But once a test is created, it can be reused in many places. Few school districts have the resources to create and validate their own tests. We would like districts to be able to choose from among a variety of tests, in order to fit with local needs. We will need a greatly increased and diverse supply of vetted, ready-to-go, exams. Once testing is widespread, the market will easily take care of increasing supply. But during the ramp-up period, the government will need to offer subsidies for test creation.

Credential validation. Any compensation scheme will surely have elements of qualification bonuses for credentials. The credentials themselves need to be validated, showing scientific evidence that at a general level the credentials predict success. Such validation needs to be independent of the group creating the credentials. It's an obvious place for an expanded role for universities in general and colleges of education in particular.

IT (Information Technology). Rewarding success means much expanded tracking of both students and teachers. Design and implementation of such systems requires care, but not technological breakthroughs. Most school systems rightfully regard themselves as being in the teaching business rather than the IT business. Costs are not terribly high for a large district—on the order of hundreds of thousands of dollars to set up. One estimate is that setup costs would average four dollars per student and operation costs about two dollars per student per year to maintain.[11]

Here, too, there is a role for the government to subsidize creation of good IT software during the rollout period. While the software may well be created by the private sector, there will be a need for quasi-public standardization efforts to make sure information exchange works between systems used by different districts. There will also be a critical need to ensure that adequate privacy safeguards are built into such systems.

Compensation system design. The nitty-gritty of designing a bonus system will differ from one state to another, from one district to another within a state, and even among schools within a district. With rare exceptions, school administrators, unions, and teachers themselves have had little experience designing compensation systems. Being lent a hand from the outside will be invaluable. Outside experts can provide a fast track for sharing information about what is being done elsewhere. Outside experts can also sometimes play a useful mediating role. This is an area in which foundations may be particularly valuable in providing funding and in helping put together such expert groups. This is also an area in which the national scope of the NEA and AFT can move information around both quickly and credibly.[12]

TALKING POINTS

As we've walked through the *Profit of Education,* I've tried hard to provide a lot of details and to be open about both the strengths and weaknesses of the arguments. Now I think it's time for some simplification. Fixing public education is a political decision. Or better, it's a whole string of political decisions made everywhere from isolated school districts to the halls of Congress. That means we have to push at many levels. Here are some talking points—sans caveat—to help get the discussion started:

Always and Everywhere

- Restoring America's educational system to preeminence is a national priority for our children and for our country's future
- Teachers are *the* key to education
- It's time to apply the American way of building a winning team to education:
  - Pay what it takes to attract great people.
  - Reward those great people when they do great things.

Local School Districts

- Here's the deal, teachers: You get seriously—and fairly—evaluated. In return, we pay you fairly—seriously raising pay (40 percent on average)

- Here's the deal, teacher unions: We need to do this together. Your participation reassures teachers that they're protected. Work with us so that your members finally get treated like professionals
- Teacher salaries take first priority in spending. We'll cut the budget in other areas where we can, use increased state and federal resources, and raise taxes as needed

States

- More money for education—but the money goes for higher teacher salaries. It doesn't get thrown into the general pot
- Insist on results, but offer maximum flexibility for how those results are measured and for the details of how results and pay get linked
- Offer support for districts willing to step out first and serve as models

Foundations, Colleges of Education, Reform-Minded Nonprofits

- Help vet success measures
  - Create a variety of tests so schools can pick ones that fit their needs
  - Provide validation for specific qualification measures such as advanced degrees
- Offer consulting services and conferences to share lessons learned

Federal Government

- The power of the purse is yours. Convert emergency stimulus money into support for teacher salaries
- Add to state efforts; don't substitute. The key is that salaries actually go up
- Fund development of data systems, test banks, and research that can be shared among the states
- Just as schools expect results but support flexibility in how teachers get those results, so too should the federal government pay for states and local districts for results, while encouraging experimentation and supporting local decision making

Always and Everywhere Redux

- Next time you see a great teacher, *say thanks*. Money's not everything, you know

FINALLY

If two decades from now our schools are no better, America will be on a downward spiral. Two decades from now our schools should be not just better, they should be *much* better—once again world class. Remembering that teachers make the difference, it's up to all of us to back up our words when we say "children are the future."

Technical Appendix

CHAPTER 1: TEACHERS MAKE THE DIFFERENCE

Researchers report the effect of an increase in teacher effectiveness using a number of different metrics. The most common method is to report the effect of a one standard deviation increase in teacher effectiveness measured as an X standard deviation improvement in student test scores. If teacher effectiveness follows a Gaussian distribution, then one-half standard deviation above the mean is the 70th percentile. Actually the 69.15th percentile, but the rounding is small enough to be innocuous.

Translating the effect on student achievement measured in standard deviations requires making some technical assumptions. First, in most cases the authors do not translate standard deviation units into academic months of achievement. The change of units does depend somewhat on grade level, on the test used, and on whether achievement is measured for reading versus math. Hanushek reports, "One standard deviation on the student tests ranges from one to one and a half grade-level equivalents, depending on the grade."[1] Looking at the National Assessment of Educational Progress tests, the difference between 4th grade and 8th grade reading scores in 2007 was 41 points, a standard deviation was 36 points. So one standard deviation comes out to 3.5 years progress.

There is no perfect reconciliation to differing systems of measurement. Since I wish to be conservative in estimating the effect of teacher quality, I am translating one student standard deviation as

1.25 grade levels where the original research doesn't give more specific guidance. As an example, the finding that one standard deviation of teacher quality translates into 0.10 standard deviations of student achievement in one year is converted into 0.125 grade levels, or in academic months $9 \times 0.125 = 1.125$ months. Since I am considering a ½ standard deviation change, this would translate into 0.625 months.

CHAPTER 2: WHO TEACHES?

Figure 1 shows a plot of adjusted AFQT scores using the author's calculations of data drawn from NLSY79. "Adjusted" scores represent percentiles. Data is limited to the NLSY79 representative sample and those observations reporting a positive AFQT score and positive wage. I then adjusted AFQT scores in order to account for the age at test taking effect by regressing AFQT on age dummies, taking the residuals, and adding back in the overall mean. Descriptive statistics of the adjusted score are:

Table 8 Descriptive Statistics for Adjusted NLSY79 AFQT Scores

		College-educated, Wage>0	
	All	**Nonteacher**	**Teacher**
Mean	50.25	74.35	68.36
Median	50.21	79.21	71.85
Max	108.13	107.13	108.13
Min	−8.24	−5.24	9.21
Standard deviation	27.83	20.74	20.48

The vertical line in the text figure shows the overall median. The distributions for teachers and nonteachers are kernel density plots.

Looking at data from the 1960s, Ehrenberg and Brewer find a strong relation between teacher performance on verbal aptitude tests and student performance. Improving teacher ability by ¾ of a standard deviation is equivalent to a 40 percent cut in class size.[2] The mean difference between teachers and nonteachers reported above is 5.75 points, or $0.288 = \frac{5.75}{20.38}$. The median difference is 6.68, giving $0.328 = \frac{6.68}{20.38}$. These translate to $15.4 = .288 \times \frac{4}{3} \times 40$ or $17.9 = .328 \times \frac{4}{3} \times 40$.

Goldhaber reports:

> [T]eachers see the largest gains in productivity during the early years of their career. Students with a teacher who has one to two years of experience outperform students with novice teachers by 3 to 7 percent of a standard deviation; students with teachers who have three to five years of experience tend to outperform students of teachers with one to two years of experience by an additional 2 percent of a standard deviation (though the difference is not statistically significant across all model specifications).[3]

Using the metric I have adopted earlier of 1.25 standard deviations per grade level, this translates into $0.33 = .03 \times 9 \times 1.25$ to $0.79 = .07 \times 9 \times 1.25$ months. The difference between beginners and the next group adds another 2 percent, $0.55 = .05 \times 9 \times 1.25$ to $1 = .09 \times 9 \times 1.25$ months.

CHAPTER 3: TEACHER PAY

Data for median and 75th percentile computations are from the March 2008 Current Population Survey. The income measure is wage and salary income. Teacher is defined as occupations coded "Elementary of middle school teacher" or "Secondary school teacher." Sample is college-educated (bachelor's degree or above), age 22 through 64, in fulltime labor force, reporting positive income. The 27 percent calculation is the ratio of the median for nonteachers to teachers. The "nearly 60 percent" number is actually 58.2 percent and is the ratio of the 75 percentile figures.

Data for Figure 7 are from King et al. (2004). Measure is Wage and Salary Income. Sample is college-educated, full-time workers, ages 22 through 64, reporting income greater than $1,000 and more than 20 hours of work per week. Ratio is calculated as a weighted average of female (.75) and male (.25) ratios.

CHAPTER 4: RAISES!

Data for 2008 for the teacher income percentile table is based on the author's calculations from the March 2008 Current Population Survey. The income measure is wage and salary income. Teacher is defined as occupations coded "Elementary of middle school teacher" or "Secondary school teacher." Sample is college-educated (bachelor's degree or above), age 22 through 64, in fulltime labor force, reporting positive income. While this is the sensible data definition for current comparisons, it isn't perfectly comparable to the older census data.

Median teacher income in 2008 was $45,000; $44,500 for women and $48,000 for men. Comparative percentiles are calculated for nonteachers.

Salaries for comparative professions reported in the boxes are median wage and salary income for the same CPS sample as used previously. The CPS sample sizes for some of the comparative professions are relatively small. However, median income calculations should be relatively robust to these sample sizes.

Cross-State Results

I report here results underlying the cross-state estimates of NAEP scores reported in the text. As mentioned in the footnote, the effects are noticeably sensitive to the definition of nonteacher income in a state. This is one reason I regard them as providing only weak evidence.

Data Definitions

Teacher Salaries: Average annual public school teacher salary 1999–2000, *Digest of Education*.

Nonteacher income: Median 1999 income from 2000 census, 1% public use sample, college-educated reporting positive income.

RatioDigest: Teacher Salaries/Nonteacher income. Note that income and salaries measure slightly different things. The mean value of RatioDigest is approximately 1.

Read4All: 2003 NAEP scores on fourth grade reading test, all students. Note that 10 points on the NAEP is roughly equivalent to one grade of progress.

Median income: 2007 CPS median wage and salary income, fulltime workers reporting positive income.

Pup2Teach: Pupil/teacher ratio Fall 2000, Table 63, *Digest of Education.* (average value is 15.6)

PercentCollege: Fraction of adult population with four-year college degree or more, March 2007 CPS (average 0.18).

The regression underlying the scatter plot in the text is given in Table 9.

Table 9 Regression Underlying the Scatter Plot in the Text

Dependent Variable: READ4ALL
Method: Least Squares
Date: 05/13/09 Time: 13:29
Sample: 1 51
Included observations: 51

Variable	Coefficient	Std. Error	*t*-statistic	Prob.
C	176.5634	11.02539	16.01425	0.0000
RATIODIGEST	41.09007	11.04360	3.720713	0.0005

R-squared	0.220288	Mean dependent var	217.4314
Adjusted R-squared	0.204375	S.D. dependent var	7.650503
S.E. of regression	6.824080	Akaike info criterion	6.717218
Sum squared resid	2281.835	Schwarz criterion	6.792976
Log likelihood	−169.2891	Hannan-Quinn criter.	6.746167
F-statistic	13.84371	Durbin-Watson stat	2.140677
Prob(F-statistic)	0.000512		

I report a more detailed multiple regression in Table 10. The reader is warned that I report the results for the sake of completeness. While they support the thesis of *Profit*, the results are not terribly robust to alternative data definitions. In any event, interpreting this kind of cross-state regression as causal raises a whole host of problems.

The estimated impact of teacher salaries in the multiple regression is lower than in the simple regression, but still large and significant. While the coefficients are all significant, the sign of PERCENTCOLLEGE is surprising. Note that the effect of a increasing the student/teacher ratio is negative but quite small.

Bond's Results

Bond presents several relevant regression results.[4] To aid in interpretation, it would be useful to know average salaries at the BA and MA level. These are not reported, but the Digest of Education reports an average BA salary of $30,200 and an average MA salary of $38,500 for 1993–1994.[5] Bond reports the average teacher/nonteacher BA salary gap to be $10,900 (page 149), which is roughly consistent.

Bond's Table 6–2 reports a coefficient of 0.000347 for the effect of the BA salary gap on 8th grade math NAEP scores, although this estimate does not control for poverty rates. A 40 percent salary increase would raise scores by $4.2 = 0.000347 \times 12,080$. Bond's

Table 10 A More Nuanced Regression

Dependent Variable: READ4ALL
Method: Least Squares
Date: 02/20/09 Time: 17:26
Sample: 1 51
Included observations: 51

Variable	Coefficient	Std. Error	*t*-statistic	Prob.
C	186.9219	14.10485	13.25231	0.0000
RATIODIGEST	28.28418	11.02102	2.566386	0.0136
PUP2TEACH	−1.080883	0.445082	−2.428506	0.0191
PERCENTCOLLEGE	−72.08114	32.51530	−2.216838	0.0316
MED_INCOME	0.000918	0.000333	2.755911	0.0084
R-squared	0.370091	Mean dependent var		217.4314
Adjusted R-squared	0.315316	S.D. dependent var		7.650503
S.E. of regression	6.330456	Akaike info criterion		6.621516
Sum squared resid	1843.435	Schwarz criterion		6.810910
Log likelihood	−163.8487	Hannan-Quinn criter.		6.693889
F-statistic	6.756606	Durbin-Watson stat		2.146258
Prob(F-statistic)	0.000230			

Table 6–3 uses master's salaries, does control for poverty and finds a coefficient of 0.0005158. A 40 percent salary increase would raise scores by $7.9 = 0.0005158 \times 15,400$. Her Table 6–4 looks at 4th grade math scores and Master's salaries. Her preferred Model 5 has a coefficient of 0.000339, which translates in a similar manner to by $5.2 = 0.000339 \times 15,400$.

In the text table, I convert 10 NAEP points into 1 grade level.

Aksoy and Link results

Aksoy and Link had three separate observations for each student. They report the effect of raising teacher salaries for subsamples using all three years, using observations 1 and 2, and observations 1 and 3. The coefficients are beginning district salaries (in thousands) are 0.61, 0.51, and 0.94, respectively. In all cases the *t*-statistics are above 3. The average teacher salary is approximately $20,000, so a 40 percent increase would be 8, for an effect on test scores of between 4.1 and 7.5. The means and standard deviations of the test scores are approximately 48 (13), 37 (13), and 46 (14), respectively. So the proposed increase is one-third to one-half a standard deviation.

The authors do not report values that would allow a conversion into grade-level equivalents. However, using similar data, Ehrenberg et al. report a 4.5 to 5 point increase in scores between grades 8 and 10.[6] This suggests gains of 1.75 to 3.15 years.

CHAPTER 6: QUALIFICATION SUPPLEMENTS: AN INPUT MEASURE THAT MATTERS

Goldhaber and Emily find "The magnitudes of the future NBCT coefficients suggest that student gains produced by NBCTs exceed those of noncertified applicants by about 4% of a standard deviation in reading and 5% of a standard deviation in math."[7] Using the same metric as earlier, that 0.1 standard deviation equals 1.125 months of schooling, 4% of a standard deviation is $1.8 = 4 \times 1.125 \times .4$ weeks of schooling.

Cavalluzzo shows that NBCTs raised ninth- and tenth-grade math test scores by about 7 to 8 percent of a standard deviation.[8] I translate this as 3 to 4 weeks, using the same translation as above.

CHAPTER 10: SOME (RECENT) HISTORY LESSONS

In 2008, total Q Comp revenue was $57,581,000.[9] In 2007, 68% of expenditures went into teacher salary payments.[10] About 30 percent of students were in Q Comp programs and Minnesota had something over 52,000 teachers. A rough calculation of the per teacher payment is $\$2,509 = \$57,581,000 \times \frac{0.68}{0.30 \times 52,000}$.

CHAPTER 11: THE MONEY TRAIL

Expenditure per student in constant 2006–07 dollars in 1965–66 was $4,183, rising to 11,643 in 2005–06 for a percentage change of 178 percent. The annual rate of change was 2.59 percent. Average teacher salary in constant 2006–07 dollars in 1965–66 was 41,489. In 2005–2006 it was 50,295.[11] This gives a percentage increase of 21 percent. The annual rate of change was 0.48 percent.

In 1965, the median family income for white, college-educated heads of households was $11,075.[12] In 2005, median family income for (all, not just white) college-educated heads of households was $91,010.[13] The July

CPIs were 31.8 in 1965 and 195.4 in 2005.[14] This gives a real percentage increase of 33.7 percent. The annual rate of change was 0.73 percent.

The figure in the text compares 8th grade NAEP reading scores to the fraction of educational spending that goes to instruction.[15] The regression results are:

Table 11 Eighth-Grade Reading Scores Versus Instructional Spending

Dependent Variable: NAEPR8
Method: Least Squares
Date: 07/24/09 Time: 13:27
Sample: 1 51
Included observations: 51

Variable	Coefficient	Std. Error	*t*-statistic	Prob.
C	219.9764	12.52480	17.56326	0.0000
INSTRUCTION/ TOTAL_SPENDING	79.65547	23.86073	3.338350	0.0016

R-squared	0.185297	Mean dependent var	261.6796
Adjusted R-squared	0.168670	S.D. dependent var	7.076463
S.E. of regression	6.452128	Akaike info criterion	6.605123
Sum squared resid	2039.868	Schwarz criterion	6.680881
Log likelihood	−166.4306	Hannan-Quinn criter.	6.634072
F-statistic	11.14458	Durbin-Watson stat	2.128805
Prob(F-statistic)	0.001616		

Roughly, a 0.1 increase in the ratio would account for 8 points on the NAEP which is about 8/10ths of a grade. Note that controlling for median household income makes no noticeable difference.

The latest official teacher salary data is for 2006–07.[16] The report shows an average annual salary of $50,816. Benefits related to instruction are one quarter of salaries.[17] I assume that one half of benefits rise with income and one half remains constant. This gives a total cost of a "40 percent increase" for the average teacher of $\$22,867 = \$50,816 \times 0.4 + (\$50,816 \times 0.4) \times 0.25 \times 0.5$. In order to bring that up to date, I will add 10 percent. I will assume that this applies to 3.2 million teachers, and then add 10 percent to cover administrators and others. This gives a total annual bill of $88.5 billion.

Total K–12 public school expenditure in 2005–06 was $529 billion. To keep dates roughly comparable, ignore the 10 percent adjustment in the preceding paragraph. That gives an increase equal to 15 percent of total spending.

CHAPTER 12: PAYBACK!

I computed the ratio of students to working-age population as follows. K–12 enrollment is 16.6 percent of the population.[18] In 2007, the total population was 301,621 (in thousands). The population under age 20 was 82,361 and the population 65 and over was 37,888.[19] Thus the working-age population was 60.1 percent of the total population. This gives a student to worker ratio of 0.276. If we assume that 1/13th of the students enter the workforce each year, the "fill-in" rate of the new cohort is 2.1 percent.

In addition, in the first year of the program graduating students will only have been trained under *Profit* for 1/13th of their schooling. In the second year, 2/13ths, etc. The combination of these two effects is shown in Figure 19. Finally, I assume that output is delayed one year.

Note that the effect of gradual cohort replacement is quite long-lasting.

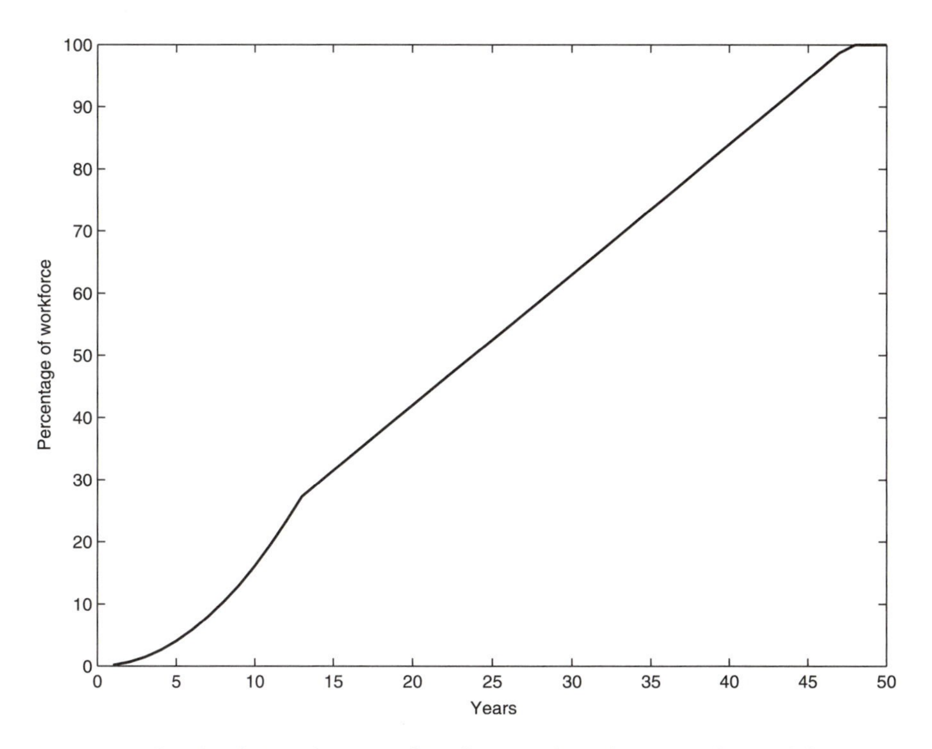

Figure 19 Gradual introduction of *Profit* trained workers into the workforce

The figures in Chapter 12, Payback! were created with the two following pieces of Matlab code. "profitPath" computes the effects of the program and "valueOfProfit" sets up the parameters for the various scenarios and displays output.

```
function [flow, govFlow, discountedFlow, effectOnDebt, breakEvenYear,...
        NPV, bcRatio, effectedPercentage] ...
   = profitPath(maxYears, r, g)
%{
Project flow from Profit of Education implementation
Dick Startz
August 2009
%}

%{
inputs:
   maxYears:  years to run simulation
   r:      discount rate
   g:      growth rate of labor productivity

outputs:
   flow:        annual net cost
   govFlow:        annual net cost to the government
   discountedFlow:  flow reduced by discount rate
   effectOnDebt:  future value of effect on government debt
   breakEvenYear:  first year NPV is positive
   NPV:      net present value of flow
   bcRatio:  ratio of extra output to cost
   effectedPercentage: fraction of the workforce with
   profit benefit

constants:
   profMargin:    percentage increase in labor productiv-
   ity due to profit
   initialCost:  first year cost of profit in billions
   initialGDP:    first year size of economy
   laborShare:  part of economic output due to labor
   replRate:    rate of entry of better educated cohort
   yearsOfSchool: K-12
   taxRate:     share of gain that goes to government.
%}
```

```
profMargin = 0.10;
initialCost = 90;
initialGDP = 14000;
laborShare = 2/3;
replRate = 0.021;
yearsOfSchool = 13;
taxRate = 0.3;

years = 1:maxYears; years = years';

% fractionAtRisk is fraction of workforce that has been
  through Profit.

fractionAtRisk = min(1.0,replRate*years);

%{
   fractionProfited is the fraction of Profit that a gradu-
   ate in a given year will have benefited by
%}
fractionProfited = min(1.0,years/yearsOfSchool);

effectedPercentage = fractionAtRisk.*fractionProfited;

%{
effectOfGrowth accounts for growth rate plus gExtra on part
of Profit
that's in effect
%}
effectOfGrowth = (1+g).^years;
%{
   extraOutput is the amount of extra output
   start with what Profit would add, cut it down for fraction
   that has
   entered workforce and the fraction of their education
   that exposed them
   to Profit.
%}
%{
effectOfGrowth accounts for growth rate on part of Profit
that's in effect

then we delay extraOutput one year to reflect not working
until after
```

```
graduation.
note that we we ignore both work during school and delay of
work for college
%}
extraOutput = initialGDP*laborShare*profMargin...
      *fractionAtRisk.*fractionProfited;
extraOutput = [0;extraOutput(1:end-1)];
extraOutput = extraOutput.*effectOfGrowth;

cost = initialCost.*effectOfGrowth;

flow = extraOutput - cost;
bcRatio = extraOutput./cost;
govFlow = taxRate*extraOutput - cost;

discount = (1+r).^(years-1);
discountedFlow = flow./discount;
effectOnDebt = zeros(maxYears,1);
effectOnDebt(1) = -govFlow(1);
for i=2:maxYears
   effectOnDebt(i) = effectOnDebt(i-1)*(1+r) - govFlow(i);
end
breakEvenYear = find(cumsum(discountedFlow)>=0,1);
NPV = sum(discountedFlow);
```

and

```
% valueOfProfit.m
%{
Plot the value of Profit of Education under various assumptions
Dick Startz
August 2009
%}

maxYears = 50;
years = 1:maxYears;
years = years';
% base case
r = 0.02;
g = 0.0186;

[flow, govFlow, discountedFlow, effectOnDebt, breakEvenYear,
NPV,...
        bcRatio, effectedPercentage]...
     = profitPath(maxYears, r, g);
```

```
plot(years, 100*effectedPercentage,'Linewidth',1.5);
xlabel('Years');
ylabel('Percentage of workforce');
title(...
'Gradual introduction of {\itProfit} trained workers into
    the workforce');
print -djpeg 'gradual introduction of profit trained workers';

figure;

plot(years, discountedFlow,'Linewidth',1.5);
hold;
plot(years,0*years,':');
xlabel('Years');
ylabel('Billions of dollars')
title('50 years of {\itProfit} - Base Case Discounted
Flows');
text(10,600,['break even year = ',num2str(breakEvenYear)]);
text(10,550,['NPV = ',num2str(NPV,5),' billion']);
print -djpeg 'discounted flow base case';

figure;

plot(years, effectOnDebt,'Linewidth',1.5);
hold;
plot(years,0*years,':');
xlabel('Years');
ylabel('Billions of dollars')
title('50 years of {\itProfit} - Base Case Effect on
Government Debt');
print -djpeg 'Govt debt base case';

figure;
plot(years, flow,'-','Linewidth',1.5);
hold;
plot(years, govFlow,'-','Linewidth',1.5);
plot(years,0*years,':');
legend('net flow','increase in budget surplus');
xlabel('Years');

ylabel('Billions of dollars')
title('50 years of {\itProfit} - Base Case Flows');
print -djpeg 'simple flow base case';
```

```
% moderately optimistic case
r = 0.00;
g = 0.0206;

[flowOp, govFlowOp, discountedFlowOp, effectOnDebtOp,
breakEvenYearOp,...
     NPVOp, bcRatioOp, effectedPercentage]...
   = profitPath(maxYears, r, g);

% moderately pessimistic case
r = 0.04;
g = 0.0186;

[flowPes, govFlowPes, discountedFlowPes,
effectOnDebtPes,...
   breakEvenYearPes, NPVPES, bcRatio, effectedPercentage]...
   = profitPath(maxYears, r, g);

breakEvenYear
breakEvenYearOp
breakEvenYearPes
NPV
NPVOP
NPVPES
```

References

Aaronson, Daniel, Lisa Barrow, and William Sander. 2007. Teachers and student achievement in the Chicago public high schools. *Journal of Labor Economics* 25 (1):95–135.

AFT (American Federation of Teachers). 2008. Differentiated pay plans, http://www.aft.org/issues/teaching/diffpay/index.cfm.

Aksoy, Tevfik, and Charles R. Link. 2000. A panel analysis of student mathematics achievement in the US in the 1990s: Does increasing the amount of time in learning activities affect math achievement? *Economics of Education Review* 19 (3):261–77.

Allegretto, Sylvia A., Sean P. Corcoran, and Lawrence Mishel. 2008. *The teaching penalty: Teacher pay losing ground*. Washington, DC: Economic Policy Institute.

Bacolod, Marigee P. 2007. Do alternative opportunities matter? The role of female labor markets in the decline of teacher quality. *Review of Economics & Statistics* 89 (4):737–51.

Baldi, S., Y. Jin, M. Skemer, P. J. Green, and D. Herget. 2007. *Highlights from PISA 2006: Performance of U.S. 15-year-old students in science and mathematics literacy in an international context (NCES 2008–016).* Washington, DC: National Center for Education, Statistics, Institute of Education Sciences, U.S. Department of Education.

Ballou, Dale. 2001. Pay for performance in public and private schools. *Economics of Education Review* 20 (1):51–61.

Barber, Michael, and Mona Mourshed. 2007. *How the world's best-performing school systems come out on top*. New York: McKinsey & Company.

Betts, Julian R. 1995. Does school quality matter? Evidence from the National Longitudinal Survey of Youth. *Review of Economics and Statistics* 77 (2):231–50.

———. 1996. Do school resources matter only for older workers? *Review of Economics and Statistics* 78 (4):638–52.

Betts, Julian R., Robert M. Costrell, Herbert J. Walberg, Meredith Phillips, and Tiffani Chin. 2001. Incentives and equity under standards-based reform. *Brookings Papers on Education Policy* (4):9–74.

Bils, Mark, and Peter J. Klenow. 2000. Does schooling cause growth? *American Economic Review* 90 (5):1160–83.

Bishop, John H., Joan Y. Moriarty, and Ferran Mane. 2000. Diplomas for learning, not seat time: The impacts of New York Regents examinations. *Economics of Education Review* 19 (4):333–49.

Bond, Constance. 2001. Do teacher salaries matter?. PhD diss., Teachers College, Columbia University.

Boyd, Donald, Daniel Goldhaber, Lankford Hamilton, and James Wyckoff. 2007. The effect of certification and preparation on teacher quality. *Future of Children* 17 (1):45–68.

Boyd, Donald, Pamela Grossman, Hamilton Lankford, Susanna Loeb, and James Wyckoff. 2006. How changes in entry requirements alter the teacher workforce and affect student achievement. *Education Finance and Policy* 1 (2):176–216.

Bureau of Labor Statistics. 2010. *Occupational outlook handbook, 2010–11 edition*. U.S. Department of Labor. Table 25–2040.

Bushaw, William J., and Alec M. Gallup. 2008. Americans speak out—are educators and policy makers listening? The 40th annual Phi Delta Kappa/Gallup poll of the public's attitudes toward the public schools. *Phi Delta Kappan* 90 (1):9(12).

Cantrell, Steven, Jon Fullerton, Thomas J. Kane, and Douglas O. Staiger. 2008. National Board Certification and teacher effectiveness: Evidence from a random assignment experiment. *National Bureau of Economic Research Working Paper Series* No. 14608.

Card, David, and Alan B. Krueger. 1992. Does school quality matter? Returns to education and the characteristics of public schools in the United States. *Journal of Political Economy* 100 (1):1–40.

Cavalluzzo, Linda C. 2004. Is National Board Certification an effective signal of teacher quality?, http://cna.org/sites/default/files/CavaluzzoStudy.pdf.

Chambers, Jay G., Thomas B. Parrish, and Jenifer J. Harr. 2004. What are we spending on special education services in the United States, 1999–2000? Special Education Expenditure Project, Center for Special Education Finance, http://www.eric.ed.gov/PDFS/ED471888.pdf.

Chicago TAP. *Chicago TAP FAQs*. 2009. http://www.chicagotapschools.org/.

Clotfelter, Charles T., and Helen F. Ladd. 1996. Recognizing and rewarding success in public schools. In *Holding schools accountable: Performance-based reform in education*, ed. H. F. Ladd. Washington, DC: Brookings Institution.

Clotfelter, Charles T., Helen F. Ladd, and Jacob L. Vigdor. 2006. Teacher-student matching and the assessment of teacher effectiveness. *Journal of Human Resources* 41 (4):778–820.

———. 2007. Teacher credentials and student achievement: Longitudinal analysis with student fixed effects. *Economics of Education Review* 26 (6):673–82.

Cooper, Samuel T., and Elchanan Cohn. 1997. Estimation of a frontier production function for the South Carolina educational process. *Economics of Education Review* 16 (3):313–27.

Corcoran, Sean P., William N. Evans, and Robert M. Schwab. 2004. Women, the labor market, and the declining relative quality of teachers. *Journal of Policy Analysis and Management* 23 (3):449–70.

Costrell, Robert M., and Michael Podgursky. 2009. Peaks, cliffs and valleys. *Education Next* Winter 2008.

———. Forthcoming. Peaks, cliffs and valleys: The peculiar incentives in teacher retirement systems and their consequences for school staffing. *Education Finance and Policy* 4 (2):175–211.

Council of Economic Advisors. 2009. Economic report of the president, http://www.gpoaccess.gov/eop/.

Crowe, Patrick H. 1978. *How to teach school and make a living at the same time.* Kansas City: Sheed, Andrews, and McMeel.

Darling-Hammond, Linda. 1996. *What matters most: Teaching for America's future.* New York: National Commission on Teaching & America's Future.

Darling-Hammond, Linda, Deborah J. Holtzman, Su Jin Gatlin, and Julian Vasquez Heilig. 2005. Does teacher preparation matter? Evidence about teacher certification, Teach for America, and teacher effectiveness. *Education Policy Analysis Archives* 13 (42).

DeArmond, Michael, and Dan Goldhaber. 2008. *A leap of faith: Redesigning teacher compensation.* Seattle: Center on Reinventing Public Education, University of Washington.

Dee, Thomas S., and Benjamin J. Keys. 2004. Does merit pay reward good teachers? Evidence from a randomized experiment. *Journal of Policy Analysis and Management* 23 (3):471–88.

———. 2005. Dollars and sense. *Education Next* 5 (1).

Duncan, Arne. 2009. Partners in reform. Remarks of Arne Duncan to the National Education Association, http://www2.ed.gov/news/speeches/2009/07/07022009.pdf.

———. 2009. Robust data gives us the roadmap to reform. Secretary Arne Duncan addresses the Fourth Annual IES Research Conference, http://www2.ed.gov/news/speeches/2009/06/06082009.html.

———. 2009. States will lead the way toward reform. Secretary Arne Duncan's remarks at the 2009 Governors Education Symposium, http://www2.ed.gov/news/speeches/2009/06/06142009.html.

Duncan, Greg J. 1976. Earnings functions and nonpecuniary benefits. *Journal of Human Resources* 11 (4):462–83.

Eberts, Randall, Kevin Hollenbeck, and Joe Stone. 2002. Teacher performance incentives and student outcomes. *Journal of Human Resources* 37 (4):913–27.

Ehrenberg, Ronald G., and Dominic J. Brewer. 1995. Did teachers' verbal ability and race matter in the 1960s? Coleman revisited. *Economics of Education Review* 14 (1):1–21.

Ehrenberg, Ronald G., Daniel D. Goldhaber, and Dominic J. Brewer. 1995. Do teachers' race, gender, and ethnicity matter? Evidence from the National Educational Longitudinal Study of 1988. *Industrial and Labor Relations Review* 48 (3):547–61.

Eide, Eric, Dan Goldhaber, and Dominic Brewer. 2004. The teacher labour market and teacher quality. *Oxford Review of Economic Policy* 20 (2): 230–44.

Federal Reserve Bank of St. Louis. 2009. FRED(R)-Federal Reserve Economic Data.

Flyer, Fredrick, and Sherwin Rosen. 1997. The new economics of teachers and education. *Journal of Labor Economics* 15 (1):S104.

Goldhaber, Dan. 2007. Everyone's doing it, but what does teacher testing tell us about teacher effectiveness? *Journal of Human Resources* 42 (4):765–94.

———. 2009. The politics of teacher compensation reform. In *Performance Incentives: Their Growing Impact of American K–12 Education*, ed. M. G. Springer. Washington, DC: Brookings Institution.

Goldhaber, Dan, and Emily Anthony. 2007. Can teacher quality be effectively assessed? National board certification as a signal of effective teaching. *Review of Economics and Statistics* 89 (1):134–50.

Goldhaber, Dan, Michael DeArmond, Albert Yung-Hsu Liu, and Daniel W. Player. 2008. Returns to skill and teacher wage premiums Seattle: Center on Reinventing Public Education, University of Washington, Working paper 8.

Goldhaber, Dan, and Michael Hansen. 2008. Is it just a bad class? Assessing the stability of measured teacher performance. Seattle: Center on Reinventing Public Education, University of Washington, *working paper # 2008_5.*

Goldin, Glauda, and Lawrence F. Katz. 2008. *The race between education and technology.* Cambridge, MA: Harvard University Press.

Gootman, Elissa. 2009. Next test: Value of $125,000-a-year teachers. *New York Times*, June 4, 2009.

Gordon, Robert, Thomas J. Kane, and Douglas O. Staiger. 2006. *Identifying effective teachers using performance on the job.* Discussion Paper 2006–01, Hamilton Project, Brookings Institution.

Gratz, Donald B. 2005. Lessons from Denver: The pay for performance pilot. *Phi Delta Kappan* 86 (8):568–81.

Hanushek, Eric A. 1986. The economics of schooling: Production and efficiency in public schools. *Journal of Economic Literature* 24 (3):1141–77.
———. 1992. The trade-off between child quantity and quality. *Journal of Political Economy* 100 (1):84–117.
———. 1994. *Making schools work: Improving performance and controlling costs.* Washington, DC: Brookings Institution.
———. 1997. Assessing the effects of school resources on student performance: An update. *Educational Evaluation and Policy Analysis* 19 (2): 141–64.
———. 2004. The economic value of improving local schools. In *Proceedings of Federal Reserve Bank of Cleveland Research Conference.*
———. 2006. Alternative school policies and the benefits of general cognitive skills. *Economics of Education Review* 25 (4):447–62.
———. 2007. The single salary schedule and other issues of teacher pay. *Peabody Journal of Education* 82 (4):574–86.
Hanushek, Eric A., Dean T. Jamison, Eliot A. Jamison, and Ludger Woessmann. 2008. Education and economic growth. *Education Next* (Vol 8. No 2).
Hanushek, Eric A., and Dale W. Jorgenson. 1996. *Improving America's schools: The role of incentives.* Washington, DC: National Academy Press.
Hanushek, Eric A., and Alfred A. Lindseth. 2009. *Schoolhouses, courthouses, and statehouses.* Princeton, NJ: Princeton University Press.
Hanushek, Eric A., and Steven G. Rivkin. 1997. Understanding the twentieth-century growth in U.S. school spending. *Journal of Human Resources* 32 (1):35–68.
———. 2004. How to improve the supply of high-quality teachers. Brookings Papers on Educational Policy, 7–25.
———. 2006. Teacher quality. In *Handbook of the Economics of Education*, ed. E. Hanushek and F. Welch.: Amsterdam: Elsevier.
———. 2007. Pay, working conditions, and teacher quality. *Future of Children* 17 (1):69–86.
Harris, Douglas N. 2006/2007. Class size and school size: Taking the tradeoffs seriously. *Brookings Papers on Education Policy*:137–61.
Harris, Douglas N., and Scott J. Adams. 2007. Understanding the level and causes of teacher turnover: A comparison with other professions. *Economics of Education Review* 26 (3):325–37.
Harris, Douglas N., and Tim R. Sass. 2009. The effects of NBPTS-certified teachers on student achievement. *Journal of Policy Analysis and Management* 28 (1):55–80.
Haveman, Robert H., and Barbara L. Wolfe. 1984. Schooling and economic well-being: The role of nonmarket effects. *Journal of Human Resources* 19 (3):377–407.
Hezel Associates. 2009. Quality compensation for teachers summative evaluation, http://www.leg.state.mn.us/docs/2009/other/090321.pdf.

Hill, Paul Thomas, and James Harvey. 2004. *Making school reform work: New partnerships for real change*. Washington, DC: Brookings Institution.

Howell, William, Martin West, and Paul Peterson. 2007. What Americans think about their schools. *Education Next* 7 (4):12–26.

Hoxby, Caroline Minter. 1996. How teachers' unions affect education production. *Quarterly Journal of Economics* 111 (3):671–718.

Hoxby, Caroline Minter, and Andrew Leigh. 2004. Pulled away or pushed out? Explaining the decline of teacher aptitude in the United States. *American Economic Review* 94 (2):236–40.

Jacob, Brian A., and Steven D. Levitt. 2003. Rotten apples: An investigation of the prevalence and predictors of teacher cheating. *Quarterly Journal of Economics* 118 (3):843–77.

Jennings, Jennifer L., and Thomas A. DiPrete. 2010. Teacher effects on social/behavioral skills in early elementary school. *Sociology of Education* 83 (2):135–59.

Jerald, Craig D., and Richard M. Ingersoll. 2002. All talk, no action: Putting an end to out-of-field teaching. Education Trust, http://www.edtrust.org/sites/edtrust.org/files/publications/files/AllTalk.pdf.

Jorgenson, Dale W., and Barbara M. Fraumeni. 1992. Investment in education and U.S. economic growth. *Scandinavian Journal of Economics* 94:S51–S70.

Kane, Thomas J. and Douglas Staiger. 2008. Estimating teacher impacts on student achievement: An experimental evaluation. Working Paper 4607, National Bureau of Economic Research, www.nber.org.

King, Miriam, Steven Ruggles, Trent Alexander, Donna Leicach, and Matthew Sobek. 2004. Integrated public use microdata series, current population survey: Version 2.0. [machine readable database]. Minnesota Population Center, http://cps.ipums.org/cps/.

Kinsler, Josh. 2008. Estimating teacher value-added in a cumulative production function. Department of Economics, University of Rochester.

Klein, Joel I., and Al Sharpton. 2009. Charter schools can close the achievement gap. It is not acceptable for minority students to be four grades behind. *Wall Street Journal*, January 12, 2009.

Koedel, Cory, and Julian R. Betts. 2007. Re-examining the role of teacher quality in the educational production function. Department of Economics, University of Missouri.

Krueger, Alan B. 1999. Experimental Estimates of Education Production Functions. *Quarterly Journal of Economics* 114 (2):497–532.

Krueger, Alan B., and Mikael Lindahl. 2001. Education for growth: Why and for whom? *Journal of Economic Literature* 39 (4):1101–36.

Ladd, Helen F., and Randall P. Walsh. 2002. Implementing value-added measures of school effectiveness: getting the incentives right. *Economics of Education Review* 21 (1):1–17.

Lavy, Victor. 2009. Performance pay and teachers' effort, productivity, and grading ethics. *American Economic Review* 99 (5):1979–2011.

Lazear, Edward P. 1995. *Personnel economics*. Cambridge, Mass.: MIT Press.

———. 2001. Educational production. *Quarterly Journal of Economics* 116 (3):777–803.

Leigh, Andrew. 2005. Teacher pay and teacher aptitude. Research School of Social Sciences, Australian National University.

Leigh, Andrew, and Sara Mead. 2005. Lifting teacher performance. Progressive Policy Institute, http://www.ppionline.org/documents/teachqual_0419.pdf.

Lemieux, Thomas, W. Bentley MacLeod, and Daniel Parent. 2009. Performance pay and wage inequality. *Quarterly Journal of Economics* 124 (1): 1–49.

Lemke, M., A. Sen, E. Pahlke, L. Partelow, D. Miller, T. Williams, D. Kastberg, and L. Jocelyn. 2004. International outcomes of learning in mathematics literacy and problem solving: PISA 2003 results from the U.S. perspective. (NCES 2005–003). Washington, DC: U.S. Department of Education, National Center for Education Statistics.

Levitt, Steven D., and Stephen J. Dubner. 2005. *Freakonomics: A rogue economist explores the hidden side of everything*. New York: William Morrow.

Lochner, Lance. 2004. Education, work, and crime: A human capital approach. *International Economic Review* 45 (3):811–43.

Lochner, Lance, and Enrico Moretti. 2004. The effect of education on crime: Evidence from prison inmates, arrests, and self-reports. *American Economic Review* 94 (1):155–89.

Loeb, Susanna, and Marianne E. Page. 2000. Examining the link between teacher wages and student outcomes: The importance of alternative labor market opportunities and non-pecuniary variation. *Review of Economics and Statistics* 82 (3):393–408.

Loeb, Susanna, Cecilia Rouse, and Anthony Shorris. 2007. Introducing the issue. *Future of Children* 17 (1):3–14.

Marshall, Ray, and Marc Tucker. 1992. *Thinking for a living: Education and the wealth of nations* New York: Basic Books.

McCourt, Frank. 2005. *Teacher man: A memoir*. New York: Scribner.

Medina, Jennifer. 2009. Charter schools weigh freedom against the protection of a union. *New York Times*, April 21, 2009.

———. 2009. Class size in New York City rises, but the impact is debated. *New York Times*, February 22, 2009.

Miller, Matthew. 2003. *The two percent solution: Fixing America's problems in ways liberals and conservatives can love*. New York: PublicAffairs.

Moulthrop, Daniel, Nínive Clements Calegari, and Dave Eggers. 2005. *Teachers have it easy: The big sacrifices and small salaries of America's teachers*. New York: New Press.

Mueller, Marnie W. 1975. Economic determinants of volunteer work by women. *Signs* 1 (2):325–38.

Murnane, R. J., and Jennifer L. Steele. 2007. What is the problem? The challenge of providing effective teachers for all children. *Future of Children* 17 (1):15–43.

Murnane, Richard J. 1996. Staffing the nation's schools with skilled teachers. In *Improving America's schools: The role of incentives*, edited by E. A. Hanushek and D. W. Jorgenson. Washington, DC: National Academy Press.

Murnane, Richard J., and Randall J. Olsen. 1990. The effects of salaries and opportunity costs on length of stay in teaching: Evidence from North Carolina. *Journal of Human Resources* 25 (1):106–24.

Murnane, Richard J., Judith D. Singer, John B. Willet, James J. Kemple, and Randall J. Olsen. 1991. *Who will teach?: Policies that matter*. Cambridge, MA: Harvard University Press.

Nadler, Carl, and Matthew Wiswall. 2009. Risk aversion and support for merit pay: Theory and evidence from Minnesota's Q comp program. Department of Economics, NYU.

National Board for Professional Teaching Standards. 2002. Raising the standard.

National Center on Performance Incentives. 2008. State-by-State Resources: State Initiatives Overview.

National Education Association. 2003. Status of the American public school teacher 2000–2001.

———. *Myths and facts about educator pay*. 2009.

New York State Education Department. 2008. Salary percentiles for classroom teachers by degree status and total educational experience.

Nye, Barbara, Spyros Konstantopoulos, and Larry V. Hedges. 2004. How large are teacher effects? *Educational Evaluation & Policy Analysis* 26 (3):237–57.

OECD (Organisation for Economic Co-operation and Development). 2003. Education at a glance: OECD indicators.

Office of the Legislative Auditor, State of Minnesota. 2009. Evaluation report, Q Comp: Quality compensation for teachers.

Podgursky, Michael J. 2006. Teams versus bureaucracies: Personnel policy, wage-setting, and teacher quality in traditional public, charter, and private schools. *Education Working Paper Archive*, http://www.uark.edu/ua/der/EWPA/Research/Teacher_Quality/TvB_files/Teams_v_B.pdf.

———. 2009. Teacher compensation reform: A market-based perspective. In *Performance incentives: Their growing impact on American K–12 education*, edited by Matthew G. Springer. Washington, DC: Brookings Institution.

Podgursky, Michael, and Matthew G. Springer. 2007a. Credentials versus performance: Review of the teacher performance pay research. *Peabody Journal of Education* 82 (4):551–73.

———. 2007b. Teacher performance pay: A review. *Journal of Policy Analysis and Management* 26 (4):909–49.

Podgursky, Michael J. 2009. Teacher compensation reform: A market-based perspective. In *Performance incentives: Their growing impact on American K–12 education*, edited by Matthew G. Springer. Washington, DC: Brookings Institution.

Raymond, Margaret, and Stephen Fletcher. 2002. The teach for America evaluation. *Education Next* Spring 2002.

Raymond, Margaret, Stephen Fletcher, and Javier Luque. 2001. Teach for America: An evaluation of teacher differences and student outcomes in Houston, Texas. Stanford, CA: Center for Research on Education Outcomes, Stanford University.

Rhee, Michelle. 2009. The toughest job. *Washington Post*, February 9, 2009.

Rivkin, Steven G., Eric A. Hanushek, and John F. Kain. 2005. Teachers, schools, and academic achievement. *Econometrica* 73 (2):417–58.

Rockoff, Jonah E. 2004. The impact of individual teachers on student achievement: Evidence from panel data. American Economic Review 94(2): 247–52.

Roza, Marguerite, and Raegen Miller. 2009. Separation of degrees: State-by-state analysis of teacher compensation for master's degrees. Seattle: Center on Reinventing Public Education, University of Washington.

Ruggles, Steven, Matthew Sobek, Trent Alexander, Catherine A. Fitch, Ronald Goeken, Patricia Kelly Hall, Miriam King, and Chad Ronnander. 2009. Integrated public use microdata series: Version 4.0 [machine-readable database]. Minnesota Population Center.

Sanders, William L., James J. Ashton, and S. Paul Wright. 2005. Comparison of the effects of NBPTS certified teachers with other teachers on the rate of student academic progress. Cary, NC: SAS Institute.

Sanders, William L., and June C. Rivers. 1996. Cumulative and Residual Effects of Teachers on Future Student Academic Achievement. Value-Added Research and Assessment Center, University of Tennessee.

Scarsdale Public Schools. 2008. Scarsdale Public Schools, Annual Report of the Superintendent, Scarsdale NY.

Schrag, Peter. 2006/2007. Policy from the hip: Class-size reduction in California. *Brookings Papers on Education Policy*:229–43.

Shanker, Albert. 1990. The end of the traditional model of schooling—And a proposal for using incentives to restructure our public schools. *Phi Delta Kappan* 71 (5):344(14).

Smith, Marshall S., Brett W. Scoll, and Jeffrey Link. 1996. Research-based school reform: The Clinton administration's agenda. In *Improving America's schools: The role of incentives*, eds. Eric A. Hanushek and D. W. Jorgenson. Washington, DC: National Academy Press.

Smith, Tracy W., Belita Gordon, Susan A. Colby, and Jianjun Wang. 2005. An examination of the relationship between depth of student learning and national board certification status. Office for Research on Teaching, Appalachian State University.

Snyder, T. D., S. A. Dillow, and C. M. Hoffman. 2008. Digest of education statistics 2007 (NCES 2008–022).

———. 2009. Digest of education statistics 2008 (NCES 2009–020).

Solmon, Lewis C., J. Todd White, Donna Cohen, and Deborah Woo. 2007. The effectiveness of the teacher advancement program. National Institute for Excellence in Teaching, http://www.tapsystem.org/.

Springer, Matthew G., Dale Ballou, and Art (Xiao) Ping. 2008. Impact of the teacher advancement program on student test score gains: Findings from an independent appraisal. National Center on Performance Initiatives, Vanderbilt University.

Springer, Matthew G., Michael J. Podgursky, Jessica L. Lewis, Mark W. Ehlert, Bonnie Ghosh-Dastidar, Timothy J. Gronberg, Laura S. Hamilton, Denis W. Jansen, Omar S. Lopez, Christine H. Patterson, Brian M. Stecher, and Lori L. Taylor. 2008. Texas Educator Excellence Grant (TEEG) Program: Year One Evaluation Report. National Center on Performance Incentives, Vanderbilt University.

Springer, Matthew G., Michael J. Podgursky, Jessica L. Lewis, Mark W. Ehlert, Timothy J. Gronberg, Laura S. Hamilton, Denis W. Jansen, Omar S. Lopez, Art (Xiao) Ping, Brian M. Stecher, and Lori L. Taylor. 2008. Texas Educator Excellence Grant (TEEG) Program: Year Two Evaluation Report. National Center on Performance Incentives, Vanderbilt University.

Summers, Anita A. 2002. Expert measures. *Education Next* 2002 (2).

Summers, Anita A., and Barbara L. Wolfe. 1977. Do schools make a difference? *American Economic Review* 67 (4):639–52.

TAP (Teacher Advancement Project). 2008. TAP brochure 2008.

Teacher Portal. *Teaching in Scarsdale union free school district* 2009. http://teacherportal.com/district/new-york/scarsdale-union-free-school-district.

Temin, Peter. 2002. Teacher quality and the future of America. *Eastern Economic Journal* 28 (3):285–300.

TEP (The Equity Project). *http://www.tepcharter.org/Redefined-Expectations.php* 2009. Available from www.tepcharter.org.

U.S. Census Bureau. 1967. *Statistical abstract of the United States: 1967*. 88 ed. Washington, DC.

———. 2008. *Statistical abstract of the United States: 2008*. 128 ed. Washington, DC.

———. 2009. *Statistical abstract of the United States: 2009*. 128 ed. Washington, DC.

U.S. Department of Education. *Teacher incentive fund, frequently asked questions* 2009 [cited July 15, 2009. Available from http://www.ed.gov/programs/teacherincentive/faq.html.

U.S. Department of Education. 2002. The condition of education, 2002. National Center for Education Statistics.

United Federation of Teachers. *School-wide bonus program agreement* 2007. http://www.uft.org/news/bonus_prog/.

———. *Voluntary school-wide bonus program q & a (updated October 2008)* 2008. http://www.uft.org/member/rights/moa/school_wide_bonus_programs_faqs/.

Vandevoort, L. G., A. Amrein-Beardsley, and D. C. Berliner. 2004. National board certified teachers and their students' achievement. *Education Policy Analysis Archives* 12 (46).

Wagner, Tony. 2008. *The global achievement gap: Why even our best schools don't teach the new survival skills our children need—and what we can do about it*. New York: Basic Books.

Walsh, Kate. 2006. If wishes were horses: The reality behind teacher quality findings. National Council on Teacher Quality. Center on Children and Families. http://www.nctq.org/p/publications/docs/wishes_horses_20080316034426.pdf.

Weingarten, Randi. 2010. A new path forward: Four approaches to quality teaching and better schools. Speech to the National Press Club, Washington, DC.

Wessel, David. 2006. It's the teachers, stupid. *Wall Street Journal*, April 6, 2006.

West, Martin R., and Matthew M. Chingos. 2009. Teacher effectiveness, mobility and attrition in Florida. In *Performance incentives: Their growing impact on American K–12 education*, ed. Matthew G. Springer. Washington, DC: Brookings Institution.

Winters, Marcus A., Gary Ritter, Joshua H. Barnett, and Jay P. Greene. 2007. An evaluation of teacher performance pay in Arkansas. Department of Education Reform, University of Arkansas, http://www.uark.edu/ua/der/.

Winters, Marcus A., Gary Ritter, Jay P. Greene, and Ryan Marsh. 2009. The impact of the Arkansas Achievement Challenge Pilot Project on student performance. In *Performance incentives: Their growing impact on American K–12 education*, ed. Matthew G. Springer. Washington, DC: Brookings Institution.

Wiswall, Matthew. 2009. Licensing and occupational sorting in the market for teachers. Working paper, New York University, Department of Economics.

Notes

Introduction

1. More about Vic's program, called WISE Individualized Senior Experience, is on the web at wiseservices.org.
2. Smith, Scoll, and Link (1996, 18).
3. Snyder, Dillow, and Hoffman (2009, Table 22).

Chapter 1: Teachers Make the Difference

1. Wessel (2006).
2. Klein and Sharpton (2009).
3. Names are real. Thanks, guys.
4. Thanks go to Jennifer Carroll and Zoë Williams for drawing Figure 2 for me.
5. Stat note: "average" in the sense of median.
6. Made up names here, again.
7. The density curve is a normal drawn parametrically. The horizontal axis and the labels below the tick mark line are simply linearly related in the ratio 9/13.
8. In years past, following the progress of thousands of students was completely impractical, but increased interest in performance metrics has led to the creation of student databases that are available to researchers. Such studies are always set up to protect student privacy, and researchers don't have any interest in particular students anyhow.

9. This is one reason that most studies look at elementary schools, where students can be more sensibly linked to a single teacher than can be done for middle school or high school students.

10. This oversimplifies the details of the computation, which differ from one research study to another. Typically, computations are based on the effect of a one standard deviation move across the teacher distribution on student test scores measured in units of within-grade standard deviations. Gaussian distributions are generally assumed. This means that translation of the results from percentiles to grade-level equivalents would be more problematic if we were focusing on the tails of the distributions. Since we're well away from the tails, the distributional assumption shouldn't matter too much.

11. Loeb, Rouse, and Shorris (2007, 3), citing work in Rivkin, Hanushek, and Kain (2005).

12. Since averages are taken over finite class sizes, researchers typically make a statistical adjustment for measurement error in the within-class student mean gain.

13. Leigh and Mead (2005).

14. Hanushek (1992, 107). Emphasis mine.

15. Hanushek (2007, 576), citing earlier work in Hanushek (1992).

16. Ehrenberg and Brewer (1995).

17. Hanushek (2007, 576), citing earlier work in Hanushek (1992).

18. Nye, Konstantopoulos, and Hedges (2004, 237).

19. Koedel and Betts (2007, Table 3).

20. Goldhaber (2007, 777).

21. Gordon, Kane, and Staiger (2006, 5).

22. Aaronson, Barrow, and Sander (2007, 97).

23. Rockoff (2004, 248).

24. Gordon, Kane, and Staiger (2006, 8). Note, however, that the gap for *low-income* black students versus *higher-income* white students is larger, so more than four years would be required.

25. Kinsler (2008).

26. Sanders and Rivers (1996).

27. For an extensive review of the relation between teacher quality, teacher characteristics, student achievement, and related issues see Hanushek and Rivkin (2006).

28. Summers and Wolfe (1977, 644).

29. Temin (2002, 285–86).

Chapter 2: Who Teaches?

1. The statistics here and in the next few paragraphs are largely drawn from Snyder, Dillow, and Hoffman (2009, Table 68). Data is for 2003–04.

2. Snyder, Dillow, and Hoffman (2009, Table 271).

3. U.S. Department of Education (2002, 92).
4. Jerald and Ingersoll (2002, 4).
5. Snyder, Dillow, and Hoffman (2009, Table 68).
6. Snyder, Dillow, and Hoffman (2009, Table 69), but note that different sources on gender ratios in Tables 68 and 69 are not entirely consistent.
7. Corcoran, Evans, and Schwab (2004).
8. For a recent review of the teacher labor market and measures of academic ability of teachers, see Eide, Goldhaber, and Brewer (2004).
9. Author's calculations based on NLSY79 data. See Technical Appendix. Data shown are age-adjusted AFQT scores, which are roughly proportional to IQ but not measured on an IQ-equivalent scale.
10. The AFQT originated with the armed forces, but is now widely used in social science research having unrelated to the military. While similar to IQ tests, the AFQT numbers aren't the same as IQ scores.
11. Bacolod (2007).
12. Bacolod (2007, 748).
13. Wiswall (2009, 56).
14. Hoxby and Leigh (2004).
15. Hoxby and Leigh (2004, 240).
16. Murnane et al. (1991, 127).
17. Harris and Adams (2007).
18. Snyder, Dillow, and Hoffman (2009, Table 73).
19. Author's calculations, compound "Left-teaching" rates from Snyder, Dillow, and Hoffman (2009, Table 73).
20. Wiswall (2009, 36).
21. Harris and Adams (2007). See also Costrell and Podgursky (2009).
22. Miller (2003, 119).
23. Murnane and Olsen (1990, Figure 2). Note that the data are a little old, although there is no reason to think the basic pattern has changed.
24. Snyder, Dillow, and Hoffman (2009, Table 73).
25. Murnane and Olsen (1990).

Chapter 3: Teacher Pay

1. McCourt (2005, 4).
2. Author's calculations of median and 75th percentile gaps from 2008 Current Population Survey. For details, see Technical Appendix. "Nearly 60 percent," is more precisely 58.18 percent.
3. Different sources and differing data definitions give somewhat different measures for teacher salaries. As a result, you'll see slight variations in how numbers are reported from one spot in the book to another. None of the differences are big enough to, well, to make any difference.

4. Hanushek and Rivkin (2004, 9). See also Hanushek and Rivkin (1997).

5. Ratio is weighted average of ratios of medians for men and women. Note that if one compares median teacher/nonteacher salaries without controlling for gender, the teacher pay gap looks much larger. Source: author's calculations based on King et al. (2004). For details, see Technical Appendix. Thanks go to Kate Walsh for suggesting the form of the graph.

6. Author's calculations from March 2008 Current Population Survey, college-educated, full-time workers, age 22–64, reporting incomes of at least $5,000 and more than twenty hours of work per week.

7. Author's calculations comparing 75th percentile to median salaries, using 2008 CPS data. College-educated, full-time workers. More precisely, the gap is 58.18 percent.

8. Author's calculations using 2008 CPS data. College-educated, full-time workers. Graph shows smoothed data using a quartic fit on age.

9. Flyer and Rosen (1997, Table 8). The authors point out one of the attractive elements of a teaching career: there is no penalty for time out for childbearing. In contrast, nonteachers who took time out from the labor force had a beginning-to-end wage increase of 35 percent, much below that those without a gap, although still a much higher gain than for teachers.

10. Goldhaber et al. (2008, 4).

11. Subject to paying a minimum, humanly decent wage; teacher pay is high enough so that simple decency isn't an issue.

12. If you look at weekly pay during the school year, that *has* changed. One estimate is that compared to other college graduates, the weekly pay of public school teachers fell 10 percent between 1996 and 2006. See Allegretto, Corcoran, and Mishel (2008, 12).

13. Darling-Hammond (1996, 54).

14. National Education Association (2003, 6).

15. National Education Association (2003, 40).

16. You can find the teachers' reaction to the short-hours story on the NEA website. National Education Association (2009).

17. Teachers average 181 days teaching, plus 7 nonteaching days a year. [Snyder, Dillow, and Hoffman (2008, Table 69). Original source: NEA survey.] Figuring that others with college educations work fifty weeks a year, five days a week, and receive eleven paid holidays, one comes up with 188 work days for teachers and 239 work days for others. So teachers work 21 percent fewer days. The teacher fifty-hour work week is equivalent to a thirty-nine-hour work week for others, which is about one hour less than the reported average. This doesn't account for course-prep work that teachers do during the summer, nor for paid vacations longer than two weeks that many college-educated workers receive after enough time with their employer.

18. Thank you, thank you.

19. Medina (2009), TEP (2009).

20. References to the scientific evidence appear in Chapter 6, Qualification Supplements.

21. Of course, some beginning teachers are good enough that they overcome the beginning teacher gap. Eric Hanushek has a nice turn of phrase on the topic: "A good teacher with experience was ... a good teacher as a rookie (just not as good as later)." Eric Hanushek, personal communication.

22. Estimates of the effect vary, and are generally a bit higher for math than for reading. The estimate of one-to-two months is based on the author's conversion of findings in Rockoff (2004). Estimates based on Clotfelter, Ladd, and Vigdor (2007) are similar. See also Rivkin, Hanushek, and Kain (2005) and Goldhaber (2007).

23. The fact that getting a master's does nothing to make a better teacher is firmly established in the scientific literature. For one example, see Rivkin, Hanushek, and Kain (2005).

24. Raymond, Fletcher, and Luque (2001, Table 3).

25. Podgursky (2009).

26. West and Chingos (2009) A friend raises a good question about this finding: how do we know that teachers regard schools with high African American enrollments or high poverty rates as undesirable? It seems reasonable to conclude this from the observation that teachers with a choice move in the other direction. Still, race and poverty are sensitive subjects, so let me be clear that we have data on teacher behavior but not on teacher motivation.

27. Raymond, Fletcher, and Luque (2001, 20).

28. Clotfelter, Ladd, and Vigdor (2006, 779).

29. Raymond, Fletcher, and Luque (2001, Graphics 4 and 5).

30. Lemieux, MacLeod, and Parent (2009, 22).

31. Podgursky (2006, Table 5). See also Ballou (2001).

32. Snyder, Dillow, and Hoffman (2009, Tables 74 and 86).

Chapter 4: Raises!

1. Miller (2003, 127).

2. Bond (2001, 153–54).

3. Miller (2003).

4. Dee and Keys (2005, 63). My italics.

5. While salaries in the past are fine as a starting point, there are changes over the last half-plus century that we need to think about. Sixty or seventy years ago the Americans who went to college were a far more select group than today. That argues that to be equally selective in the overall population in choosing teachers as we were in the past, we need to be even more

selective within the college-educated population today. On the other hand, college attendance is more meritocratic now than pre-G.I. Bill. Since it's not so clear that selectivity pre-World War II was tightly associated with merit, the change in ability in the college-educated pool may or may not be that important. I'll go with the data as is, without making any changes for changing college selectivity.

6. Hanushek and Rivkin (1997, Table 6). Calculations include all income.

7. Author's calculations from March 2008 Current Population Survey. See Technical Appendix.

8. Author's calculations from March 2008 Current Population Survey. See Technical Appendix.

9. Economists call this a "compensating wage differential." As a practical matter, significant compensating wage differentials are very hard to find in the scientific literature. Nonetheless, one perk of being a teacher probably is important to a subset of teachers; that's having a schedule that lets you be at home with your own kids when they get out of school. Not many other jobs offer the equivalent of getting to grade papers at the kitchen table.

10. Leigh (2005).

11. Hanushek and Rivkin (2004) provide a thorough review of teacher pay, and the relation between measurable teacher characteristics and student achievement.

12. Loeb and Page (2000).

13. Classic reviews are Hanushek (1986, 1997). Hanushek (1986); Betts (1996) finds mixed results. Betts (1995) finds no significant effect of teacher salaries. Card and Krueger (1992) find that higher teacher salaries lead to higher income for students later in life.

14. Hoxby (1996) finds a qualitatively similar, but smaller effect.

15. Author's calculations. For details, see Technical Appendix. Markings on Figure 12 of grade levels other than fourth grade are based on author's calculations. Results using math scores are similar.

16. Details of the multiple regression appear in the Technical Appendix. If you use the line in Figure 12 without adjustment the leap is about one-and-a-half grades.

17. Bond (2001).

18. Bond (2001).

19. In other words to account for the length of an entire K–12 education, I multiplied grade eight results by 1.5 and grade four results by three.

20. Bond (2001, 80). When Bond wrote "present time," she was referring to 2001.

21. Aksoy and Link (2000). For those statisticians reading, the authors had panel individual longitudinal data allowing them to estimate fixed effects.

22. *t*-statistics are all above 3.2. See their Table 3.

23. The tests the researchers studied aren't normed as grade-level equivalents. So I've made the best translation I can. This translation is somewhat rougher than others in the book and the translation is my responsibility, not that of the original research team. See the Technical Appendix for details.

24. Author's calculations based on base BA salaries for public school teachers, 2003–04, in Snyder, Dillow, and Hoffman (2008, Table 73).

Chapter 5: Paying for Success: The View from Thirty Thousand Feet

1. Marshall and Tucker (1992).
2. Recently we've (re)learned that aligning financial incentives with undesirable goals is pretty effective at getting undesirable results too.
3. Barber and Mourshed (2007).
4. Shanker (1990, 53).
5. Moulthrop, Calegari, and Eggers (2005, 252).
6. Klein and Sharpton (2009).
7. National Education Association (2003, Table 29).
8. See Lemieux, MacLeod, and Parent (2009).
9. Hill and Harvey (2004, 5).
10. Lazear (1995, 13).
11. At the national level both the NEA and the AFT support differential pay, at least in some circumstances, with the NEA wanting more limits than the AFT. Local unions fall everywhere from actively participating in differential pay experiments to being unalterably opposed to the concept.
12. Podgursky and Springer (2007) give a careful review of the literature on credentials versus performance pay. The same authors focus on performance pay.
13. Ballou (2001, 51).
14. Ballou (2001, 54).
15. The Denver ProComp experiment.
16. Gratz (2005, 573–74).
17. Clotfelter and Ladd (1996, 35–36).
18. Lavy (2009).
19. Winters et al. (2007).
20. Winters et al. (2007) and Winters et al. (2009) plus author's calculations.
21. Hanushek (1994, 86).

Chapter 6: Qualification Supplements: An Input Measure That Matters

1. National Board for Professional Teaching Standards (2002, 2).
2. Goldhaber and Anthony (2007, 134).

3. Applicants pay part of the costs. The rest comes from donor and government contributions.

4. Goldhaber and Anthony (2007, 134).

5. Goldhaber and Anthony (2007, 141).

6. Author's calculations; see Technical Appendix.

7. Compared to the previous study, Goldhaber (2007, 777) found a smaller, although still statistically significant, advantage for NBCTs.

8. Clotfelter, Ladd, and Vigdor (2007, 681).

9. Author's calculations based on Table 6 and page 681 of Clotfelter, Ladd, and Vigdor (2007).

10. See Technical Appendix for author's calculations based on Cavalluzzo (2004).

11. Vandevoort, Amrein-Beardsley, and Berliner (2004).

12. Smith et al. (2005).

13. Harris and Sass (2009).

14. The authors also find suggestive evidence that teachers board certified before 2001 do get better student results, while more recent recipients don't—a worrisome result.

15. Sanders, Ashton, and Wright (2005, 4).

16. Cantrell et al. (2008).

17. Dee and Keys (2004, Tables 1 and 2).

18. Dee and Keys (2005).

19. Cooper and Cohn (1997).

20. Data from 2003–04 in Snyder, Dillow, and Hoffman (2009, Tables 68 and 74).

21. Author's calculations; see Technical Appendix, based on Goldhaber (2007, 777).

22. McCourt (2005, 11).

23. Author's calculations based on Snyder, Dillow, and Hoffman (2009, Table 73).

24. Boyd et al. (2006, 193).

25. Rivkin, Hanushek, and Kain (2005, 447).

26. Some of the master's degrees go to students who already have a college degree in a subject other than education. More precisely, the ratio is 1.68. Snyder, Dillow, and Hoffman (2009, Table 272).

27. Studies with this result include Rivkin, Hanushek, and Kain (2005); Murnane (1996); Clotfelter, Ladd, and Vigdor (2007); Boyd et al. (2007); Aaronson, Barrow, and Sander (2007); and Hanushek (1997).

28. Snyder, Dillow, and Hoffman (2009, Table 272).

29. Snyder, Dillow, and Hoffman (2009, Table 67).

30. Murnane and Steele (2007, 23).

31. Roza and Miller (2009, 1).

32. Loosely, "Who will guard the guardians?"

Chapter 7: Effectiveness Pay: We Grade Students, Don't We?

1. Crowe (1978, 52–54).
2. Eberts, Hollenbeck, and Stone (2002).
3. Moulthrop, Calegari, and Eggers (2005, 202–3).
4. Bishop, Moriarty, and Mane (2000, 333).
5. Jennings and DiPrete (2009).
6. Walsh (2006).
7. American Federation of Teachers (2008).
8. Betts et al. (2001, 15).
9. Wagner (2008, 6).
10. Eventually, the marine science course received a reprieve.
11. Rhee (2009).
12. Springer, Podgursky, Lewis, Ehlert, Gronberg et al. (2008).
13. Springer, Podgursky, Lewis, Ehlert, Ghosh-Dastidar et al. (2008).
14. Value-added measures are not perfect. In particular, they imperfectly control for issues such as the level of school resources and peer effects. For a careful discussion, see Ladd and Walsh (2002). When single test scores are used for evaluation, the average score for a particular teacher can bounce around considerably from one year to the next. Goldhaber and Hansen (2008) report "estimated effectiveness in math is considerably more stable over time than in reading; however, estimates did not support the notion of 'stable' performance over time in either subject." Yet another reason to prefer multiple rather than single tests.
15. Summers (2002, 16).
16. See Jacob and Levitt (2003) or Chapter 1 of Levitt and Dubner (2005).
17. Weingarten (2010).

Chapter 8: Team Bonuses: We're All in This Together, Sometimes

1. Springer, Podgursky, Lewis, Ehlert, Ghosh-Dastidar et al. (2008).
2. The intuition for this example is drawn from Lazear (2001).
3. United Federation of Teachers (2008).
4. United Federation of Teachers (2007). Author's emphasis.

Chapter 9: Compensation: Keeping Your Eye on the Ball

1. Legal note: Permission to copy verbatim the check list for a differential pay system is hereby granted. Go for it!

2. Hanushek (1994, xvi).

3. Murnane et al. (1991, 119). For an opposing view to *Profit*, note that the Murnane and coauthors feel strongly that merit pay for individual teachers does not work.

4. Summers (2002, 19).

5. Hanushek and Rivkin (2007, 82).

Chapter 10: Some (Recent) History Lessons

1. As one prominent example, Matthew Miller made a similar argument in the "Millionaire Teachers" chapter of his *The 2 % Solution* (2003).

2. While this is a Mechanism I method, because so few teachers are affected, most of the gain probably comes from skimming the best teachers out of the existing teacher pool rather than improving the overall pool quality.

3. Scarsdale Public Schools (2008).

4. Teacher Portal (2009).

5. More precisely, it was $115,538 in 2007–08. It's gone up since then. Source: New York State Education Department (2008, 3795).

6. National Center on Performance Incentives (2008).

7. U.S. Department of Education (2009).

8. Duncan (2009).

9. Duncan (2009).

10. Duncan (2009).

11. Duncan (2009).

12. Duncan (2009).

13. As of summer 2009.

14. Duncan (2009).

15. Online at http://www.talentedteachers.org/.

16. Hanushek (2006, 459).

17. Solmon et al. (2007).

18. Springer, Ballou, and Ping (2008).

19. Solmon et al. (2007, 6).

20. Teacher Advancement Project (2008).

21. Teacher Advancement Project (2008).

22. http://www.chicagotapschools.org/.

23. Chicago TAP (2009).

24. http://education.state.mn.us/MDE/Teacher_Support/QComp/index.html.

25. Hezel Associates (2009, iii).

26. Office of the Legislative Auditor (2009).

27. Office of the Legislative Auditor (2009, Table 2.2).
28. Office of the Legislative Auditor (2009, Table 3.2).
29. My calculations suggest payments are a bit higher, perhaps about $2,500 a teacher. See Technical Appendix.

Chapter 11: The Money Trail

1. An unfortunately high fraction of decisions about school spending is being made by courts rather than states or local school districts. To learn more about this see Hanushek and Lindseth (2009).
2. Inflation adjusted, author's calculations; see Technical Appendix.
3. On the other hand, we devote the same fraction of the economy to education as we have for a long time—just under 5 percent. Elementary and secondary education were 4.6 percent of GDP in 2007 and in 1970, having dipped slightly during the low enrollment years of the 1980s. Source: Snyder, Dillow, and Hoffman (2009, Table 25).
4. Hanushek and Jorgenson (1996, 35).
5. Building new schools is not included. Capital budgets are calculated separately from current spending. Other than responding to fluctuations in the number of school-age children, the fraction of the budget devoted to capital expenditure hasn't changed a great deal.
6. Snyder, Dillow, and Hoffman (2009, Table 174), 2005–06 data.
7. Snyder, Dillow, and Hoffman (2009, Table 80), Fall 2006 data.
8. Interestingly, the number of instructional coordinators rose even faster than the number of aides, doubling over the same period. However, aides outnumber instructional coordinators ten to one, so coordinators aren't that important in the budget picture. Source: Snyder, Dillow, and Hoffman (2009, Table 80).
9. National Education Association (2003, 29).
10. National Education Association (2003, Table 19).
11. OECD (Organisation for Economic Co-operation and Development) (2003, Table D2.3).
12. Krueger (1999).
13. Hanushek (1994, 35).
14. Chambers, Parrish, and Harr (2004, 7).
15. Chambers, Parrish, and Harr (2004, 7).
16. Hanushek and Rivkin (1997, 45).
17. Some years in figure interpolated. From Snyder, Dillow, and Hoffman (2009, Table 64).
18. For a completely accessible read on both the politics and economics of California's massive experiment in class-size reduction, take a look at Schrag (2006/07).

19. Howell, West, and Peterson (2007).
20. Hanushek (1994, xx).
21. Rivkin, Hanushek, and Kain (2005).
22. Krueger (1999).
23. Medina (2009).
24. Harris (2006/07, 147).
25. One explanation for the discrepancy between public perception and the scientific evidence is that the anecdotes which inform the public debate are about very large classes where there is a benefit from class-size reduction, but such large classes are sufficiently rare so as to not have much effect on the statistical evidence.
26. Snyder, Dillow, and Hoffman (2009, Table 67).
27. There are about 450,000 special education teachers in U.S. schools, but this includes private as well as public schools. Bureau of Labor Statistics (2010).
28. National Education Association (2003, Tables 21 and 23).
29. National Education Association (2003, Table 24).
30. National Education Association (2003, Table 33).
31. Snyder, Dillow, and Hoffman (2009, Table 67).
32. TEP (The Equity Project) (2009).
33. DeArmond and Goldhaber (2008, Table 1).
34. Author's calculations. See Technical Appendix.
35. Snyder, Dillow, and Hoffman (2009, Table 182).
36. Snyder, Dillow, and Hoffman (2009, Table 171).
37. Bushaw and Gallup (2008, Table 7).

Chapter 12: Payback!

1. Hanushek (2004, 19).
2. Loeb, Rouse, and Shorris (2007, 3).
3. This omits the part of proprietor's income that should be attributed to labor rather than capital. Council of Economic Advisors (2009, Table B-29).
4. I give a more nuanced calculation later in the chapter, but if you remember "nine-to-one payoff," not much will be missed.
5. Krueger and Lindahl (2001, 1101).
6. Federal tax receipts are 17.6 percent of GDP. Federal spending is 20.5 percent of GDP. State and local receipts are 13.6 percent of GDP. Federal aid to state and local governments, which needs to be netted out, is 2.1 percent of GDP. So the share of government in the economy is 29.1 percent of GDP figured as receipts and 32 percent figured as expenditure. U.S. Census Bureau (2009, Tables 451, 453, and 463).

7. One reason for choosing the Haveman and Wolfe (1984) list is that the authors reported research results supporting each item.

8. See also Duncan (1976).

9. See also Mueller (1975).

10. Haveman and Wolfe (1984).

11. Lochner (2004, 828).

12. Author's calculations based on Lochner and Moretti's (2004) report that 0.5 to 0.7 percent and that a year of schooling reduced this by 0.1.

13. Lochner and Moretti (2004, 154).

14. Lochner and Moretti (2004).

15. Goldin and Katz (2008, 52).

16. Leigh and Mead (2005).

17. Good teachers sometimes advocate for "their kids" with the kids' parents. My wife and I certainly learned from some of our daughters' most excellent teachers.

18. Snyder, Dillow, and Hoffman (2009, Table 403).

19. Snyder, Dillow, and Hoffman (2008, Table 389).

20. Snyder, Dillow, and Hoffman (2009, Table 415).

21. If you're not an American, consider this a challenge to a (friendly) brain race. We'll even spot you the lead you already have.

22. Goldin and Katz (2008).

23. Goldin and Katz (2008, 324–26).

24. Murnane and Steele (2007, 16–17).

25. Lemke et al. (2004, iv).

26. Baldi et al. (2007, iii).

27. Baldi et al. (2007, 11).

28. Rounded to the nearest dollar, applying compound interest.

29. Over the last fifty years, average labor productivity has risen at 2.06 percent per year; over the last twenty-five years the rate has been 1.86 percent. Author's calculations using data on GDP per capita from Federal Reserve Bank of St. Louis (2009).

30. Author's calculations. See Technical Appendix.

31. One of the first articles to look at the link between education and economic growth was by Jorgensen and Fraumeni (1992).

32. Hanushek et al. (2008, 66).

33. Bils and Klenow (2000, 1160).

34. Krueger and Lindahl (2001, 1130).

35. The base case assumes a discount rate of 2.0 percent and a growth rate of 1.86 percent. Further details appear in the Technical Appendix.

36. Eighteen trillion dollars times 30 percent to the government comes to $5.4 trillion, which is half of the current national debt.

37. Author's calculation of asymptotic ratio of annual benefit to annual cost comes to 10.37. See Technical Appendix.

Chapter 13: Getting There

1. Hill and Harvey (2004) Although the quote ought not be taken as endorsing the approach here.
2. TEP (The Equity Project) (2009).
3. Gootman (2009).
4. In states in which almost all funding is statewide, California, Hawaii, and Washington for example, it's even harder to make a local change without state participation.
5. Author's calculations from the 2000 Census 1 percent sample. Ruggles et al. (2009).
6. Author's calculations. Data source: Snyder, Dillow, and Hoffman (2009, Table 171).
7. Wagner (2008).
8. For a good review of the politics of teacher pay reforms, see Goldhaber (2009).
9. Nadler and Wiswall (2009).
10. See Boyd et al. (2007); Raymond, Fletcher, and Luque (2001), Raymond and Fletcher (2002). For a dissenting view, see Darling-Hammond et al. (2005).
11. Gordon, Kane, and Staiger (2006).
12. I need to interject a moment of greater-than-usual wonkishness in regard to one final element—the interaction between bonus systems and teacher retirement plans. Payouts on teacher retirement plans are almost universally weighted to reflect salaries towards the end of a teaching career. [See Costrell and Podgursky (2009) and Costrell and Podgursky (2009)) In a world in which teacher pay is inflexible, such a system more or less works. In some public sector retirement plans, it's common for an employee's pay to skyrocket in the year or two before retirement. This boosts pensions, at taxpayer expense, in a way that doesn't correspond to the employee's career earnings. This is not an issue for teachers precisely because their pay scale is inflexible. Under *Profit,* we want a teacher's pension to reflect bonuses earned throughout the career. One possibility is that the retirement share of *Profit* payments should be set aside in a separate, defined contribution plan.

Arguably, the traditional arrangement of defined benefit pension plans for teachers has become dysfunctional in a world in which people no longer follow a single, lifelong career. These plans accumulate benefits almost entirely in the last few years of a long-term teacher's career. As a result, traditional pensions do little to attract younger teachers, while at the same time trapping older teachers who might be ready for one more career switch before retirement. (Personal communication: Joel Klein.)

Technical Appendix

1. Hanushek (1992, 107).
2. Ehrenberg and Brewer (1995).
3. Goldhaber (2007, 777).
4. Bond (2001).
5. Snyder, Dillow, and Hoffman (2009, Table 74).
6. Ehrenberg, Goldhaber, and Brewer (1995, Table 1b).
7. Goldhaber and Anthony (2007, 141).
8. Cavalluzzo (2004, 25).
9. Office of the Legislative Auditor (2009, Table 1.2).
10. Office of the Legislative Auditor (2009, Table 1.4).
11. Snyder, Dillow, and Hoffman (2009, Table 78).
12. U.S. Census Bureau (1967, Table 477).
13. U.S. Census Bureau (2008, Table 676).
14. Federal Reserve Bank of St. Louis (2009) Series CPIAUCNS, Consumer Price Index for All Urban Consumers: All Items.
15. Snyder, Dillow, and Hoffman (2009, Tables 122 and 177).
16. Snyder, Dillow, and Hoffman (2009, Table 75).
17. Snyder, Dillow, and Hoffman (2009, Table 179).
18. 2005–06. Snyder, Dillow, and Hoffman (2009, Table 32).
19. U.S. Census Bureau (2009, Table 8).

Index

About the Author

Dick Startz is Castor Professor of Economics and Adjunct Professor of Statistics at the University of Washington. He is the coauthor of the internationally acclaimed textbook *Macroeconomics* (in its 11th edition) and author of three books on personal computing, as well as many articles in the areas of econometrics, macroeconomics, and labor economics. Professor Startz is long-time contributor to public policy discussions, including a syndicated op-ed column in Washington State. His two daughters are graduates of the Seattle public school system.